IMAGES
of America

BULLHEAD CITY

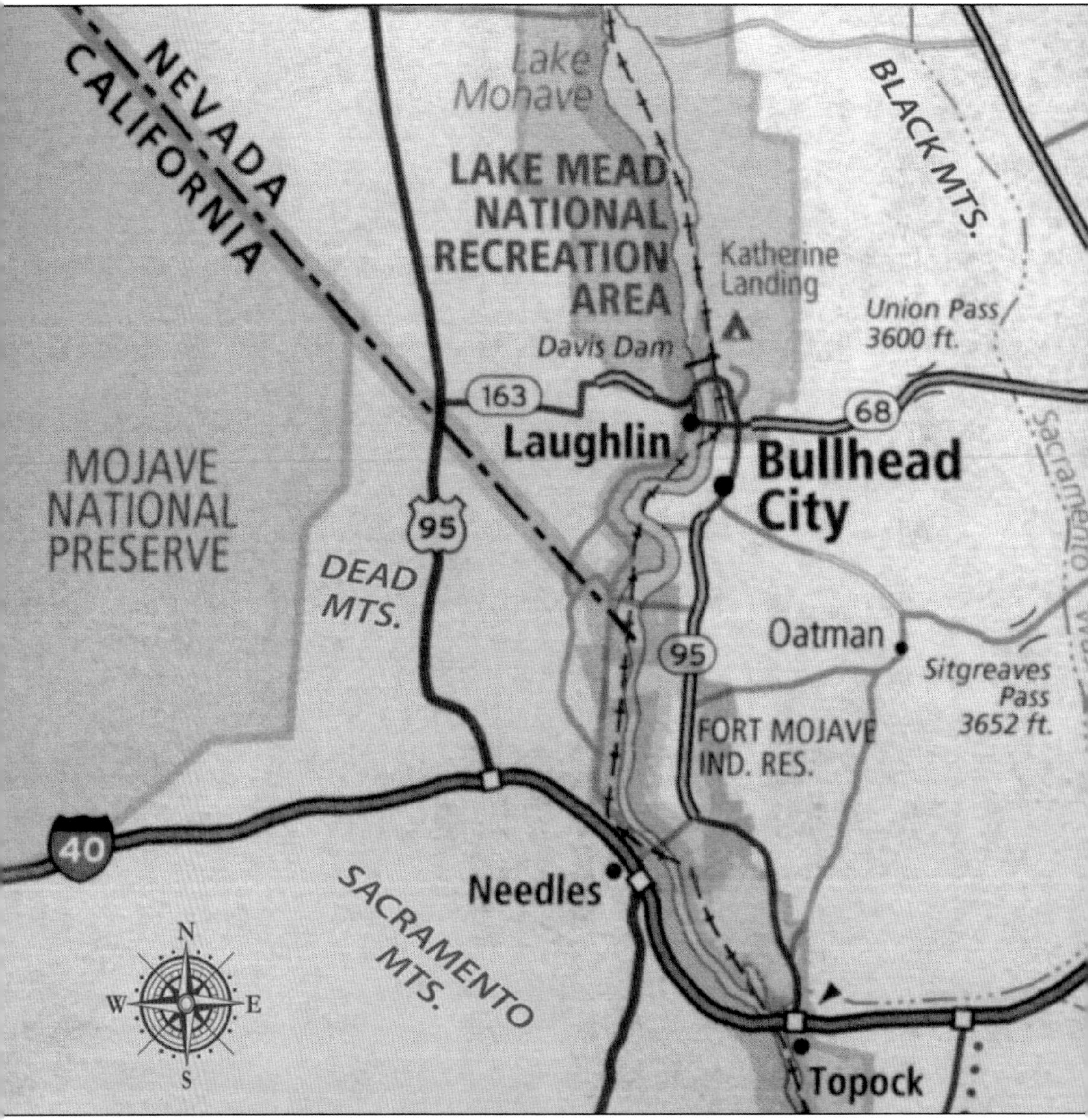

Bullhead City, Arizona, is situated on the east bank of the Colorado River in the Mohave Valley. It dominates the northern third of the valley, occupying 57 square miles from Pyramid Canyon and Davis Dam in the north to Fort Mohave in the south. The valley is approximately 27 miles long, flanked on the east by the Black Mountains, the longest mountain range in Arizona, and on the west by the Newberry Mountains and the Dead Mountains. The Mohave Valley's terminus is below the point where the borders of Arizona, Nevada, and California meet, near the town of Needles, California. (Courtesy of Terry Leclerc.)

ON THE COVER: A 1920s survey party is seen ferrying across the Colorado River in one of many such expeditions seeking an appropriate site for a dam to be built in what is now Bullhead City. The man at right is believed to be William Mulholland of Los Angeles. (Courtesy of Colorado River Historical Society; donated by Lloyd and Gloria Simons, Anaheim, California.)

IMAGES
of America

BULLHEAD CITY

Shirín McGraham

ARCADIA
PUBLISHING

ISBN 978-1-4671-3246-6

Published by Arcadia Publishing
Charleston, South Carolina

Printed in the United States of America

Library of Congress Control Number: 2014937945

For all general information, please contact Arcadia Publishing:
Telephone 843-853-2070
Fax 843-853-0044
E-mail sales@arcadiapublishing.com
For customer service and orders:
Toll-Free 1-888-313-2665

Visit us on the Internet at www.arcadiapublishing.com

Dedicated to my two high school history teachers,
Russell Camarda and Alex Pottetti, who encouraged me to view
historical events within their own time and frame of reference

Contents

ACKNOWLEDGMENTS

I want to thank everyone who has assisted me by sharing photographs and memories. Special thanks go to the people who have generously supplied most of the material for this book: Elsie Needles and the late Harold Reed of the Colorado River Historical Society; Cheryl Mangin of the Needles Regional Museum; Andy Sansom with the Mohave Museum of History and Arts; Larry Ford, former publisher and owner of the *Mohave Valley News*; and Greg Thornton of the US Department of the Interior, Bureau of Land Management. To the authors who selflessly shared their knowledge and photographs with a stranger—Jere Baker, Dennis Casebier, and Dan Messersmith—I am grateful for your help.

I would like to thank, too, all of the individuals who provided me with their photographs: Mike Conner, Donna Zurcher, Toby Cotter, Rodney Head, Tom and Karla Brady, Louise Zaborsky, John Masterson, Joe Heath, Damian Holther, Marilyn Bridges, Robert Dell, and anyone else I might have forgotten. Even if I did not have space to use your material, thank you for your generosity.

Importantly, I would like to thank my husband, Thom, for his encouragement, help, and support, and my dear friend, Jeanette Sendry, for her excellent editing of this book. I would also like to thank my staff at our newspaper, the *Bullhead City Bee*, for their support: Jimena Asigliano Vargas, Eileen Galante, and Bryan Hood. And special thanks to my son, Mark Randall, for staying out of my hair so I could finish on deadline. I cannot forget Alyssa Jones, my acquisitions editor at Arcadia Publishing who made this process as easy as possible.

Unless otherwise noted, sources for photographs and other material are credited with the following acronyms: Colorado River Historical Society (CRHS), Mohave Museum of History and Art (MMHA), Needles Regional Museum (NRM), and US Department of the Interior, Bureau of Land Management (BLM).

INTRODUCTION

The history of Bullhead City and the Mohave Valley reads like an old-time Western novella—it truly was the Wild West. A series of expeditions seeking a route to California along the 35th parallel set in motion a tide of pioneers crossing through Indian territory. Skirmishes between the Indians and the white intruders and attacks on wagon trains, including the massacre of some parties of early settlers, led to the establishment of a military garrison, Fort Mohave, to protect the pioneers. The discovery of gold, silver, and other precious metals in the mountains and desert fueled the influx of pioneers and miners looking to strike it rich. Early steamboats operated on the river, carrying passengers and freight and bringing supplies to the fort and mines. The advent of the transcontinental railroad further defined the valley as a crossroad to the Pacific Coast.

But it was the quest for water, the endeavor to tame the wild Colorado River to supply water and power to California, that would lead to the construction of Davis Dam and the creation of Bullhead City.

The Mohave Valley was home to indigenous Indian tribes for thousands of years before the Euro-Americans arrived. It is believed the prehistoric Paleo-Indians came from Eurasia to the Americas, perhaps hunting herds of wild animals. They likely arrived by way of the Beringia, a land bridge between Asia and North America spanning what is now the Bering Strait. The time frame of these migrations is debated, but generally, it is accepted that the Indians were living in North and South America more than 11,000 years ago. The earliest evidence of Indians in the Mohave Valley is found in Big Horn Cave of the Black Mountains, which was excavated by the University of Arizona. Archaeologists were hampered in attempting to date the find because these Indians did not use stone spear points and arrowheads as weapons, only sharpened sticks and clubs.

The Pipa Aha Macav (or Amacava) tribe, meaning "People by the River," are now known by the name given to them by the Spanish—Mojave. The Euro-Americans who came later used the altered spelling of Mohave with an "h." The Mojaves chiefly hunted small game; their primary food was fish and vegetables, such as corn, pumpkins, melons, beans, and later, wheat. They heavily relied on mesquite pods as well. Without the practice of irrigation, they were at the mercy of the annual inundation of the Colorado River to supply the needed moisture for crops. When there was no overflow, their crops failed. The land the Colorado River traverses is one of the driest and harshest desert regions on earth.

The Mojaves' first recorded encounters with outsiders were Spanish explorers Juan de Onate in 1604 and Fr. Francisco Garces, a Franciscan priest, in 1776. Both explorers reported that the Amacava were a friendly and hospitable people. Garces described them as healthy and robust, stating, "The women are the most attractive of any along the river." He reported being visited by some 2,000 persons. Garces was traveling to the Pacific Ocean and the Mojaves offered to accompany him, for they traded extensively with the coastal Indians and knew the way. The Mojaves were fast runners, able to make the nearly 300-mile-trip to the coast in three days, traveling from watering hole to watering hole on a route that later became known as the Mohave Road.

The next exposure to the white man came after the 1821 transfer of southwest lands from Spain to Mexico. When trade restrictions were eased, fur traders and trappers invaded the Southwest. The first trapper to enter Mojave territory was the renowned Jedediah S. Smith, who was scouting for beaver streams, in 1826. He and his men were half-starved when they encountered the Mojaves, who fed them and treated them well. After staying with them for eight days, Smith and his party set out for San Gabriel Mission. Indian guides led Smith across the desert by way of the old trail over which they had guided Garces 50 years earlier into the San Bernardino Valley, then on to San Gabriel Mission.

When Smith returned to the Mojaves a year later, it was a far different reception. In his absence, another trapping party, under the direction of Ewing Young, had reached the Mojaves' valley and, laden with beaver pelts, marched through a Mojave village. The Indians, who hunted only for food and revered the beaver, were outraged by these intruders with guns who were invading their land. When their chief demanded a horse as payment for the beaver, a quarrel erupted and the chief was killed. A battle ensued with casualties on both sides. Thus, Smith and his men were met with hostility upon their return. As the party was attempting to cross the river, the Indians attacked, killing 10 of Smith's men and capturing two French Indian women.

Capt. Lorenzo Sitgreaves of the US Army Corps of Topographical Engineers led the first government-sponsored expedition through the virtually unknown Indian-inhabited territories in 1851. Sitgreaves was to follow the Zuni River to its junction with the Colorado River, then proceed down the Colorado to its terminus in the Gulf of California, thereby reporting the navigability of these rivers and the nature of the country through which they ran. His report would give the country its first picture of the Mojave homelands and pave the way for further surveys across the Colorado River, including the Whipple, Beale, and Ives surveys, all before 1859.

Sitgreaves and his party traveled in a year of drought when the land was parched. They traversed a pass in the Black Mountains (Union Pass) that led them to the Colorado River. Sitgreaves described the scene as follows: "The presence of water seemed to afford the only relief from our former privations, for the soil—an almost impalpable sand—bore nothing but dry weeds and bushes, and the whole scene presented the most perfect picture of desolation I have ever beheld, as if some sirocco had passed over the land, withering and scorching everything to crispness."

The year 1851 was also when Yavapai Indians attacked the Oatman family, which included seven children, as they traveled by wagon across the Mojave Desert toward Yuma. Roys Oatman and his wife, Mary Ann, were massacred and brutally bludgeoned to death, along with their infant son, daughters Lucy and Charity, and Roys Jr. The Indians beat 16-year-old Lorenzo with their clubs and threw his body off a cliff onto a pile of boulders, then kidnapped 10-year-old Mary Ann and 14-year-old Olive. The girls were made to march barefoot across the desert for two days to the Yavapai village. There, they were enslaved and treated harshly by the Indians. After two years, they were traded to the Mojaves, who treated them with kindness, although they were still captives. They lived with the Chief Cairook and his family, who undoubtedly protected them.

Lorenzo had astonishingly survived the Indian attack and later searched for his sisters. Mary Ann had died in captivity during a year of famine, but Olive was able to reunite with her brother when the tribe released her in 1856. The Mojaves had tattooed her chin with vertical blue lines, a ritual they believed would help one cross over to the other side after death; otherwise, they thought the soul would disappear down a rat's hole. Lorenzo took Olive to relatives in California, where they began work on a book about her life in captivity. Olive also went on tour, speaking about her experiences with the Indians. She eventually married a wealthy banker.

The Whipple Expedition (1853–1854), commanded by Lt. Amiel Weeks Whipple and Bvt. 2nd Lt. Joseph C. Ives, traveled from Arkansas to Los Angeles, seeking a practical route for a railroad across the 35th parallel. The expedition consisted of scientists interested in astronomy, meteorology, biology, and minerals, including German-born H. Balduin Möllhausen, who was not only a topographer but also an artist and ethnographer. His drawings, paintings, and musings make his diary of the expedition a priceless source of information about the Mojaves and their country. The route Whipple surveyed is approximately that of the Santa Fe Railway today.

The first steamboat on the Colorado River, the *Uncle Sam*, was brought into service by Capt. George A. Johnson in 1852. In 1854, he added the *General Jesup*, which was the first steamboat to navigate the Colorado River all the way north to the area of present-day Davis Dam. Captain Johnson later brought two more steamboats into service in 1855, the *Colorado* and the *Mohave*. Soon, there would be more steamboats as river trade flourished during the mining era, until the coming of the transcontinental railroad.

Pres. James Buchanan appointed Brig. Gen. Edward Fitzgerald Beale to survey a wagon road along the 35th parallel, from Fort Defiance, New Mexico, to the Colorado River, on the border between Arizona and California. The survey also incorporated an experiment Jefferson Davis, secretary of war, had first proposed four years earlier to test camels as pack animals. In 1858, Beale, along with his survey party and more than two dozen camels imported from Tunis, crossed the Colorado River with the help of the steamboat *General Jesup*. The camels would not swim the river and had to be carried across on the deck of the boat. The purported location of Beale's Crossing is the site where Fort Mohave was built. The crossing was detailed in sketches by Möllhausen, who was also part of the expedition.

Lt. Joseph C. Ives was sent up the Colorado River in 1859 to develop potential routes of supply in the event of a war between the government and the Mormon settlements in Utah. His expedition included John Strong Newberry as naturalist, Möllhausen as artist and unofficial diarist, and F.W. Egloffstein as topographer.

The Rose-Udell wagon trains, as they are called today, were actually two trains of emigrants who left Santa Fe in 1858. Bound for California by way of the trail through Mojave territory, one was headed by L.R. Rose, and the other was led by Gillum Bailey. One member of the Bailey train was John Udell, who had previous experience traveling in the West. It was late August and the heat was intense. By the time the two wagon trains had reached the summit of Sitgreaves Pass in the Black Mountains, they were exhausted, hungry, and thirsty, having been troubled by Yavapai and Havasupai Indians along the way. One group, including L.R. Rose, who wrote the only eyewitness account of the next few days, pushed forward to the river. When the wagon train reached the river, the men set up camp and drove the livestock to the river to drink. The Mojaves, who had learned that yet another party would be coming through, began to drive off and kill the cattle, then cook and eat them. According to Rose's account in his journal, the Mojaves treated the matter as a huge joke, even laughing when caught in the act.

In the meantime, the Bailey party had passed through Sitgreaves Pass and camped at the edge of the valley. On August 30, the Rose party moved its camp downriver to the crossing place, using the grasses there for grazing the cattle, and cutting the cottonwood trees to build rafts to cross the river. The trees were considered valuable property of the Mojaves, and the grasses were their farmland. In the evening, the enraged Mojaves attacked, coming within 15 feet of the wagons to discharge their arrows. Of the 25 men in the party, one was killed and 11 were wounded. The Mojaves lost 17. Both wagon trains decided to turn back.

All four members of the Bentner family traveling with the Rose party had stayed behind in the mountains and were subsequently killed by Walapais, among whom were seven renegade Mojaves. The murder of this family was interpreted as a massacre—the Rose-Udell massacre—and news of it resulted in the establishment of Fort Mohave and the US military control of the Mojaves.

When Fort Mohave was established in 1859, it was briefly under the command of Maj. William Hoffman, then that of Maj. Gen. Lewis A. Armistead, who later became a famous Confederate general. When the Civil War began in 1861, the fort was abandoned, then razed by order of Gen. Edwin V. Sumner, for fear of capture by the Confederacy. The site was regarrisoned in 1863 under the command of Capt. J. Ives Fitch, who called it Camp Colorado, although it was soon renamed Fort Mohave. The soldiers spent most of their spare time exploring for gold in the vicinity of the fort.

One of the most colorful characters of that time was John Moss, the man responsible for the first major discovery of gold in the Mohave Valley. Moss was an adventurer, prospector, and promoter with a larger-than-life personality, just in his early twenties when he arrived in the Arizona Territory and the future Mohave County. Born in Utica, Iowa, in 1839, he was fascinated by the local Indians as a boy and discovered he had a gift for learning their language. Because the Indians both respected and liked him, Moss was influential in keeping peace between them and the white man. He traveled to California in 1857 as a Pony Express rider and, in 1861, headed to the new gold discoveries in Arizona. In 1863, he discovered a fabulously rich gold deposit in the Black Mountains. It was a Mojave Indian who had led him to the site that he later developed as the Moss Mine.

The next year, Moss took Chief Iretaba to Washington, DC, to see the "white chief," Pres. Abraham Lincoln. While he was in New York, Iretaba was visited by Olive Oatman. Chief Cairook, with whom Olive had lived during her captivity, was Iretaba's brother. Upon returning to his tribe, Iretaba's stories about the land of the white people were met with disbelief by some of the Mojaves.

During a time of Indian unrest, Moss signed a treaty with the Piute Indians, which permitted him unrestricted access to their territory. In 1868, a Piute chief brought Moss a piece of metallic copper, and after some searching, Moss found the source. He then headed to San Francisco with samples to garner the interest of potential investors. On the strength of his report, the Piute Company was organized in San Francisco on April 13, 1869. The company soon discovered silver in addition to the copper, staking some 130 claims.

Another adventurous businessman, William H. Hardy, purchased a ferry operation six miles north of Fort Mohave, where he constructed a trading post and toll road to Prescott. This new city of Hardyville was now the "practical" head of navigation on the Colorado River. By 1883, however, the Atlantic & Pacific Railroad, now known as the Burlington Northern Santa Fe (BNSF), had reached Needles, California, and Hardy moved his ferry there to service the newly arrived railway. Soon, the town of Hardyville fell into ruin, but it would become the future site of Bullhead City.

On September 25, 1890, Fort Mohave was turned over to the secretary of the US Department of the Interior, who directed the Indian agency to establish a school for the Mojave tribe. It remained in use as an Indian school until 1935. Abandoned, its demolition was ordered in 1942.

Cattle ranches and farms were established to help feed the growing population of settlers and miners. The advent of railroads and the development of windmill technology, used to fill ponds, brought a bonanza of ranches and cattle speculators from the East Coast. By the 1890s, about 1.5 million cattle were grazing in Arizona. The cattle boom faded quickly, however. The rapid growth of the cattle industry did not consider the limits of the land. Ranchers overgrazed the pastures in only 20 years.

Arizona became the 48th state on February 14, 1912. In that same year, the national Old Trails Highway was established, bringing an ever-increasing amount of automobile traffic to Mohave County. By 1926, US Route 66 had opened the West to more traffic and tourism from the East.

During the 1930s, the Hoover and Parker Dams were completed. Davis Dam construction was authorized in 1941 and work was started, but ceased in December 1942, as all construction resources were diverted to the war effort. Work was finally resumed in 1946, a year after World War II ended, and was completed in 1953.

It was not until the completion of Davis Dam that the idea of "Bull's Head," named for an iconic rock in the river, began to emerge when some workers from the dam project and their families remained to put down roots. Meanwhile, land developers recognized the potential of promoting Bull's Head as a recreational destination. Soon it would be a boomtown.

Across the river, on the west bank of the Nevada shore, a modern, adventurous businessman, Don Laughlin, developed a casino resort in 1965. Soon, more casinos were constructed, and an influx of tourists followed, enjoying the attractions of the river and gaming in the new Nevada township of Laughlin. This substantial tourism created thousands of jobs for Bullhead City residents. In 1980, Interstate 40 was completed through Mohave County.

On August 28, 1984, Bullhead City was officially incorporated. At that time, the city encompassed 28.5 square miles. In 1987, Don Laughlin funded and built a bridge across the Colorado River, connecting Bullhead City, Arizona, and Laughlin, Nevada. He then donated the $3.5 million bridge to the two states.

One

Early Inhabitants
The Mojave Indians

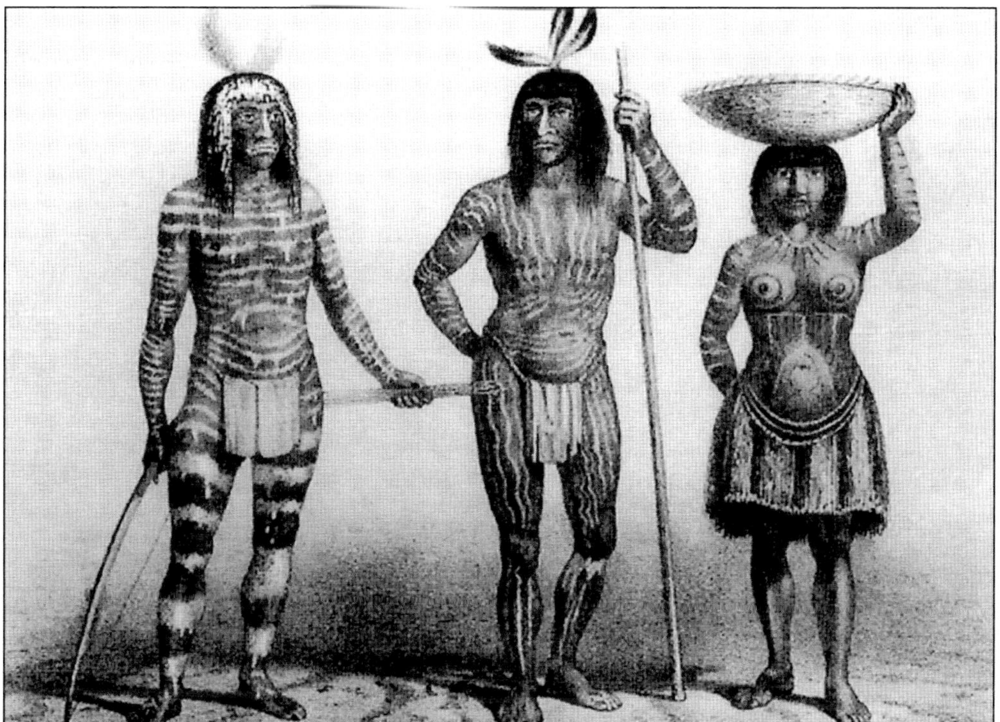

This illustration depicts two Mojave (Amacava) men and a woman, all painted in ceremonial designs. The men, in characteristic fashion, wore nothing but loincloths, sometimes adding a long cape for warmth. The woman's skirt was constructed from strips of material made of bark and attached to a belt around her waist, which was customary dress for the women. (Watercolor by H. Balduin Möllhausen; courtesy of CRHS.)

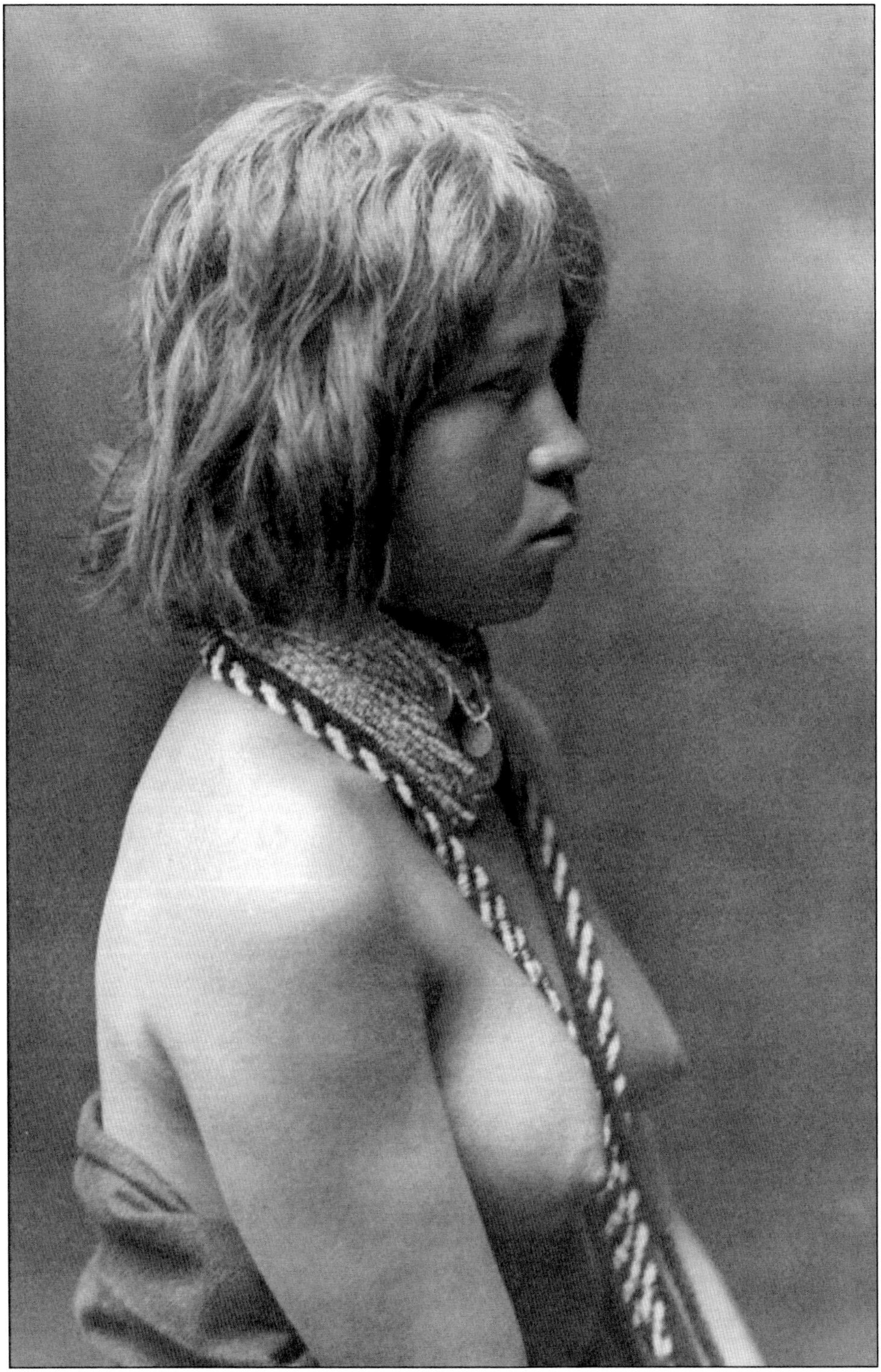

Judith is the name given to this Mojave maiden by the unidentified photographer. Mojave women went bare-breasted in all seasons except winter, when they wore a short cape made from rabbit fur. (Courtesy of NRM.)

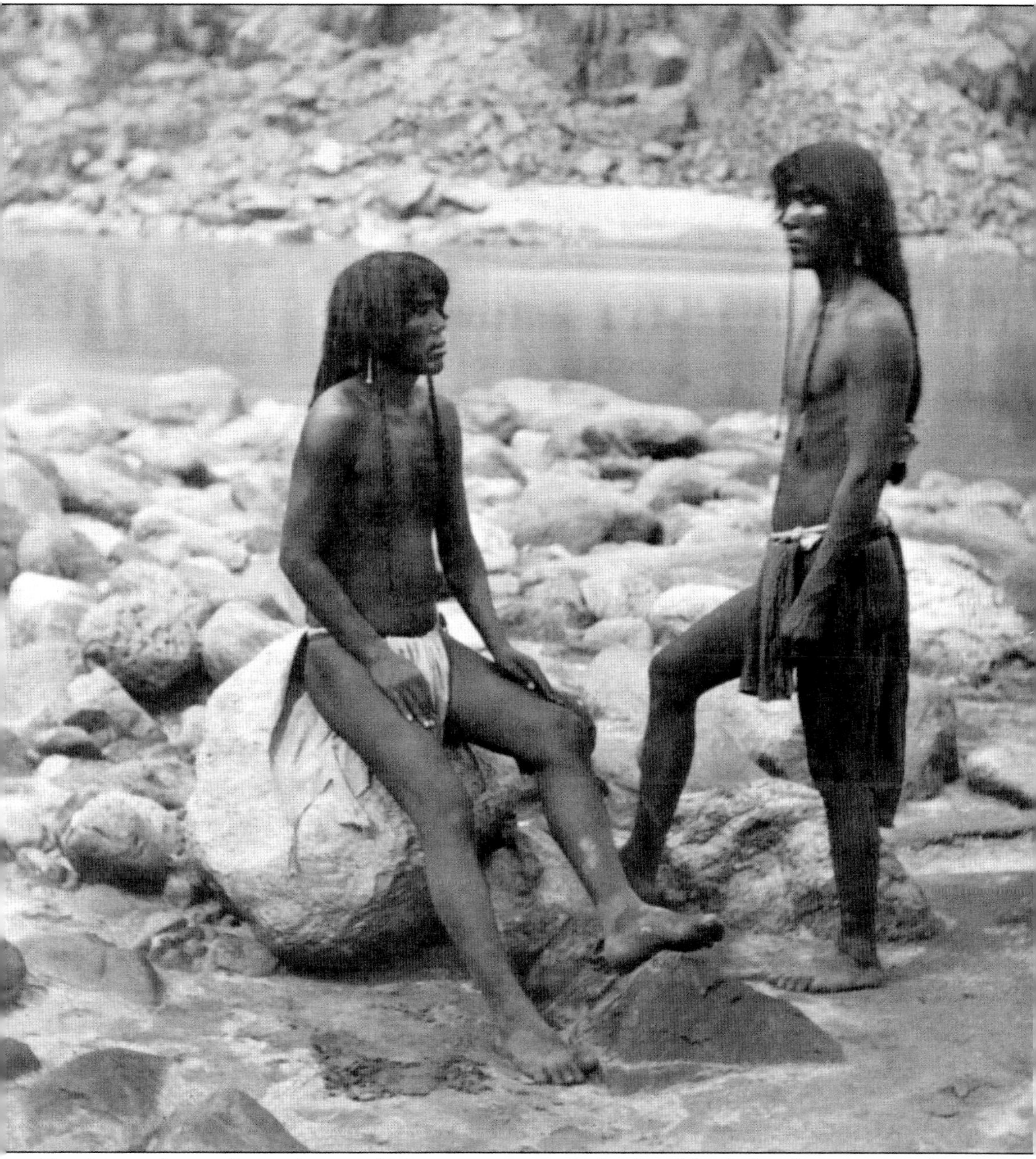

Two Mojave braves, Panambona and Mitinara, pose on the banks of the Colorado River around 1871. Their hair is worn long, tied in back and braided in front; both appear to have either a hair ornament or earring of sorts. (Courtesy of NRM.)

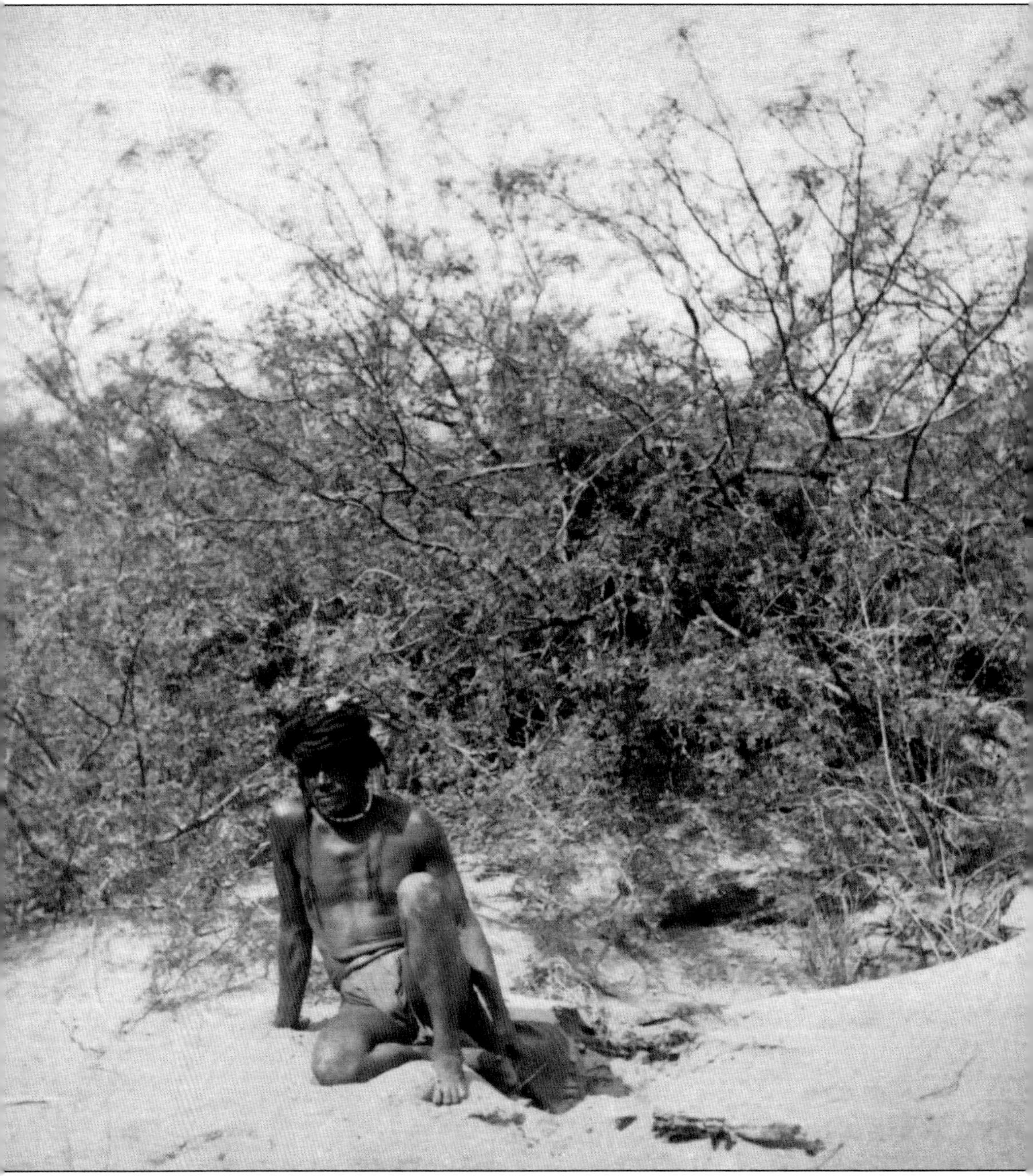

Pictured here in 1871 is Mojave brave Nee-chi gua-ra, with his hair coiled up and packed with mud to keep it out of his eyes and control lice. It was not only practical but also a stylized look considered fashionable. Often, other layers of hair were woven in, creating a towering fashion statement much like modern hair extensions. (Courtesy of NRM.)

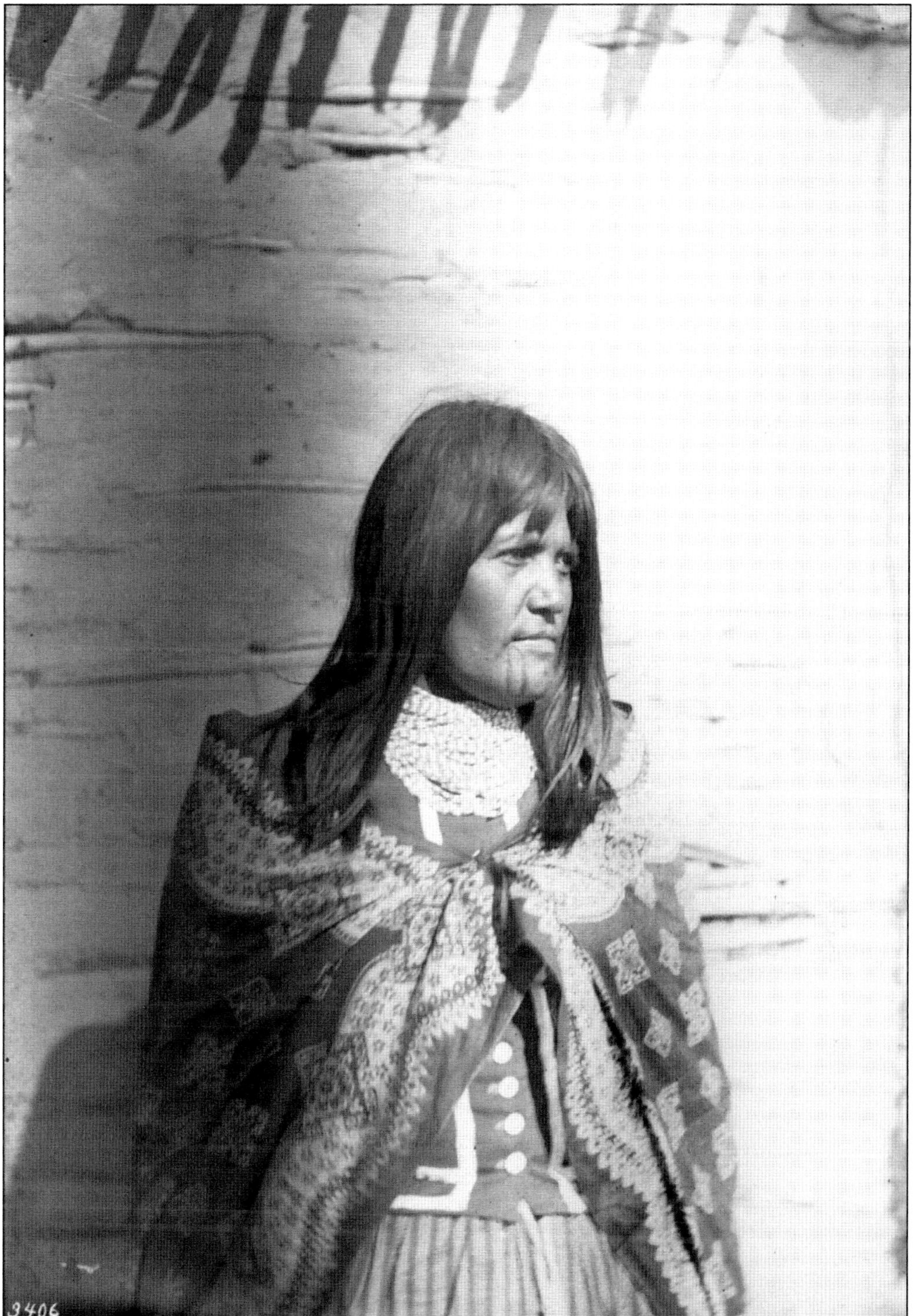

This Mojave matron with a blue tattoo on her chin was photographed around 1900. There are three possible explanations for the tattoo: it helps one make the transition to the other side after death, marks women upon marriage, or possibly indicates a slave. (Courtesy of NRM.)

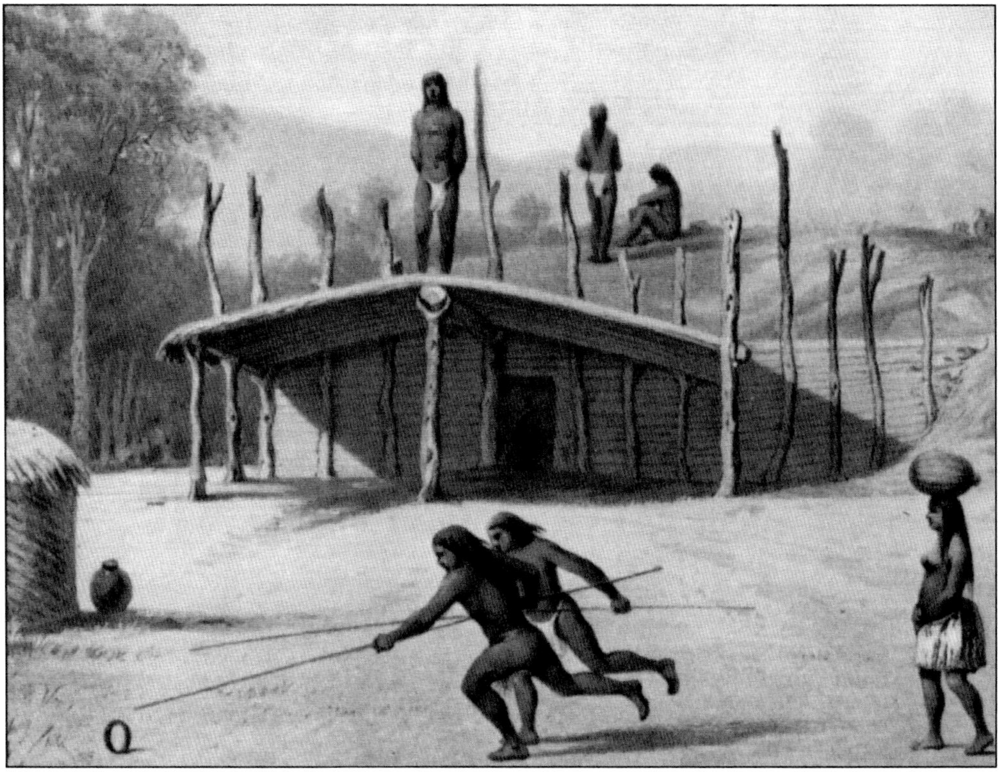

An old Mojave dwelling such as this was built into the side of a hill to keep it cool in summer and warm in winter. Families often spent time on the roof, keeping cool in the evenings. The boys with sticks and a hoop are competing in shinny, a game that is still played to this day. (Sketch by H. Balduin Möllhausen; courtesy of CRHS.)

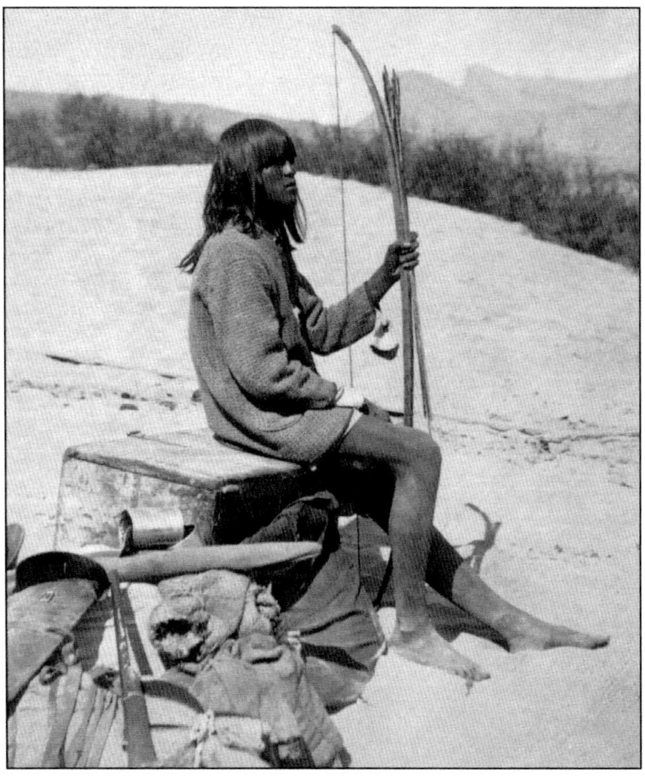

Maiman, a Mojave brave, displays his bow and arrow. Note the rifle at his feet. By the time of this 1871 photograph, the Mojaves were adopting the white man's manner in both dress and behavior. (Courtesy of NRM.)

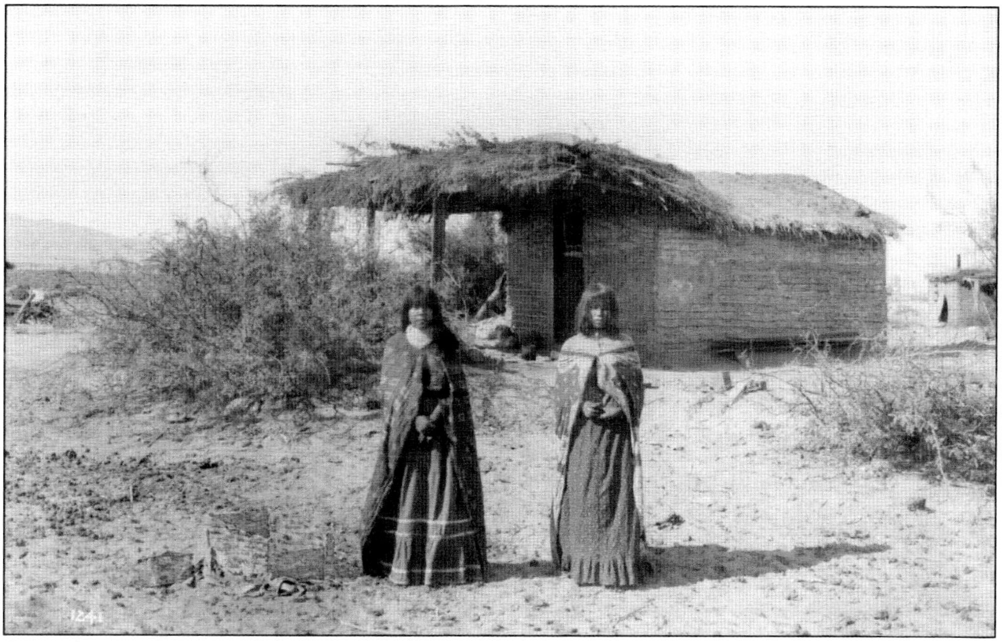

Seen above is a c. 1900 image of a typical Mojave dwelling with a thatched roof and covered porch. The two girls are wearing Western-style, store-bought skirts or dresses and capes made from imported material. Their hair, however, remains in the traditional tribal style, with bangs and a shoulder-length cut. Below, the method of the dwelling's construction involves weaving branches around posts in the ground, then filling in the structure with grasses and mud to make the walls. (Both, courtesy of NRM.)

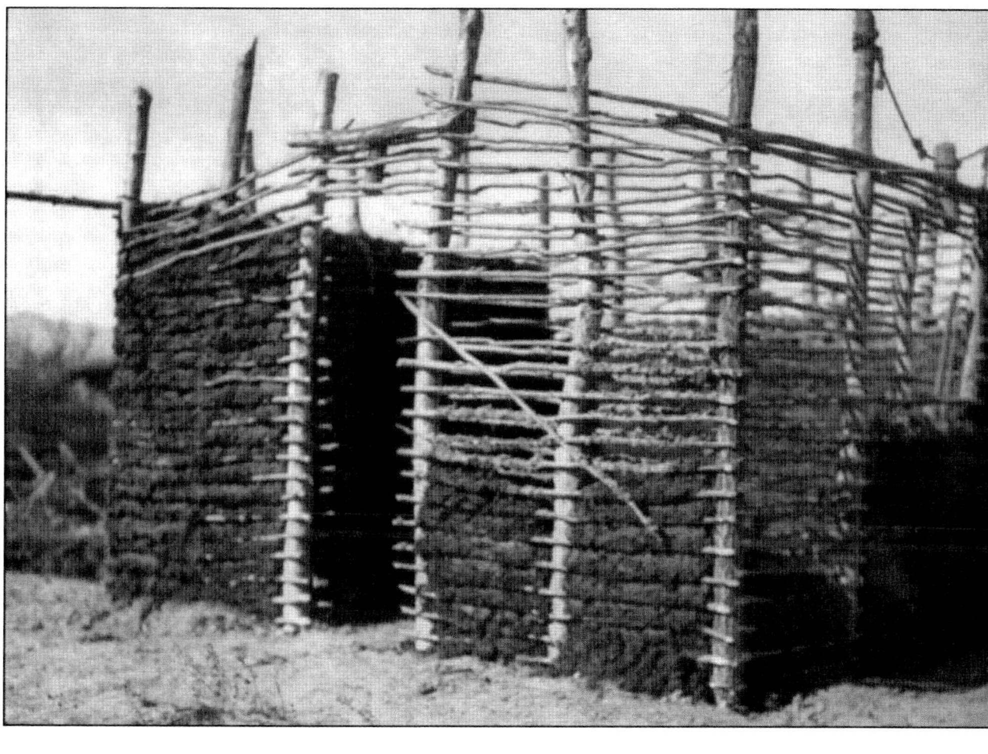

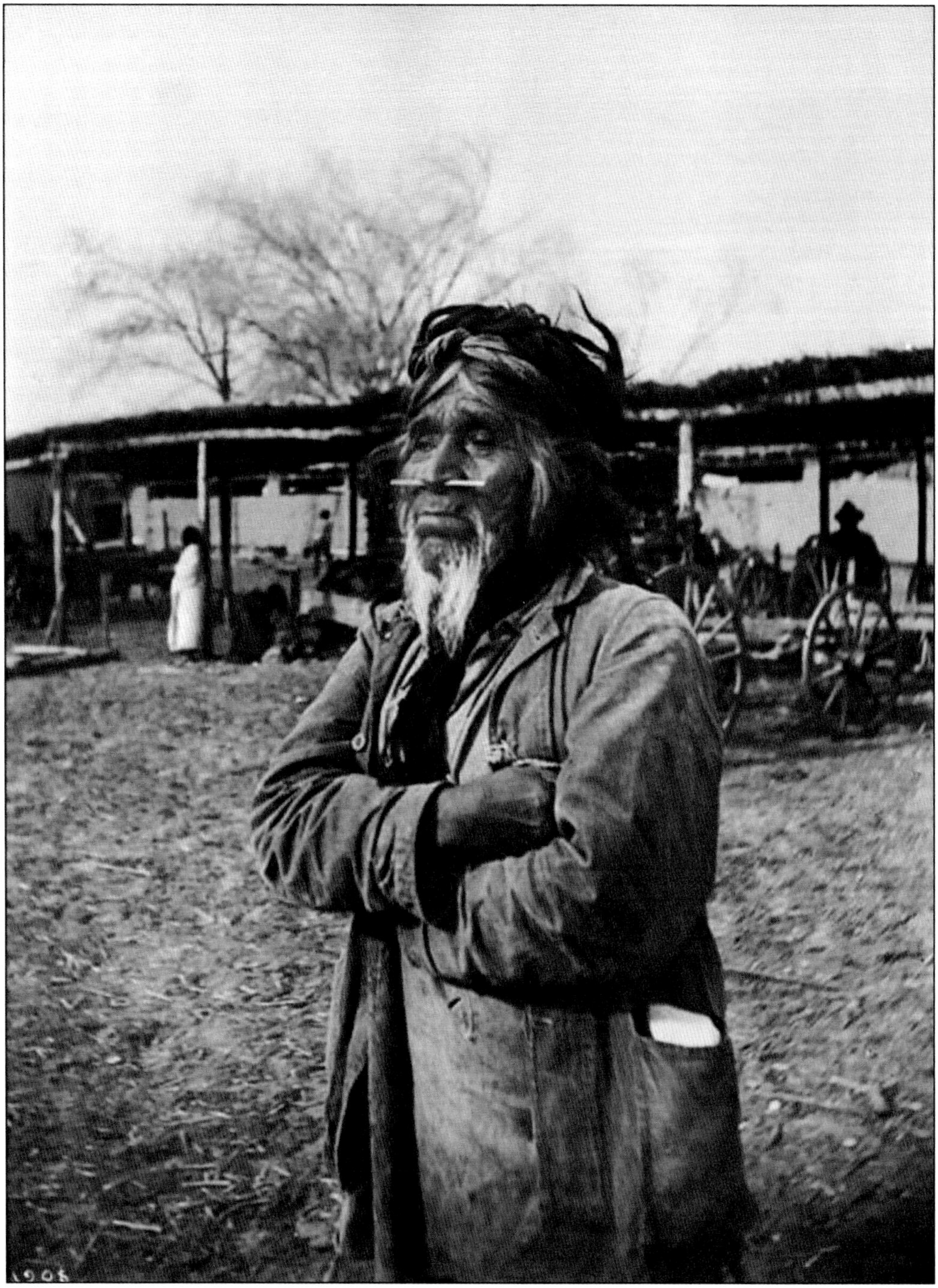

An older Mojave, with his nose pierced, stands in his village around 1871. Piercing, tattooing, and body painting were popular with the Mojaves; both men and women adorned themselves with tattoos and ceremonial paint, but there is no evidence that the women practiced piercing. (Courtesy of NRM.)

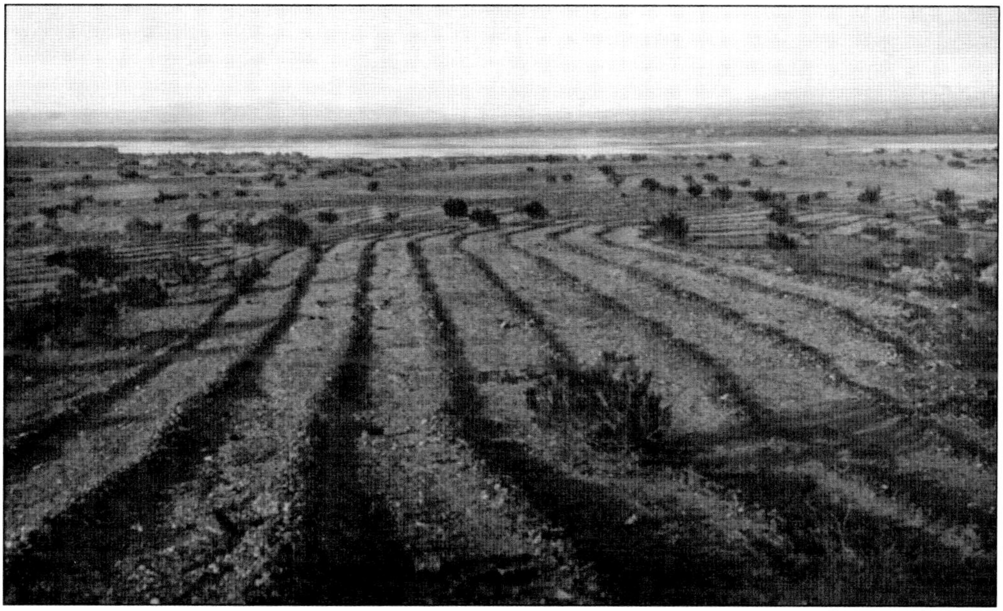

The Mystic Maze, seen above around 1900, is a series of unexplained parallel ridges of stone four to five feet apart near the Needles Mountains at the south end of the Mohave Valley. There is a spiritual significance to the maze for the Mojave Indians: upon death, natives had to proceed through the maze to the afterlife. The Mystic Maze is also believed to have played a role in ancient Mojave purification rituals, including those of Indian runners who purified themselves by passing through the maze before entering the valley. The age of the maze is uncertain but might have been created in prehistoric times. Originally, the maze was much larger than it is today; parts were destroyed when the railroad came through in the late 1800s and again when Interstate 40 was constructed in 1980. The remaining maze, seen below as it appears today, covers only 18 acres and has suffered considerable damage in recent years. (Above, courtesy of CRHS; below, author's collection.)

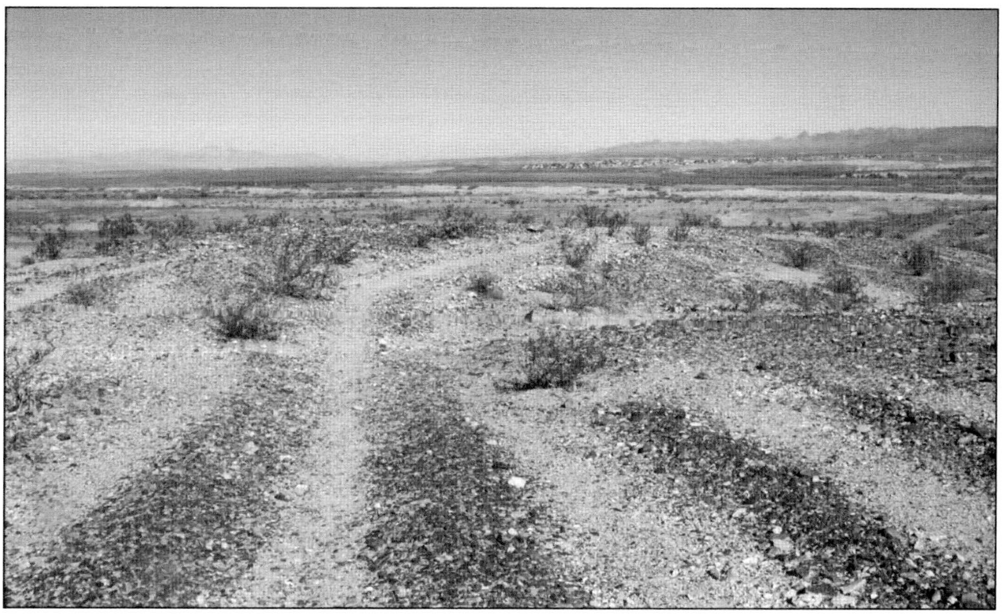

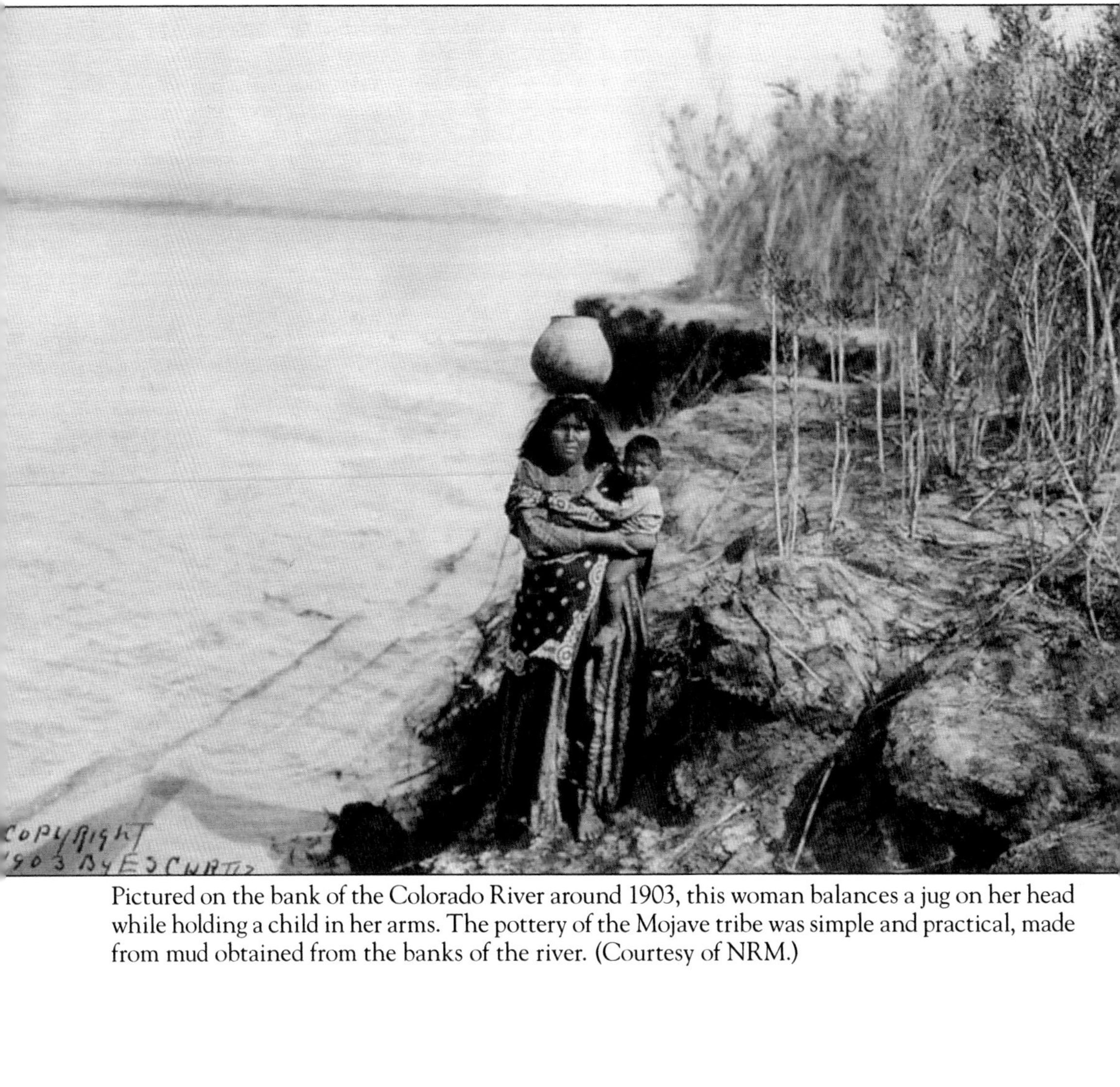

Pictured on the bank of the Colorado River around 1903, this woman balances a jug on her head while holding a child in her arms. The pottery of the Mojave tribe was simple and practical, made from mud obtained from the banks of the river. (Courtesy of NRM.)

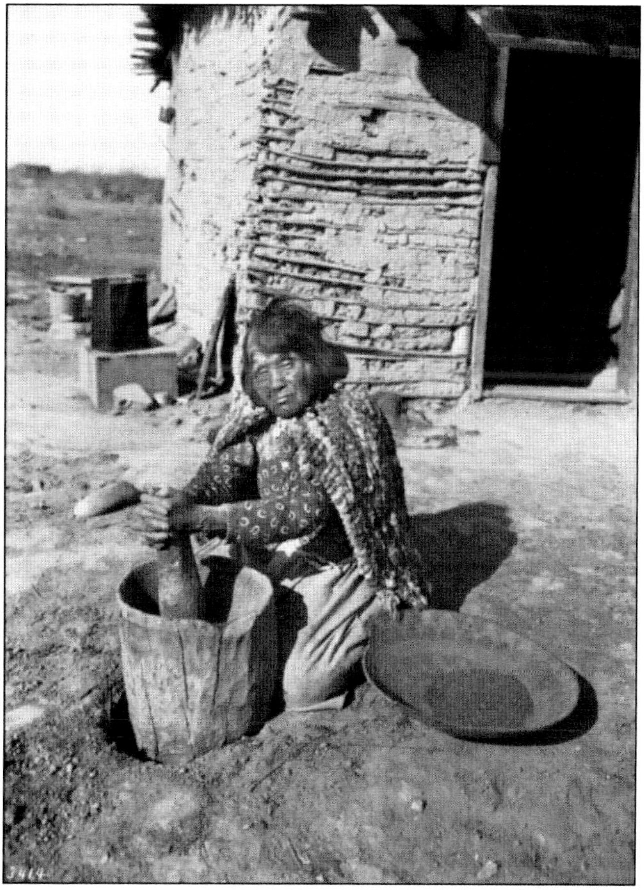

An elderly Mojave woman grinds mesquite pods (or beans) to make a flour-like substance. The mesquite tree was of great importance to the Mojaves as a source of food, especially in times of drought. The tree produces a straw-colored pod resembling a string bean that has a high nutritional value. They were eaten fresh or dried and pounded into a meal to make small sun-dried cakes. The meal also could be mixed with water to produce a refreshing drink. The image below depicts Mojave children and adults dressed in Western attire outside their home around 1903. Mesquite wood was used to fuel fires, make bows and arrows, and construct dwellings. (Both, courtesy of NRM.)

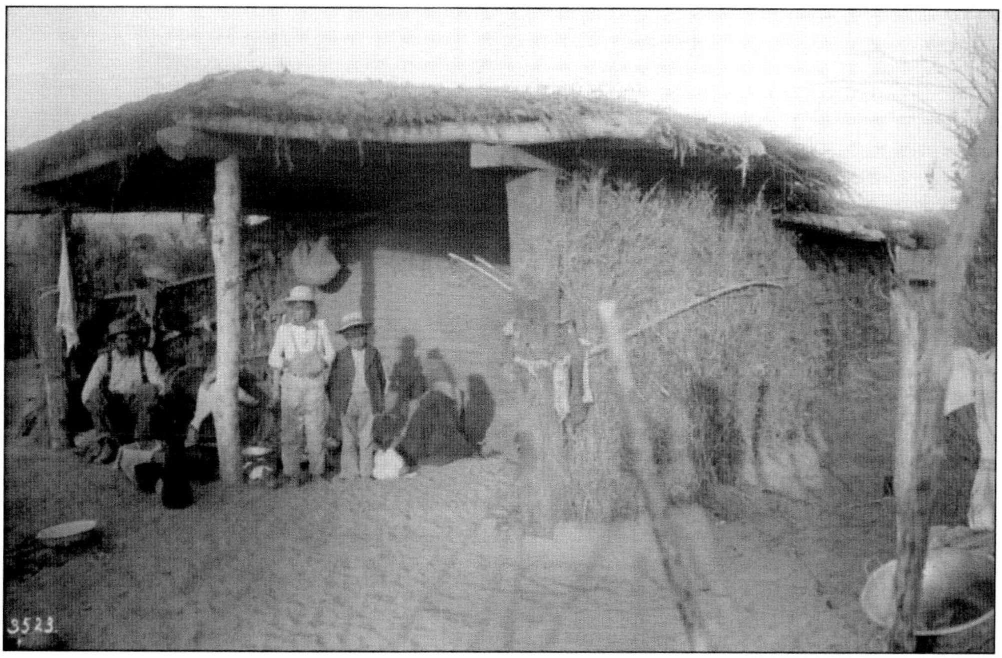

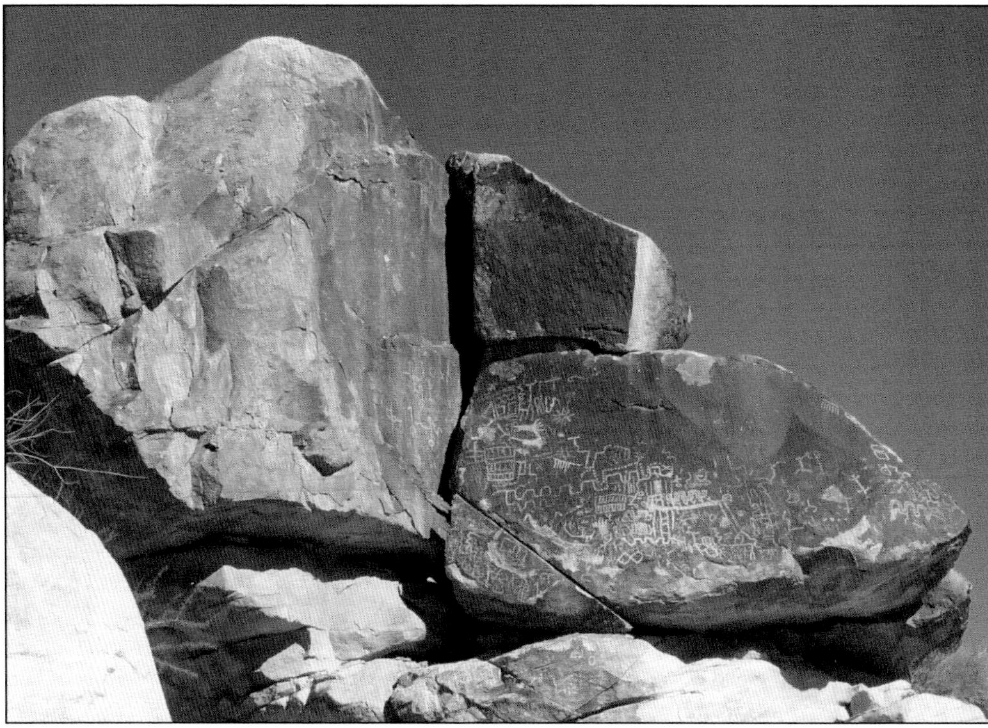

Petroglyphs and pictographs, known as "talking rocks," have been found in great profusion in the Mohave Valley, both below the sacred Spirit Mountain on the north end of the valley in the Newberry Mountains and in the Dead Mountains west of Fort Mohave on the Nevada side of the river. Huge boulders strewn with ancient symbols tower 30 to 40 feet above the dry riverbed that runs through the narrow pass below Spirit Mountain. There are two different types of ancient writings: abstractions carved into the stone (petroglyphs) and images painted on the surface (pictographs). Petroglyphs are durable and therefore more common. The petroglyphs of the Mojaves were formed by cutting away the "desert patina" that coats these ancient rocks to reveal the lighter-colored surface beneath. (Both, author's collection.)

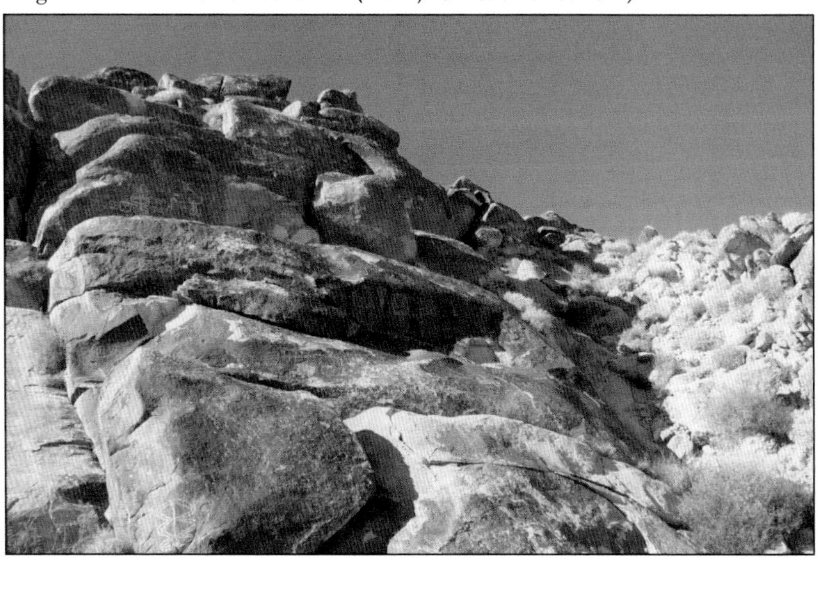

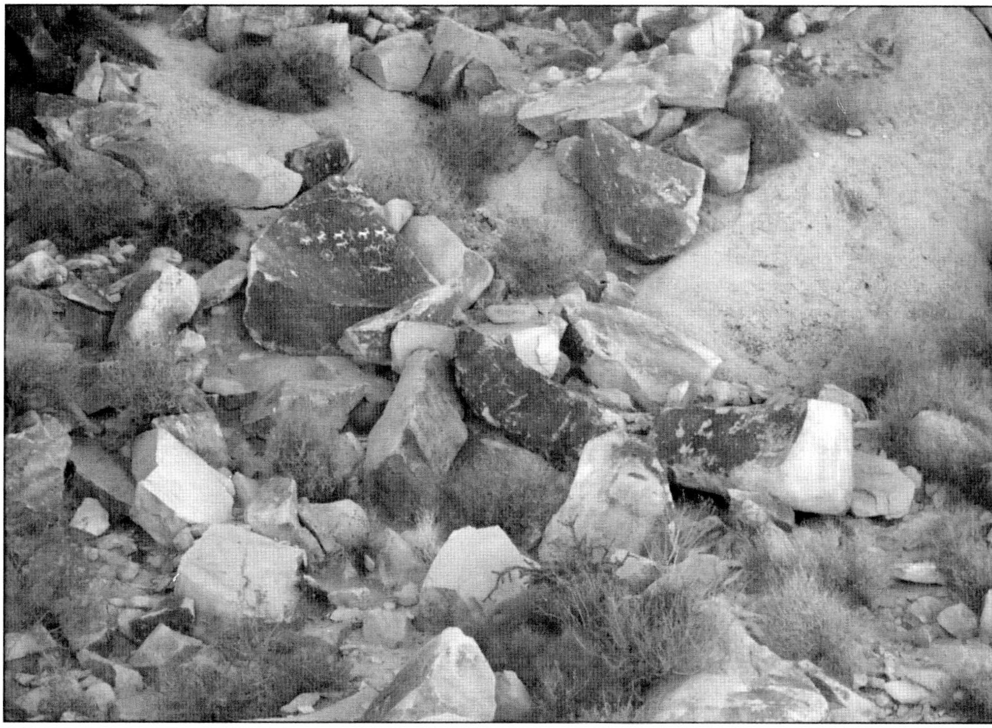

These images of antelope high atop a ridge in the Newberry Mountains are ancient in origin, possibly depicting the successful outcome of a hunt. The Mojaves were not prone to hunting for large game in recent history, instead relying on the bounty of the land and fishing. It is said there was a dispute between the Mojave tribe and the neighboring Hualapai tribe, who were fishing the Colorado River while the Mojaves were hunting game in the Hualapais' mountains. To end the conflict, both tribes agreed to stay in their own territory. (Both, author's collection.)

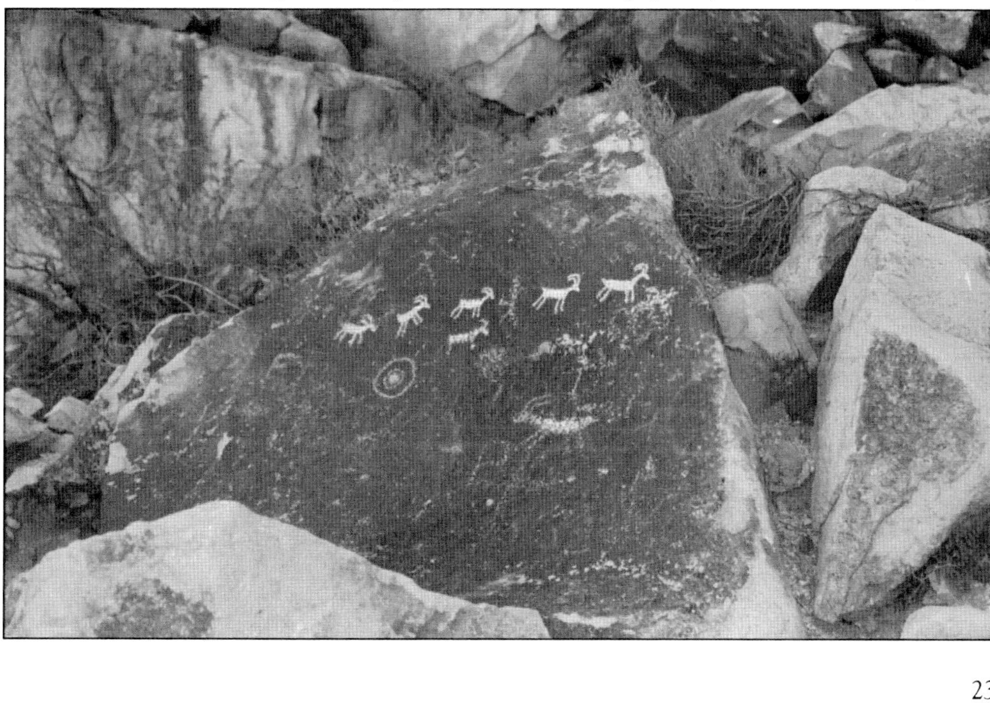

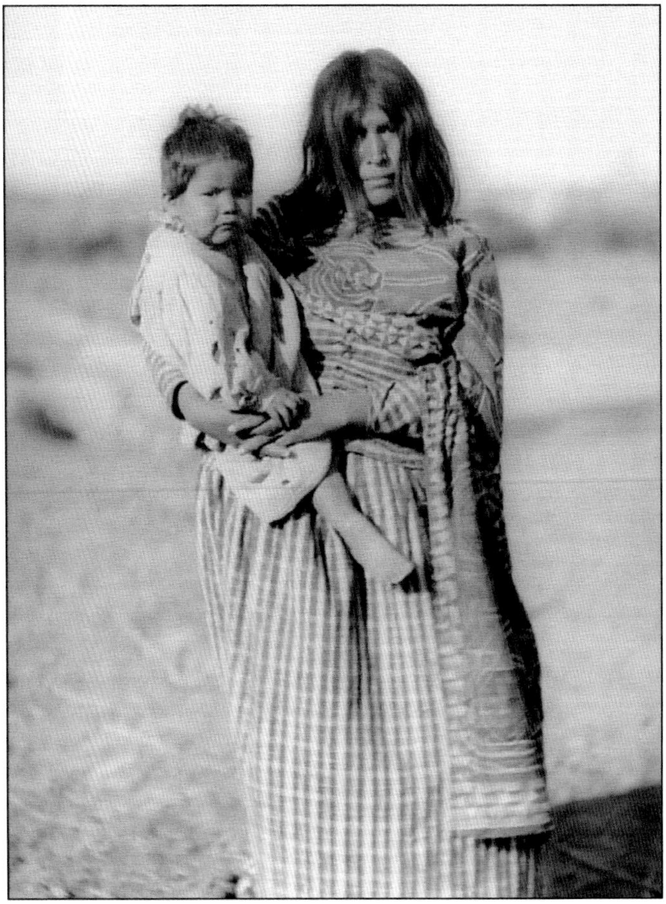

At left is an image of a young mother holding her child around 1871, and below is a postcard, dated 1911, of a Mojave Indian hauling wood. Civilization has truly arrived; the native population is featured as an attraction to tourists. (Both, courtesy of NRM.)

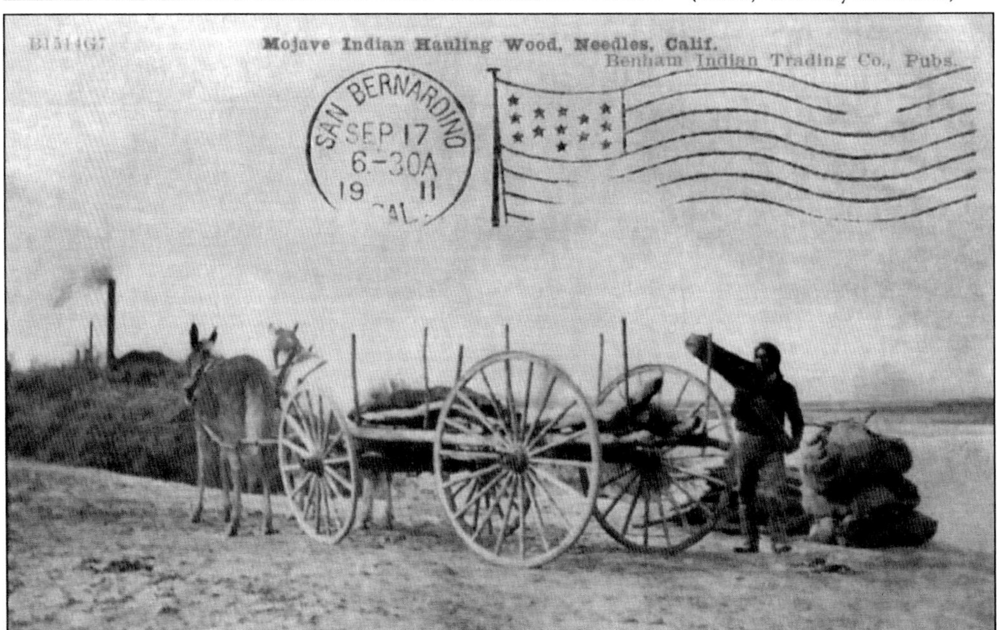

The Mojave Twins geoglyph is located just south of Bullhead City. Geoglyphs, or intaglios, are prehistoric figures created by removing the earth's hard rock face to expose the lighter rock just below the surface. These images can best be appreciated from the air. (Photograph by Marilyn Bridges.)

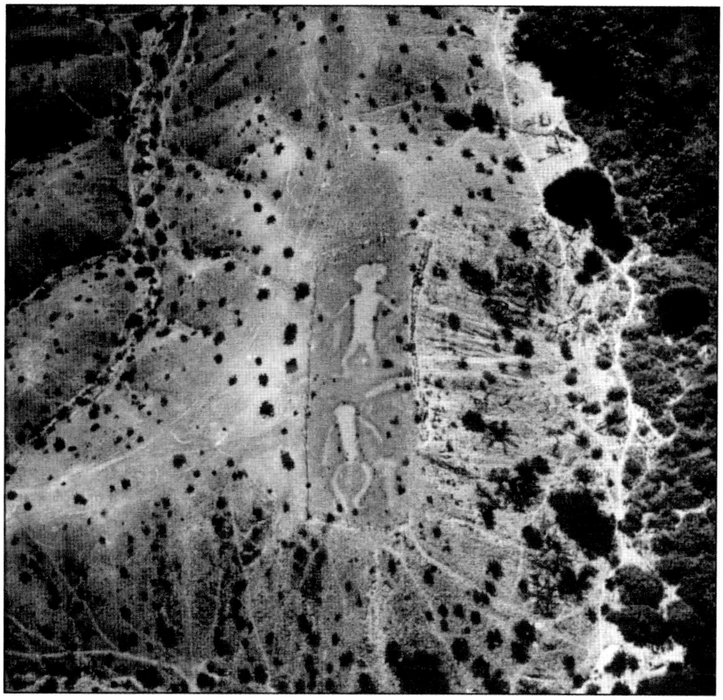

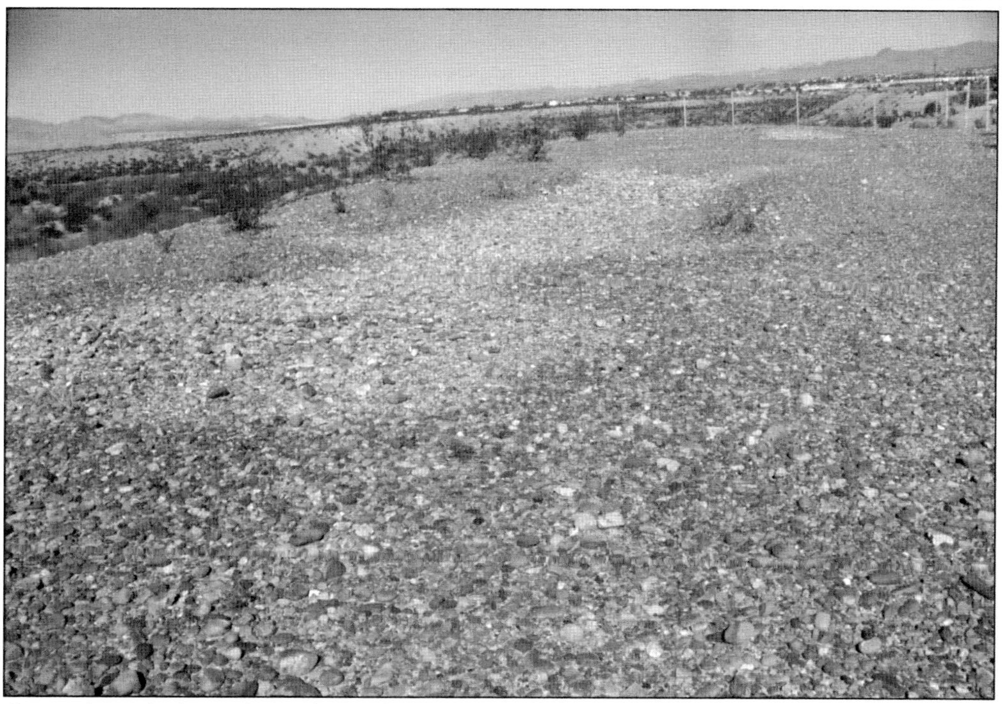

Over 120 geoglyphs are located near the California-Arizona border, from Yuma to Spirit Mountain along the Colorado River. It is no coincidence that they are all found along the 114-degree line of longitude. The Twins, barely discernible from the ground, are said to signify good and evil. The Good Twin, seen here, has a large head with attached limbs and may be their god. The Evil Twin, the smaller of the two figures, has no head and detached arms. (Author's collection.)

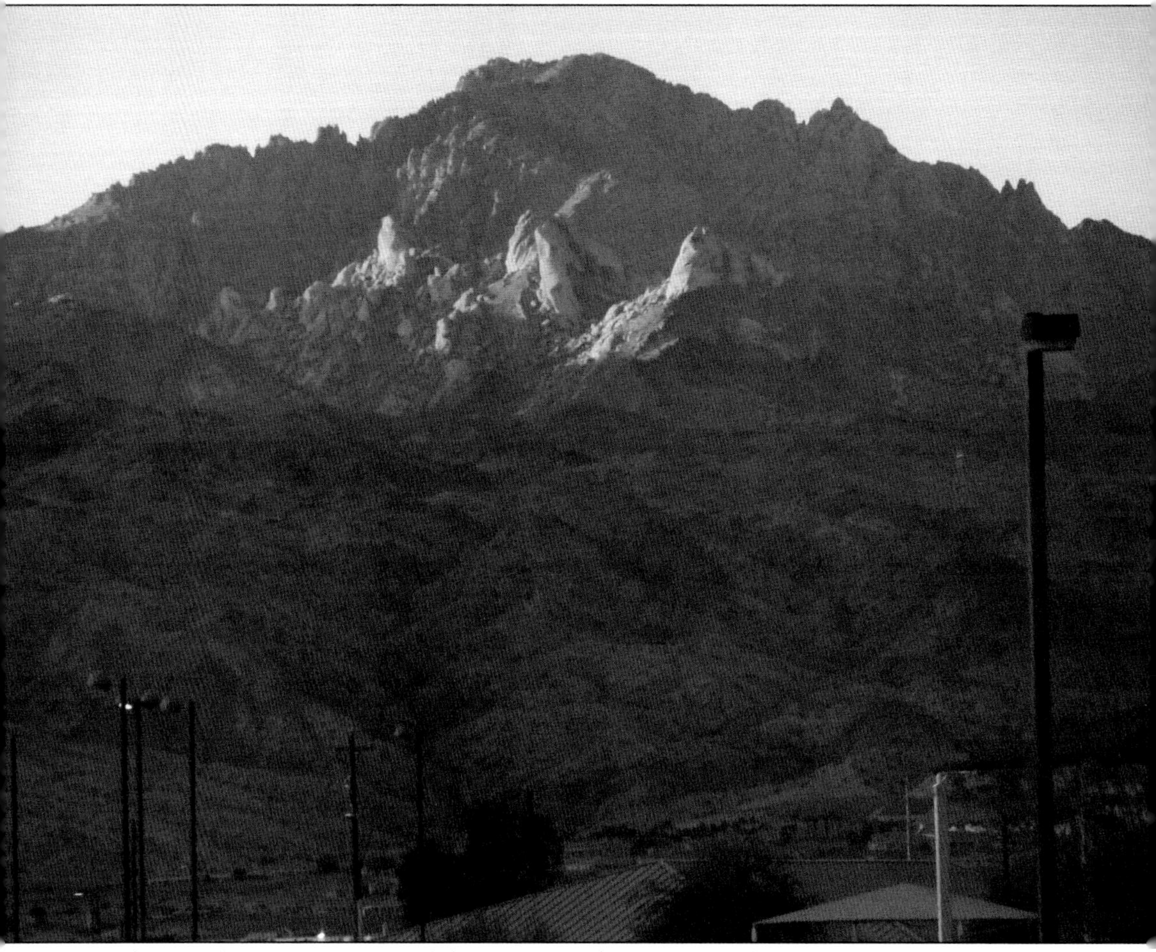

The sacred Spirit Mountain of the Mojave Indians is located at the north end of the Mohave Valley, in the Newberry Mountains. Looming above Bullhead City at 5,642 feet, the mountain is the origin of the Yuman linguistic people from whom the Mojave and Quechan tribes descended. The people emerged from the mountain, the home of Mastambo, their god. Mastambo also gave the Colorado River to the Mojaves and taught them to how to plant crops, catch fish, build fires, and survive in the desert. (Author's collection.)

Two

CROSSROADS
EARLY EXPEDITIONS

Renowned fur trapper Jedediah S. Smith was the first white man known to reach the Mojave people after the explorations of Juan de Onate in 1604 and those of Fr. Francisco Garces in 1776. The Mojaves lived undisturbed for another 50 years after Garces's departure, until the arrival of the fur trappers and traders in 1826. Smith and his men, half-starved by the time they reached the Mojave village, were treated kindly by the tribe. The Mojaves later guided Smith and his party to San Gabriel Mission, following the ancient trail they used to reach the Pacific Coast. When Smith returned a year later, his party was attacked by the Mojaves in retaliation for their poor treatment from another trapping party, under the leadership of Ewing Young. During the onslaught, 10 of his men were killed, and two women were kidnapped. (Courtesy of CRHS.)

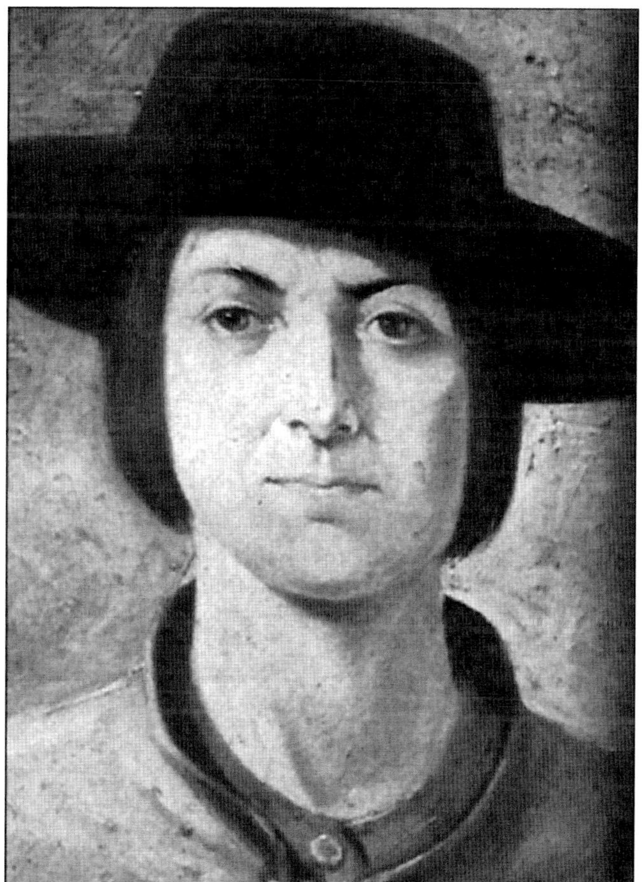

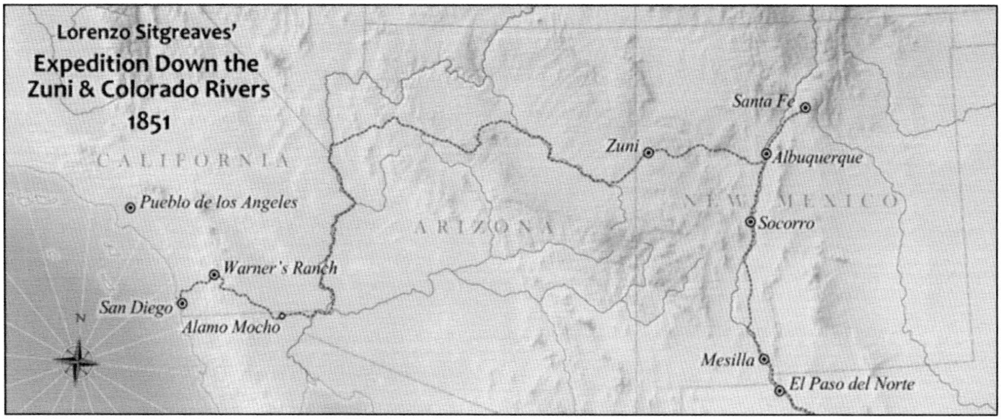

Capt. Lorenzo Sitgreaves of the US Army Corps of Topographical Engineers was sent on an expedition in 1851 to explore the unmapped, newly acquired land in the territories. There was concern that there would be a war with the Mormons in Utah, and the government wanted to know if the waterways were navigable by river steamers. After an arduous trip on the Zuni River and over the Black Mountains, Sitgreaves's party had their first view of the Colorado River. When they finally arrived in the area of present-day Bullhead City, Mojaves visited the party's camp to trade and exchange gifts. After some disagreement, the Indians left and fired arrows into the camp, slightly wounding the expedition's doctor in the leg. Sitgreaves broke camp and his party moved on, but the next day, the Indians attacked. Armed with bows and arrows, a party of braves in war paint killed one soldier who was lagging behind. Sitgreaves's troops fired upon and killed four Mojaves and wounded others before the Indians fell back. Despite a difficult journey, the expedition was a success. The intelligence Sitgreaves was able to deliver led to other expeditions and provided westward-bound settlers with a route for migration. (Both, courtesy of CRHS.)

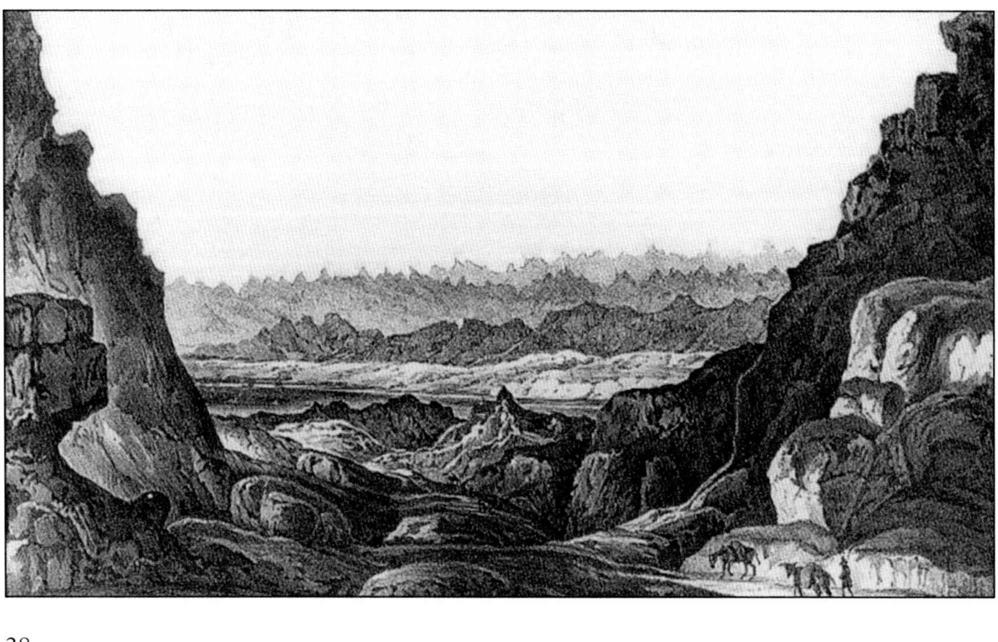

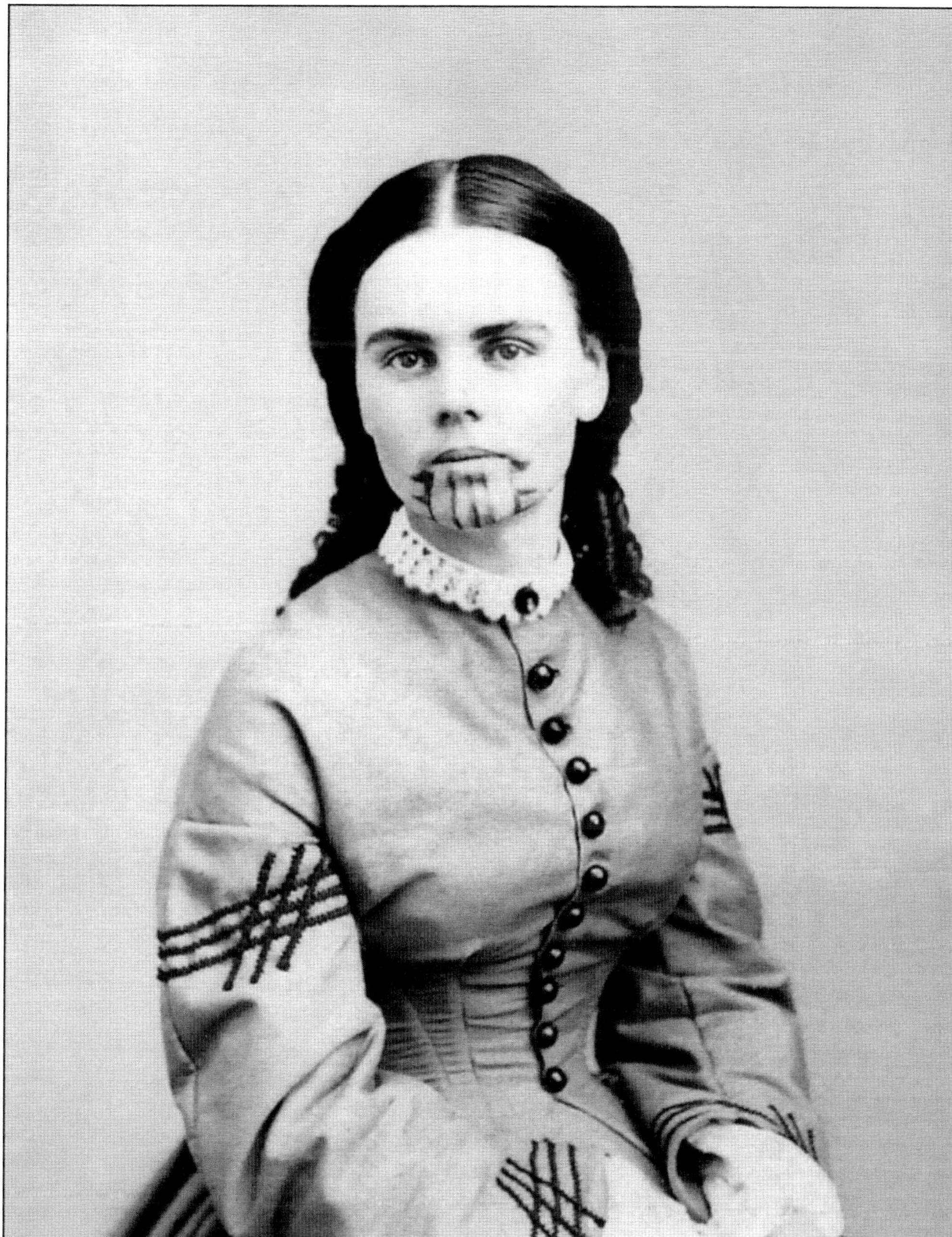

Olive Oatman was 14 when Yavapai Indians kidnapped her and 10-year-old sister Mary Ann as they traveled west across Indian territory in 1851. The rest of the Oatman family was massacred, with the exception of the girls' older brother Lorenzo, who was left for dead. The Yavapais enslaved the girls and treated them cruelly. After two years, they were sold to Chief Cairook of the Mojave tribe. The Mojaves treated them more fairly, but they were still captives. Mary Ann died during a year of famine; Olive was released in 1856 and reunited with her brother. She wrote a book and went on tour around the country, speaking about her experiences with the Indians. (Courtesy of NRM.)

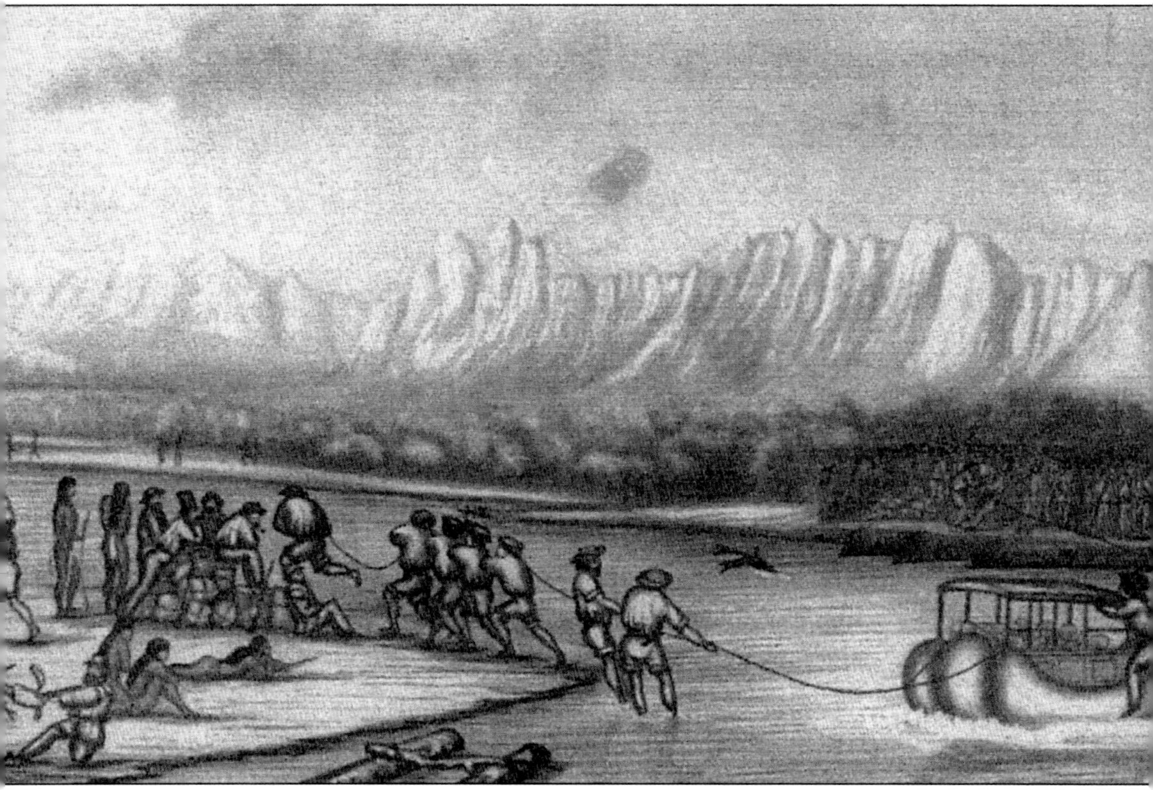

This sketch portrays Lt. Amiel Weeks Whipple's expedition party in February 1854 as they attempt to cross the Colorado River by towing supplies on an inflatable boat with a carretela perched on top. Whipple fared well with the Indians, establishing good relations with them. Ruminating on the Mojaves, Whipple later wrote, "There is no doubt that, before many years pass away, a great change will take place in their country. The advancing tide of emigration will soon take possession of it and, unless the strong arm of the government protects them, the native population will be driven to the mountains or be exterminated." (Courtesy of CRHS.)

Brig. Gen. Edward Fitzgerald Beale (pictured) was commissioned to survey a wagon road along the 35th parallel, from Fort Defiance, New Mexico, to the Colorado River. The survey incorporated an experiment Jefferson Davis, secretary of war, had proposed—the use of camels as pack animals in the desert terrain. Beale felt the camels performed well, but they were not well liked by the soldiers and they scared the horses and mules, so the Army decided to discontinue the experiment. (Courtesy of CRHS.)

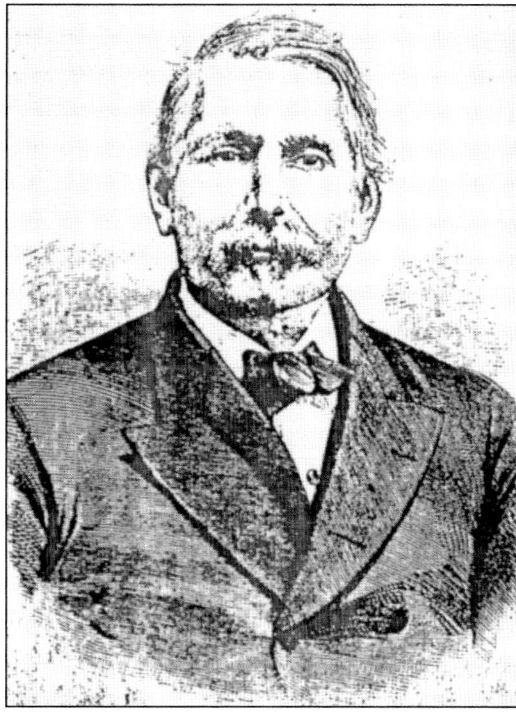

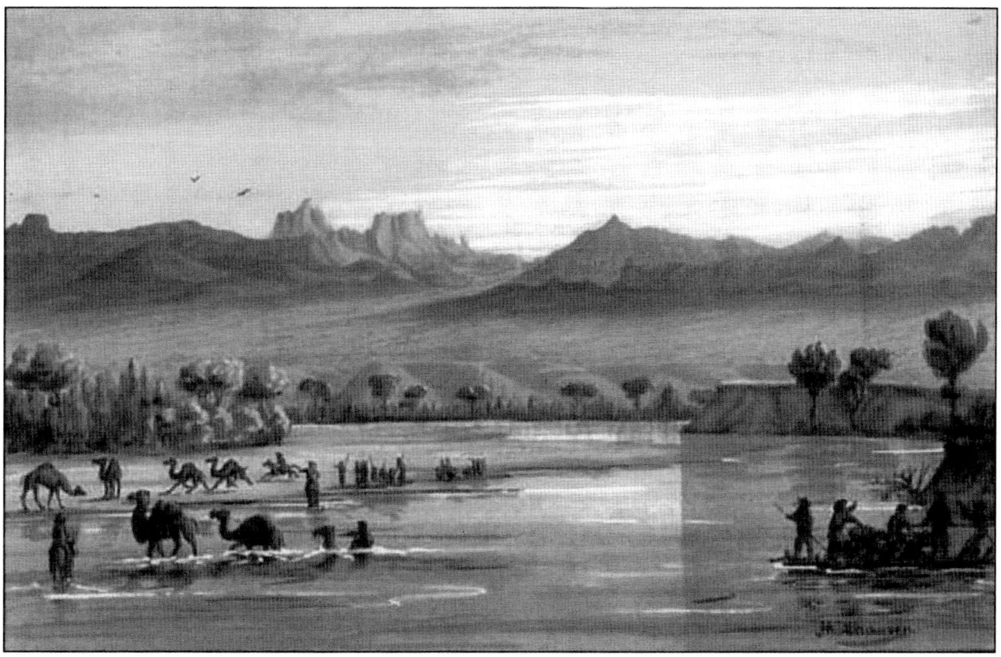

Beale, his survey party, and his camels crossed the Colorado River—at what is now known as Beale's Crossing—with the help of the *General Jesup* in 1858. On board was a Lieutenant White, who wrote the first military report on the navigability of the Colorado River: "Picture the meeting! Soldiers, Indians, horses, mules, camels and a noisy, smoke-belching steamboat! It is not hard to imagine the amazement of the Indians at such a sight." (Sketch by H. Balduin Möllhausen; courtesy of CRHS.)

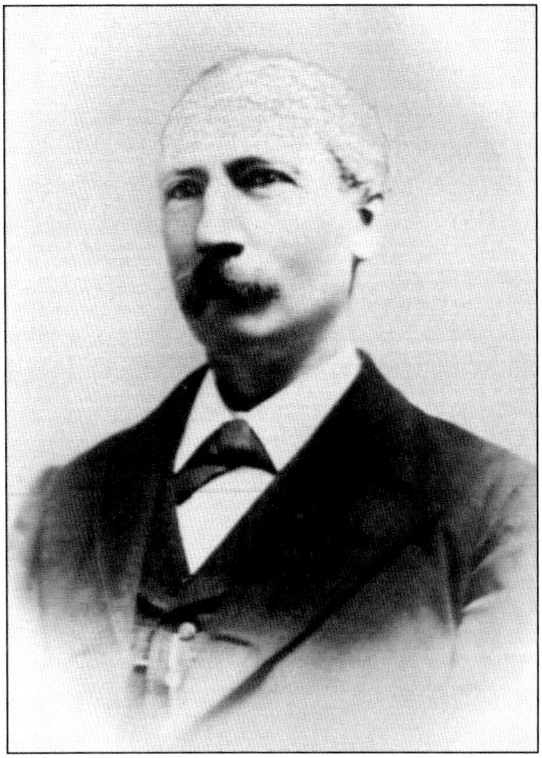

Steamboat navigation of the Colorado River was Capt. George A. Johnson's dream. He brought the *Uncle Sam* into service in 1852, followed by the *General Jesup* in 1854. In 1855, he added the *Colorado* and the *Mohave* steamboats to the fleet. (Courtesy of CRHS.)

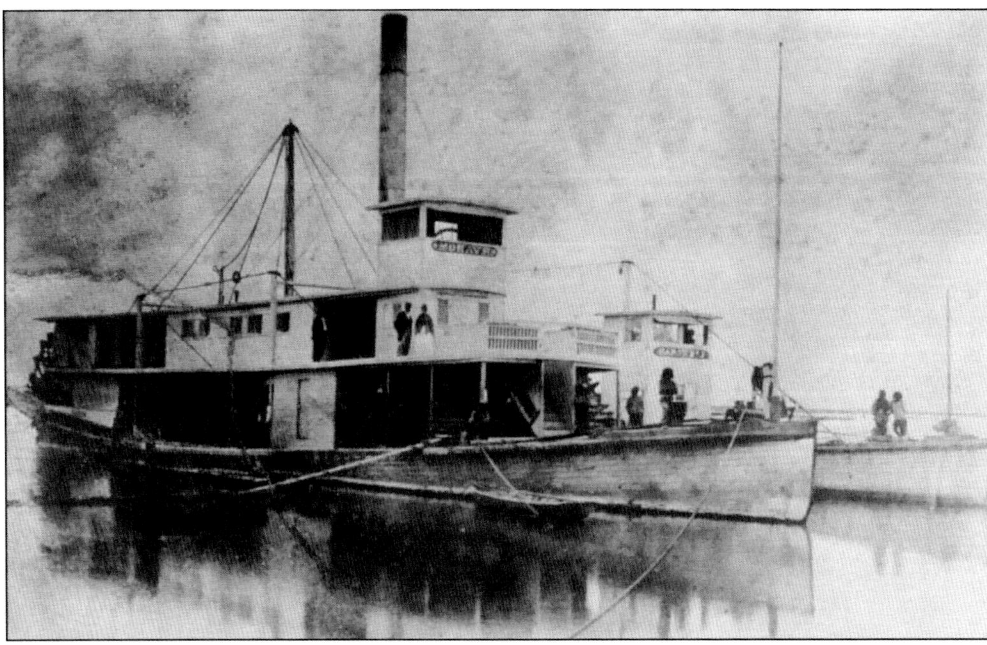

The *Mohave*, like all steamboats of the Colorado River, was more of a workhorse than a pleasure craft. The boats were designed to draw very little water, for the river was often shallow. During its low stages, the Colorado River was once described as "too thick to drink and too thin to plow." Sandbars were crossed with the help of Indian deckhands or by turning the boat around and using the paddle wheel to dig through the mire. (Courtesy of CRHS.)

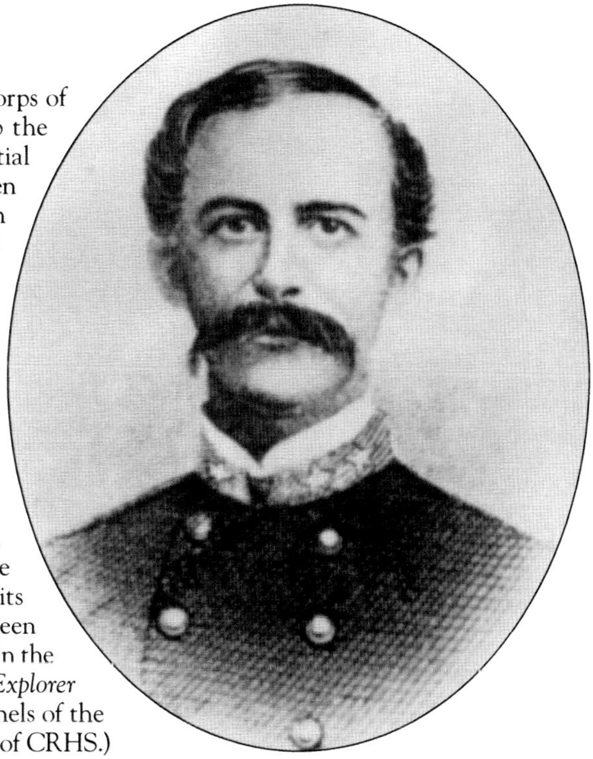

Lt. Joseph C. Ives of the US Army Corps of Topographical Engineers was sent up the Colorado River in 1859 to develop potential supply routes in the event of a war between the government and the Mormon settlements in Utah. Ives commissioned the *Explorer* for the first "official" survey of the Colorado River. The boat was built in Philadelphia, then shipped to the mouth of the Colorado and reassembled. The little steamship made it as far north as Explorer Rock, where it hit a submerged rock and was severely damaged. It was floated downstream to Yuma and converted to a barge to haul garbage. According to one anecdote, this duty was too demeaning for the proud little boat, so one night, it broke its moorings and floated away, never to be seen again. It was listed as sunken vessel, but in the 1920s, a rust-corroded hull rib of the *Explorer* was found in one of the now dry channels of the Colorado River Delta. (Both, courtesy of CRHS.)

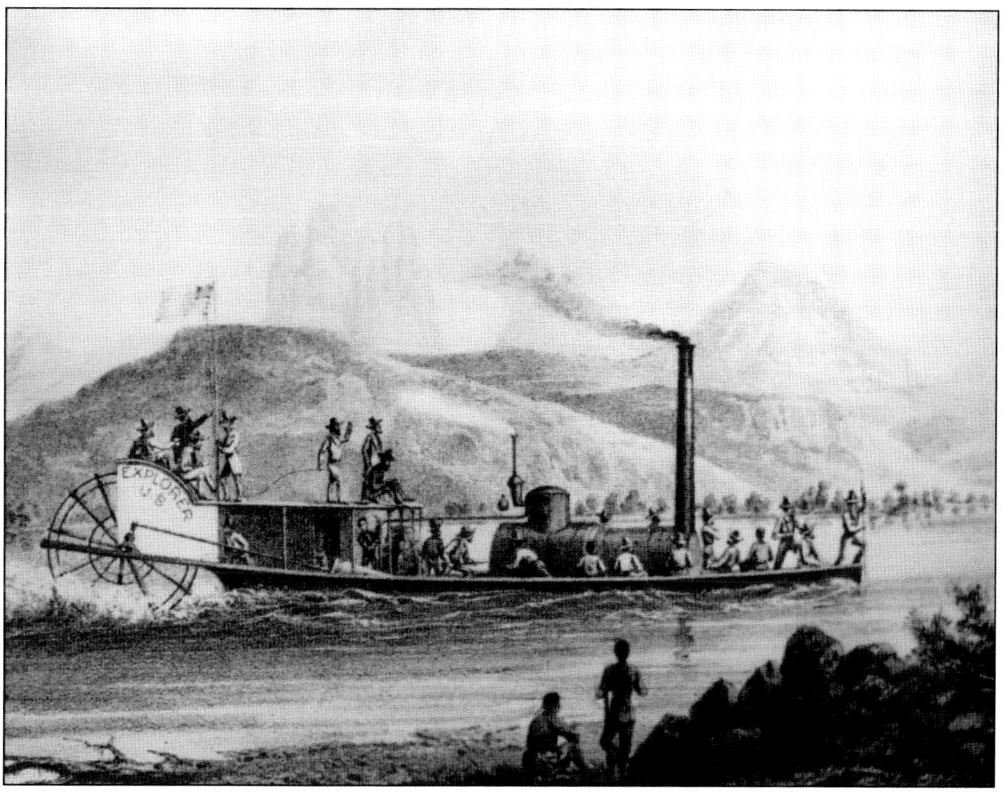

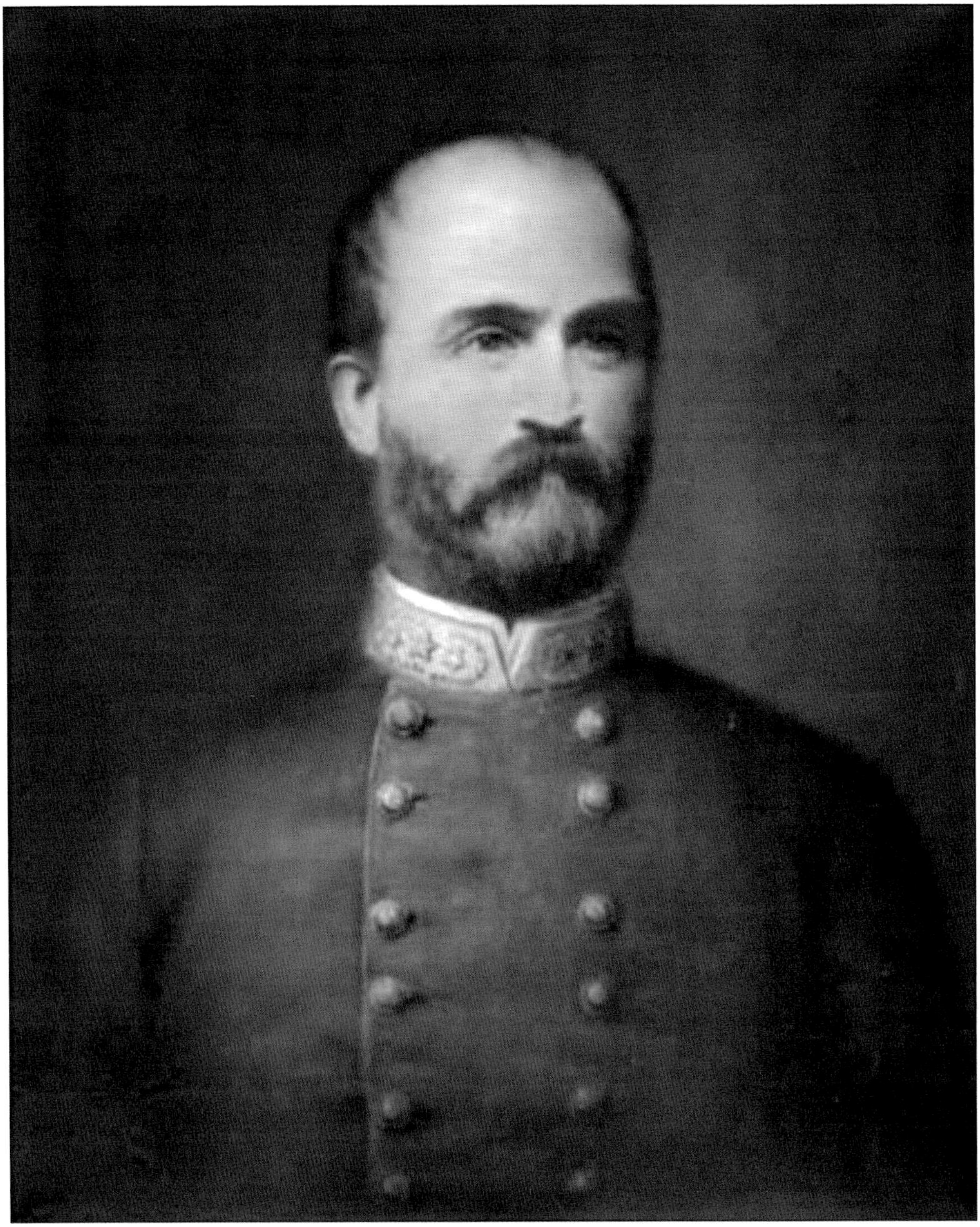

Pictured here is Maj. Gen. Lewis A. Armistead. After members of the Rose-Udell wagon train were massacred in August 1858, an army post was established in April 1859 to protect settlers from the Indians. Its first leader, Maj. William Hoffman of the 6th Infantry, named it Camp Colorado, but when Armistead took command, he renamed it Fort Mohave. Armistead later became a famous Confederate general. (Courtesy of CRHS.)

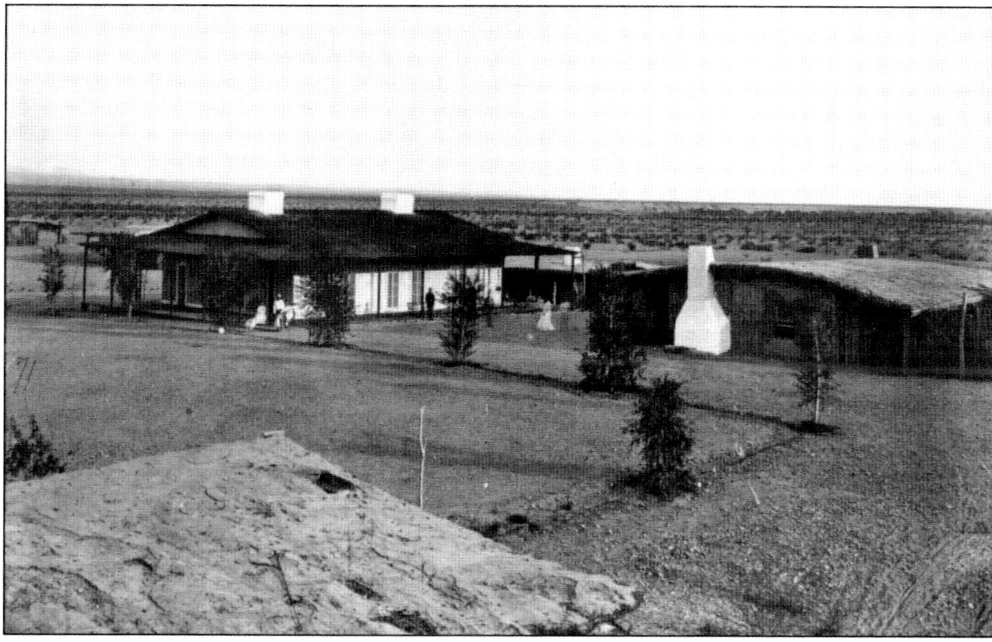

With Fort Mohave established, the government attempted to pacify and control the Mojaves, which strained relations even further. A battle ensued between the Mojaves and Major Armistead's troops, and many Mojaves were killed, including women and children. The chieftains sued for peace after their first and last battle with the Federal Troops, and on August 31, 1859, Armistead reported to his superiors that he had made peace with the Mojaves. These photographs taken at the fort in 1871 show a view to the southwest of the officers' quarters (above) and one to the northeast at the enlisted men's quarters (below). (Both photographs by Timothy H. O'Sullivan; courtesy of Jere Baker, National Archives.)

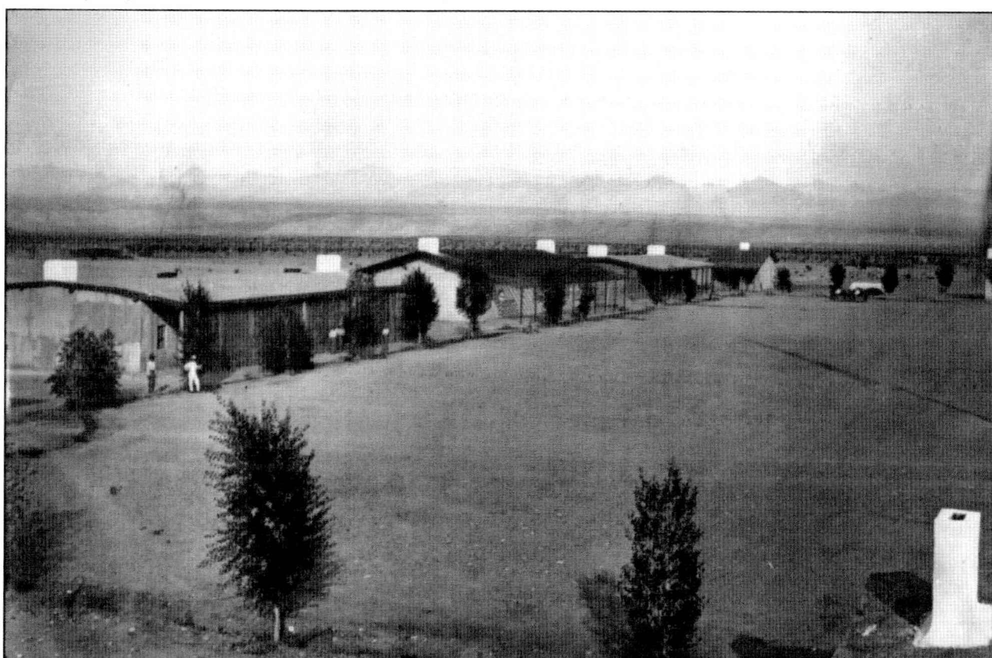

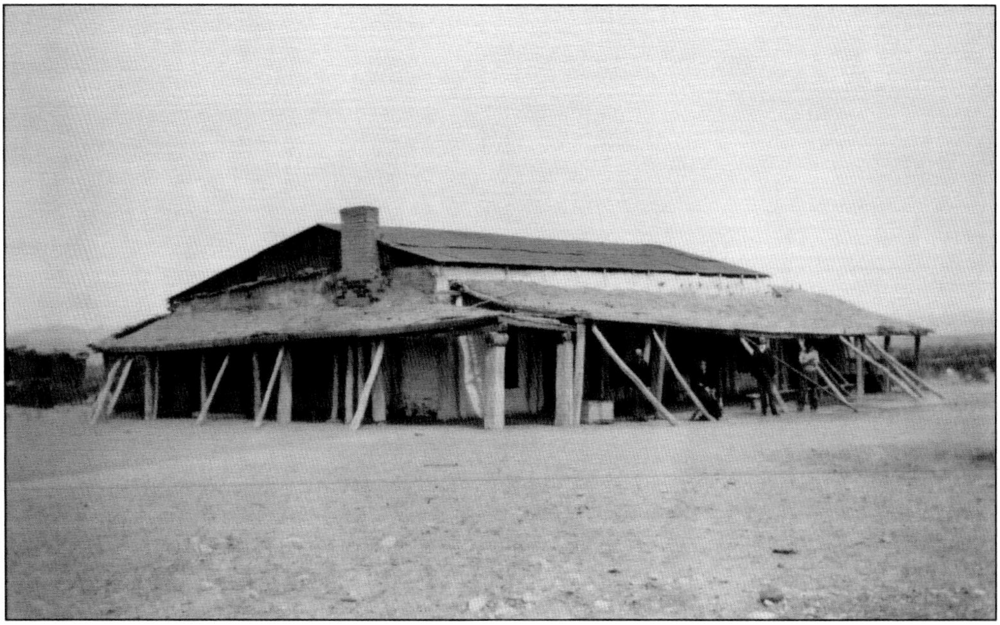

After the establishment of Fort Mohave, the trading post seen above was established to sell supplies to the soldiers and local Indians. In 1863, soldiers stationed at the fort founded Mohave City to serve as a recreational outpost, with thriving saloons and brothels for the soldiers and miners. It also included a post office, blacksmith, and ferry service. In 1864, when the Arizona Territory was first divided into four counties, Mohave City had the honor of being the first county seat, primarily because there was no alternative. The town was so troublesome that, in 1869, Fort Mohave extended its boundaries to include it and thereby condemn it. By the 1890s, all that was left is pictured below, including the trading post, two small houses, several sheds, and a barn. (Above, courtesy of NRM; below, courtesy of NRM, Ron Ross Collection.)

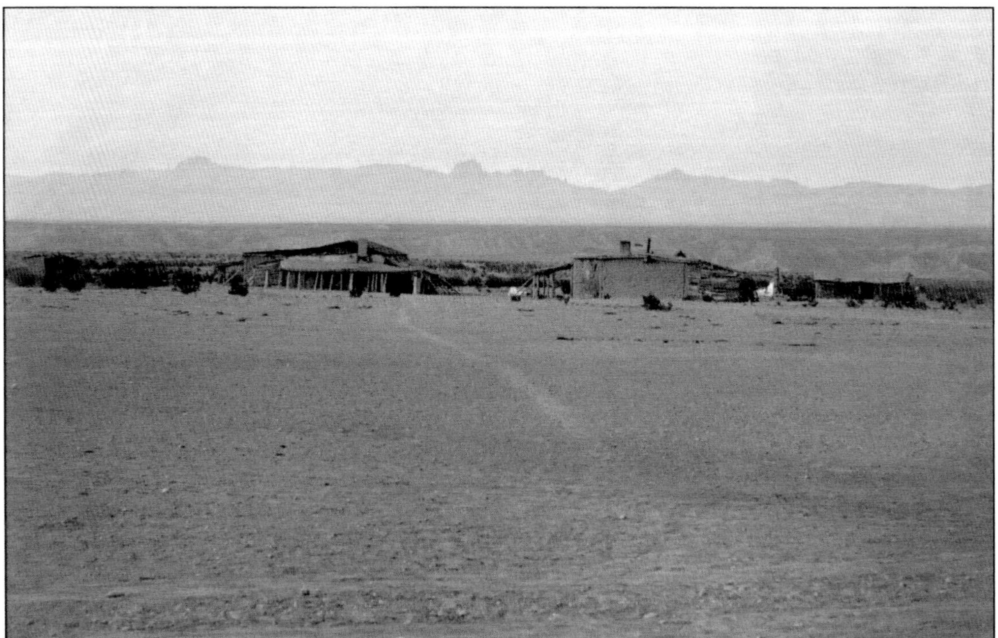

Three

Age of Adventure
The Wild West

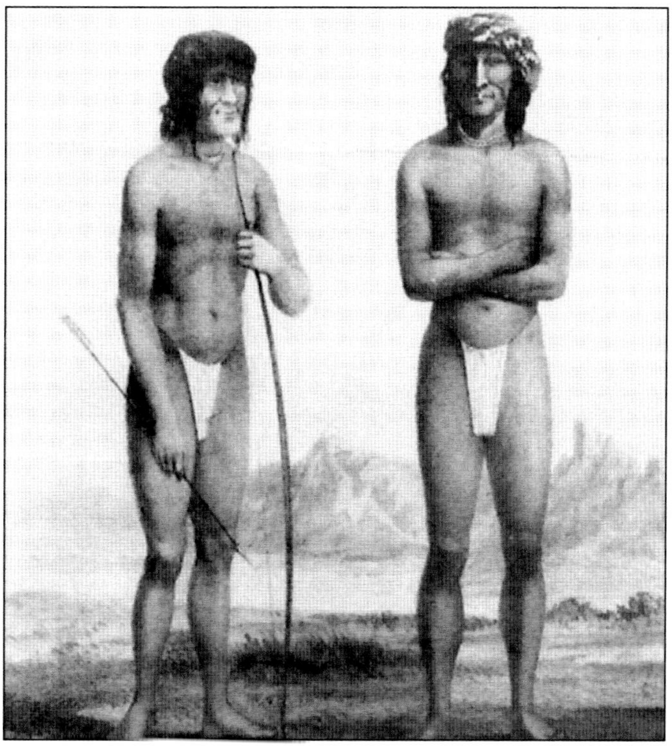

Chief Iretaba and his predecessor, Chief Cairook, were two of the most respected chiefs of the Mojaves in the 19th century. Chief Cairook volunteered to be a hostage when Maj. William Hoffman required the Mojaves to turn over hostages as a show of good faith after the Rose-Udell massacre. Languishing in the Yuma prison, Cairook sacrificed himself by keeping the guards occupied while his braves attempted an escape. Two were killed, but the rest made it back to the tribe. Iretaba, the great chief, traveled to Washington, DC, with adventurer John Moss to meet the "white chief," President Lincoln. They also visited New York and San Francisco. After seeing those mighty cities and the extent of the white man's influence, Iretaba knew the Mojave Nation could never win in a war with the Americans; however, many of his tribesmen refused to believe his "Big Lie" about the outside world. (Courtesy of CRHS.)

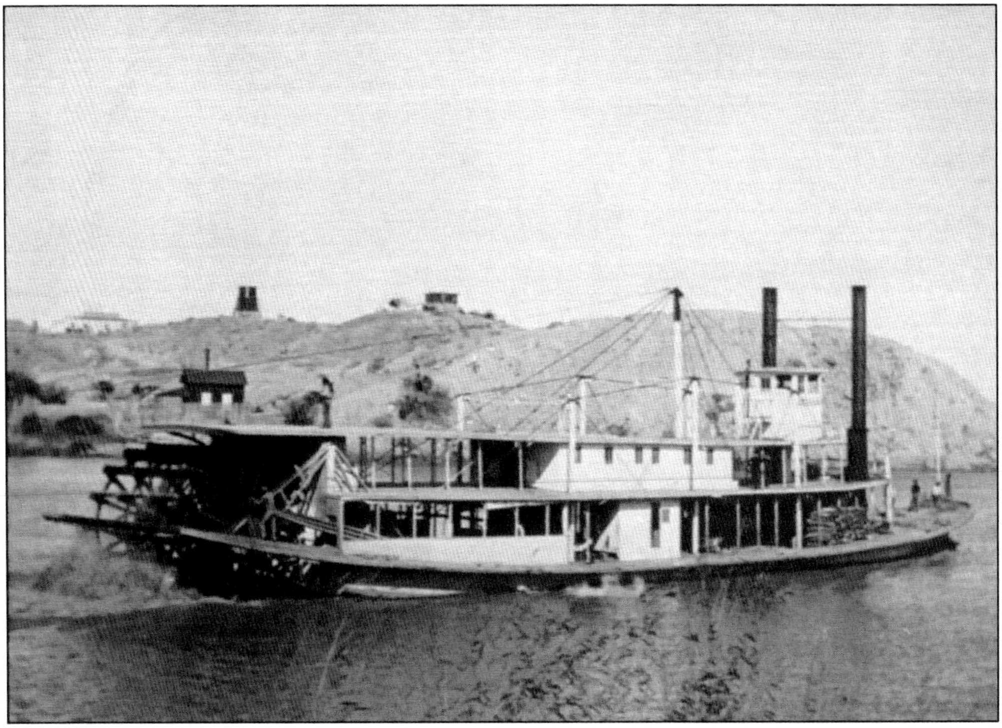

The *Mohave II* was launched in 1876 as a successor to the *Mohave*. At 149.5 feet long, the sternwheeler was the longest steamboat to ever run the river. It was the pride of the fleet for many years and held the distinction of being the only two-stacker on the Colorado. (Courtesy of NRM.)

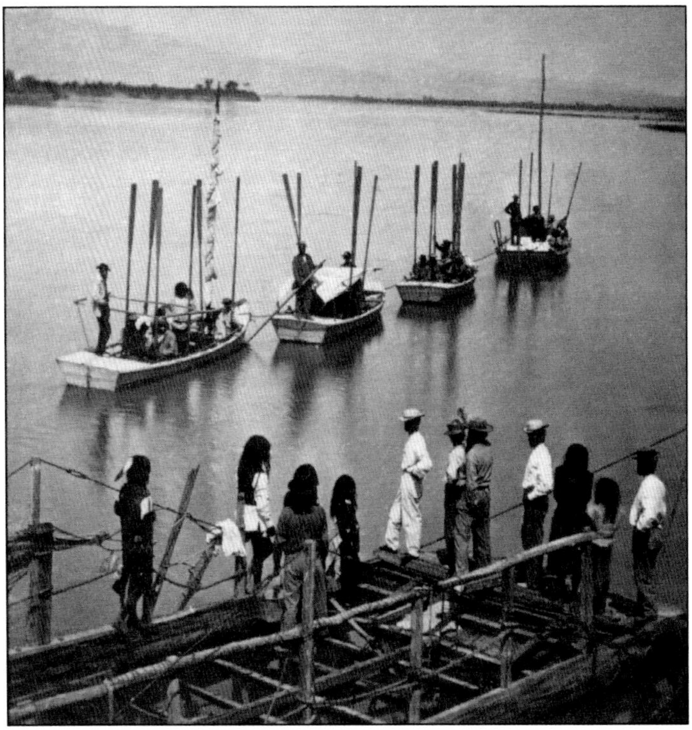

The Fort Mohave–Mohave City ferry located at the point of Beale's Crossing was the first established ferry crossing in Mohave County. It was the main crossing point for traffic on the Mojave Road, which became the Beale Wagon Road. A convoy of small boats, possibly military, is seen here leaving the Fort Mohave dock in this image dated September 15, 1871. The last boat, with flag unfurled, contains a group of Indians, while an assembly of natives watch from the dock as they depart. (Courtesy of NRM, Ron Ross Collection.)

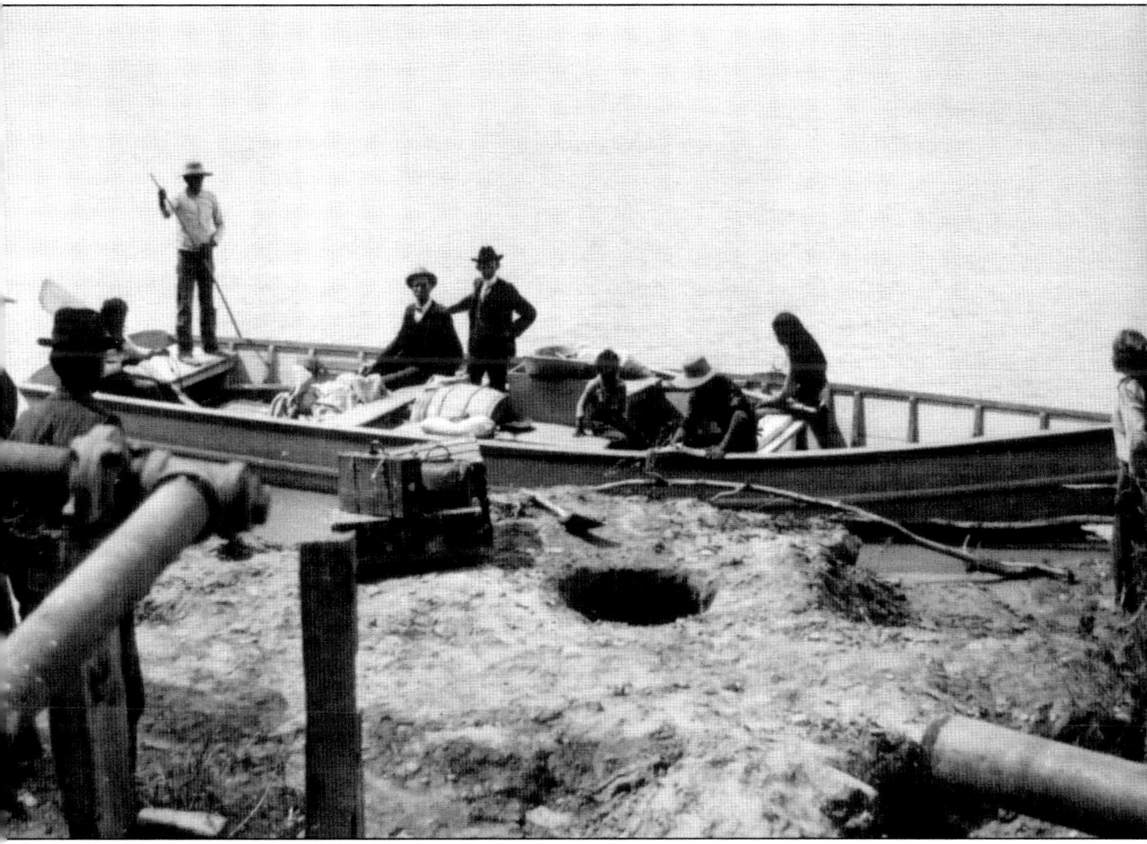

Claude Compton, proprietor of the Mohave Trading Post, is seated at center in his new 30-foot-long, flat-bottomed rowboat used to haul store supplies upriver from Needles. (Courtesy of Jere Baker.)

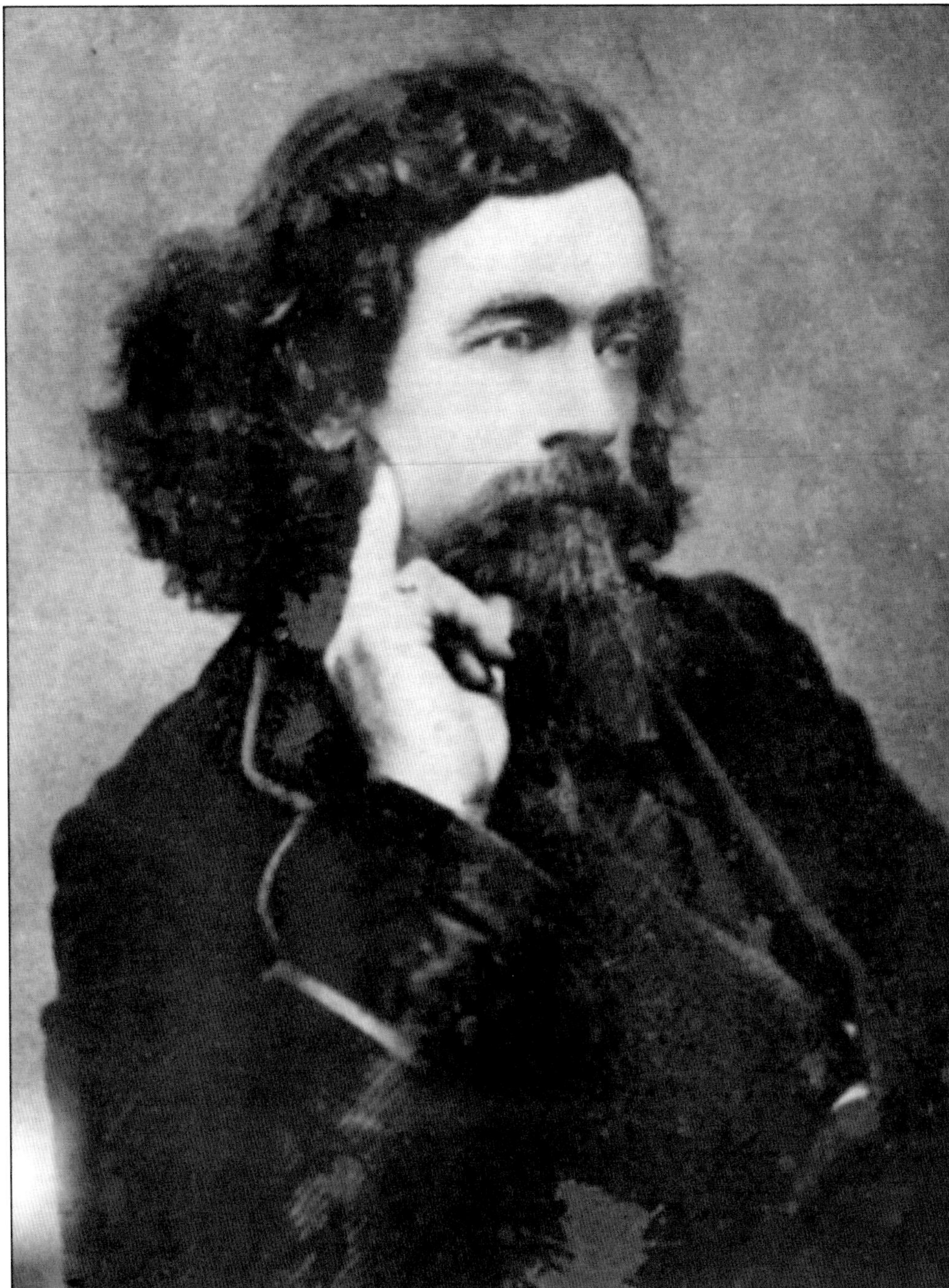

Adventurer, frontiersman, promoter, and businessman John Moss arrived in what would become the Arizona Territory in 1861. A larger-than-life character, Moss had an affinity for the Indians and became instrumental in negotiating between the tribes and the white men. Moss is responsible for the first major discovery of gold in the Mohave Valley. In 1863, he discovered a rich deposit of gold in the Black Mountains from which he established the Moss Mine. He became wealthy by promoting the mine and selling claims but never personally did much actual mining. (Courtesy of CRHS.)

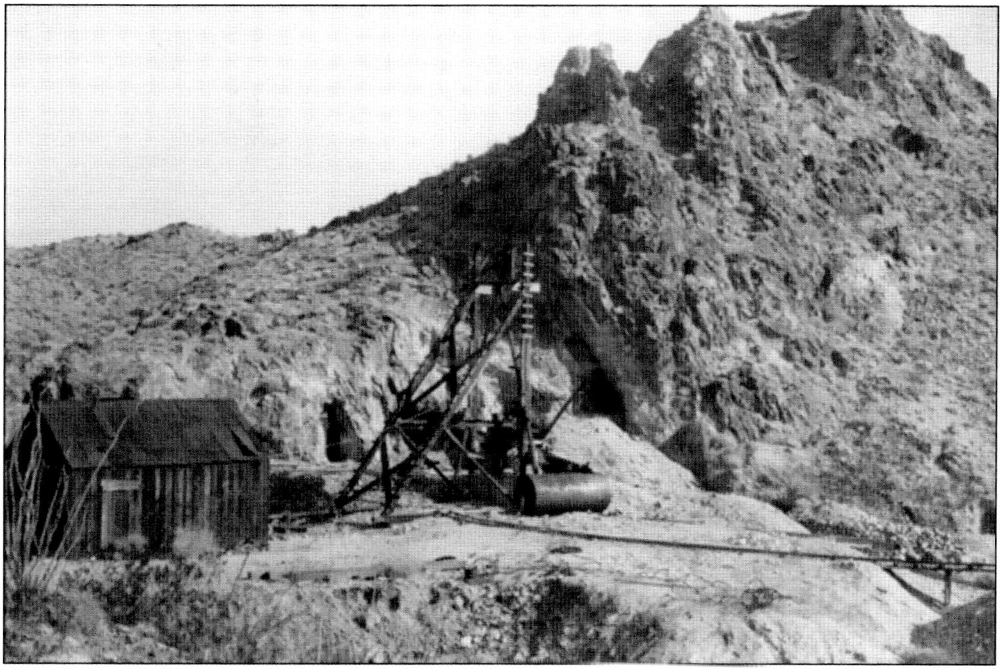

The Moss Mine was in existence from the time of its discovery in 1863 until the 1930s. The Moss property then lay idle until the early 1980s, when a number of mining companies explored the district. It is estimated that the Moss Mine project hosts the largest known gold resource in the state of Arizona. (Courtesy of John Masterson, Golden Vortex Mining.)

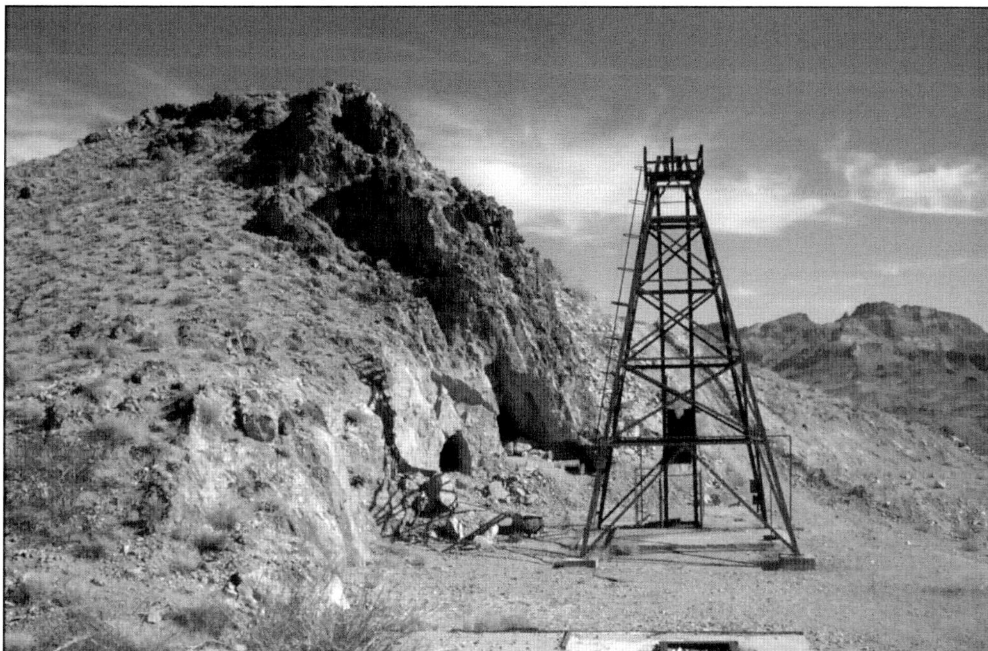

The head frame of the Moss Mine is pictured here in the late 1800s. Located at the entrance to the mine, the head frame (or winding tower) is the most visible feature of a mine shaft. It uses a hoisting mechanism to allow men and materials to enter and exit the mine. (Courtesy of CRHS.)

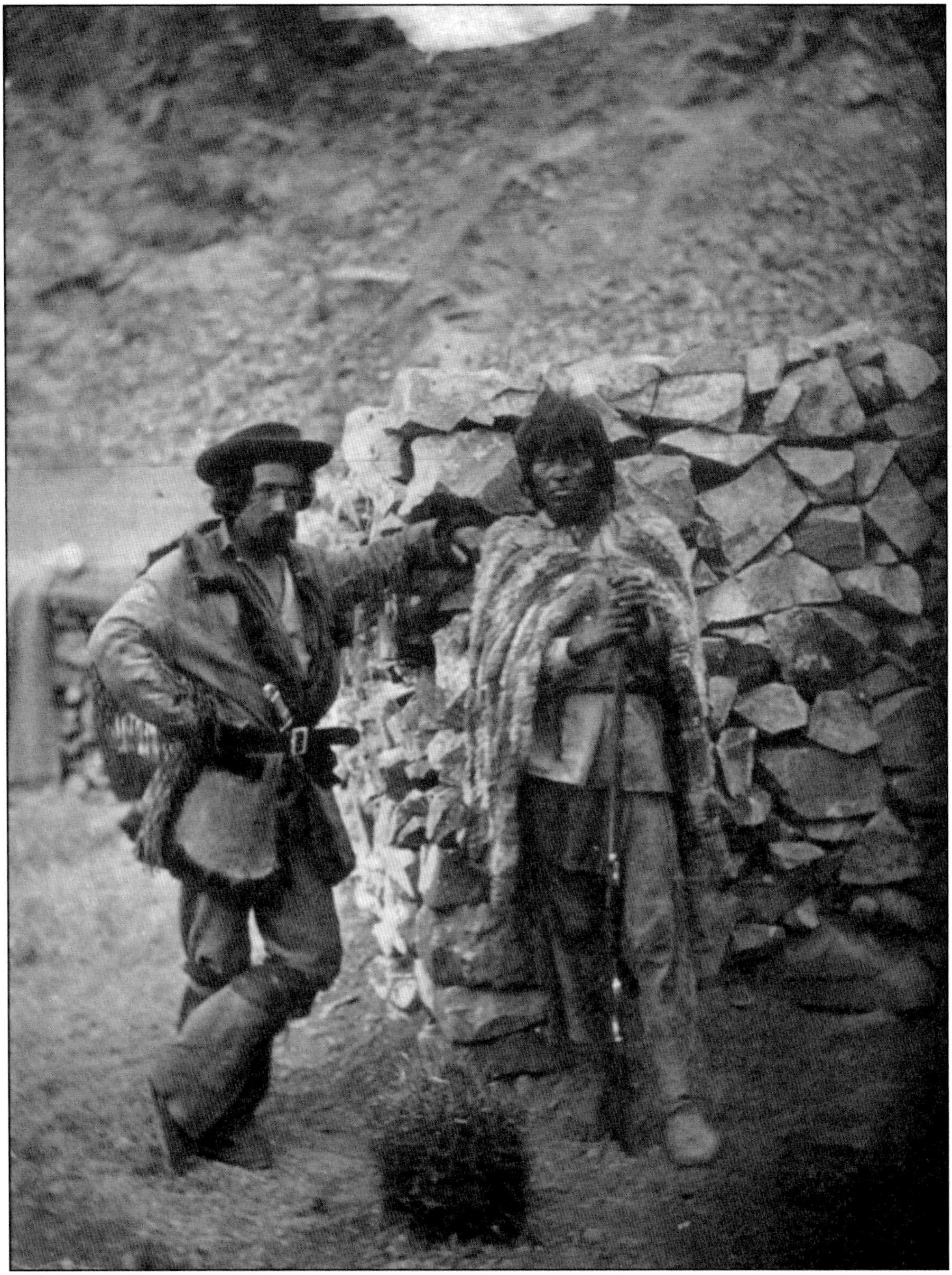

John Moss is pictured with Piute chief Tercherrum around 1863. Popular with the Indians, Moss had great influence over them, eventually getting them to agree not to kill white men. When two Germans were killed by the Indians, he met with the tribes and asked them why they had violated their agreement. They responded that the men were Germans, not white men. Moss then redefined white men to encompass Europeans as well. (Courtesy of CRHS.)

In 1864, entrepreneur William H. Hardy purchased a ferry operation six miles north of Fort Mohave. There, he established a trading post and other improvements to create the town of Hardyville. Generally accepted as the head of navigation on the Colorado River, Hardyville served as an important steamboat port as well as a ferry crossing. From 1867 to 1873, it served as Mohave County's second county seat in the new Arizona Territory, and it had one of the first post offices in the county. Hardy also developed a toll road from Hardyville to Prescott. By 1883, the Atlantic & Pacific Railroad had reached Needles, California, and Hardy moved his ferry there to service the new railway. After his departure, the town fell into disrepair, and by 1903, there was nothing left but the remains of the adobe buildings in what had once been Hardyville. (Both, courtesy of Dan Messersmith.)

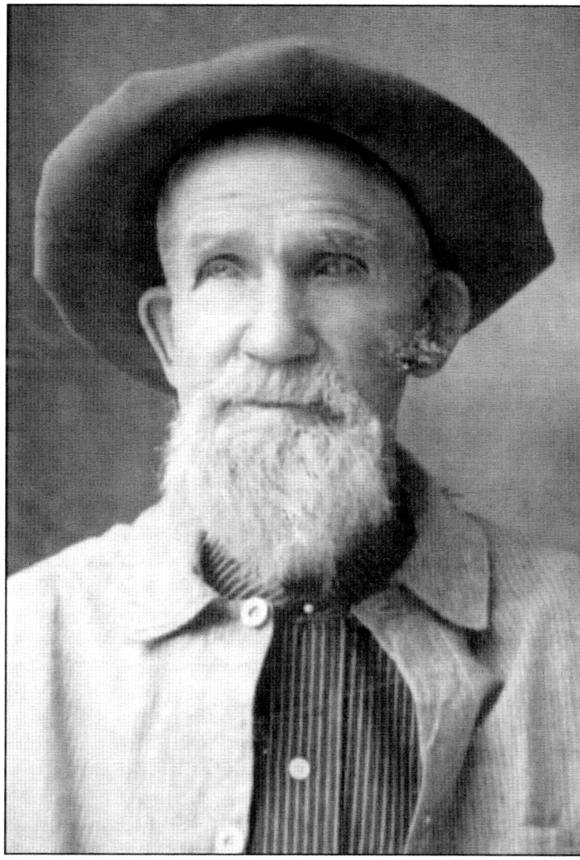

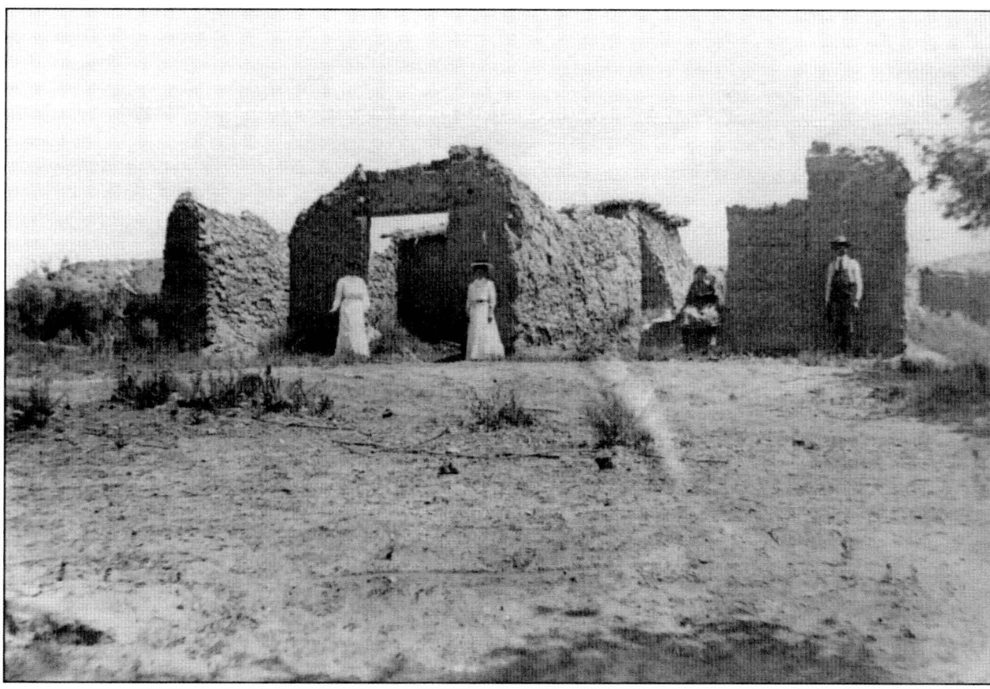

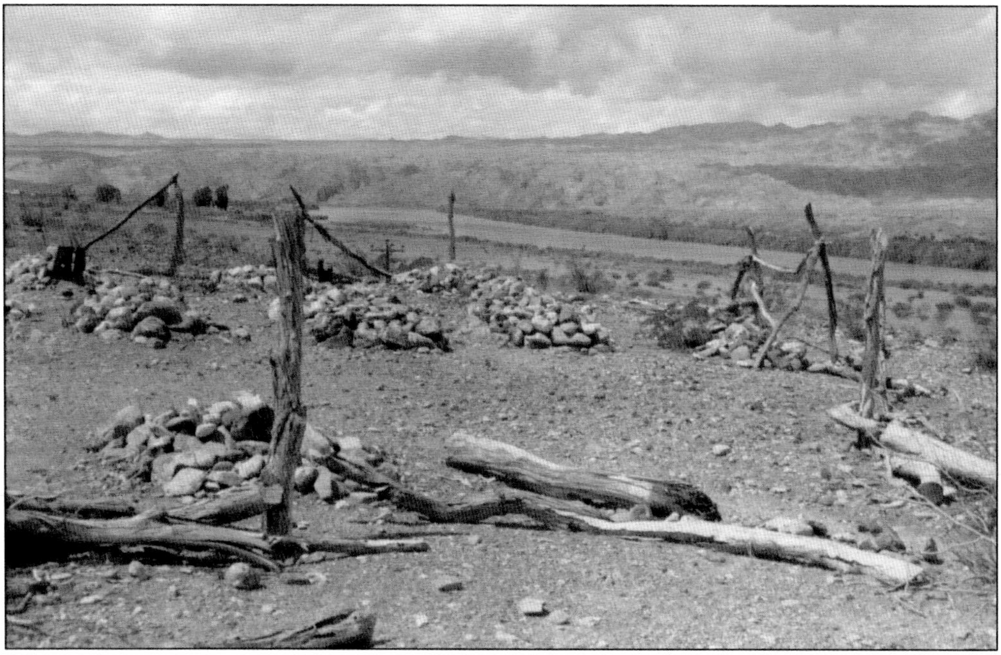

The Hardyville cemetery was built at the highest point of a mesa overlooking the Colorado River where Bullhead City sits today. Rocks were piled on top of the graves to protect them from wild animals and fierce winds. They remained in place until 1976, when a large storm and resulting flood damaged many of the graves. It is said that some of the earth was washed down the embankment onto Highway 95, exposing portions of the remains. As seen below, the cemetery today has fewer graves, but it is fenced and maintained. A strip mall has been built across the highway, obscuring the river view. (Above, courtesy of Dan Messersmith; below, author's collection.)

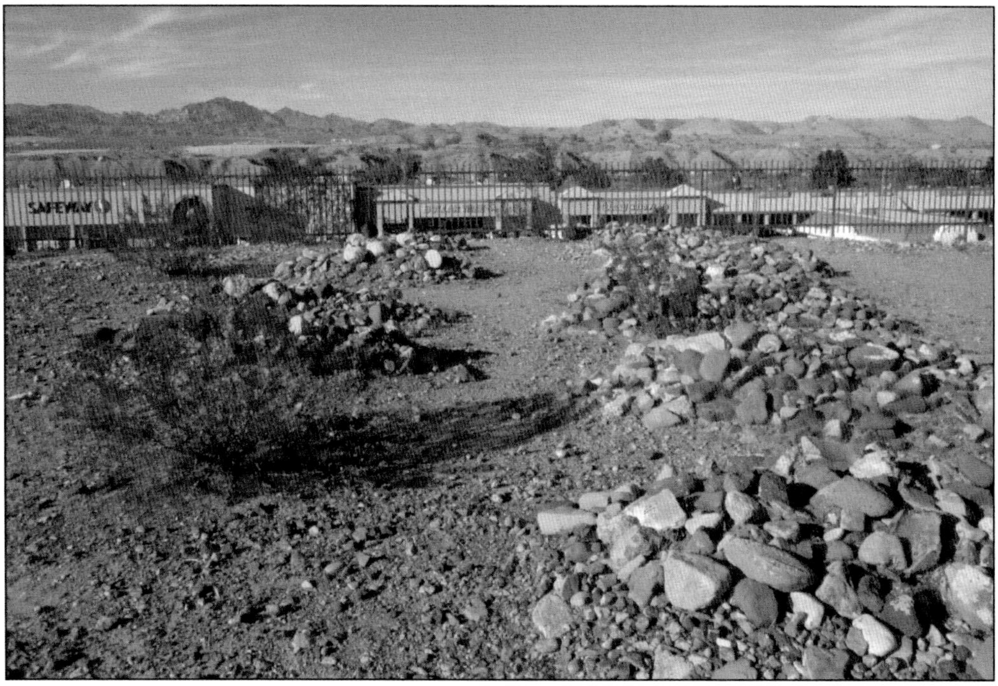

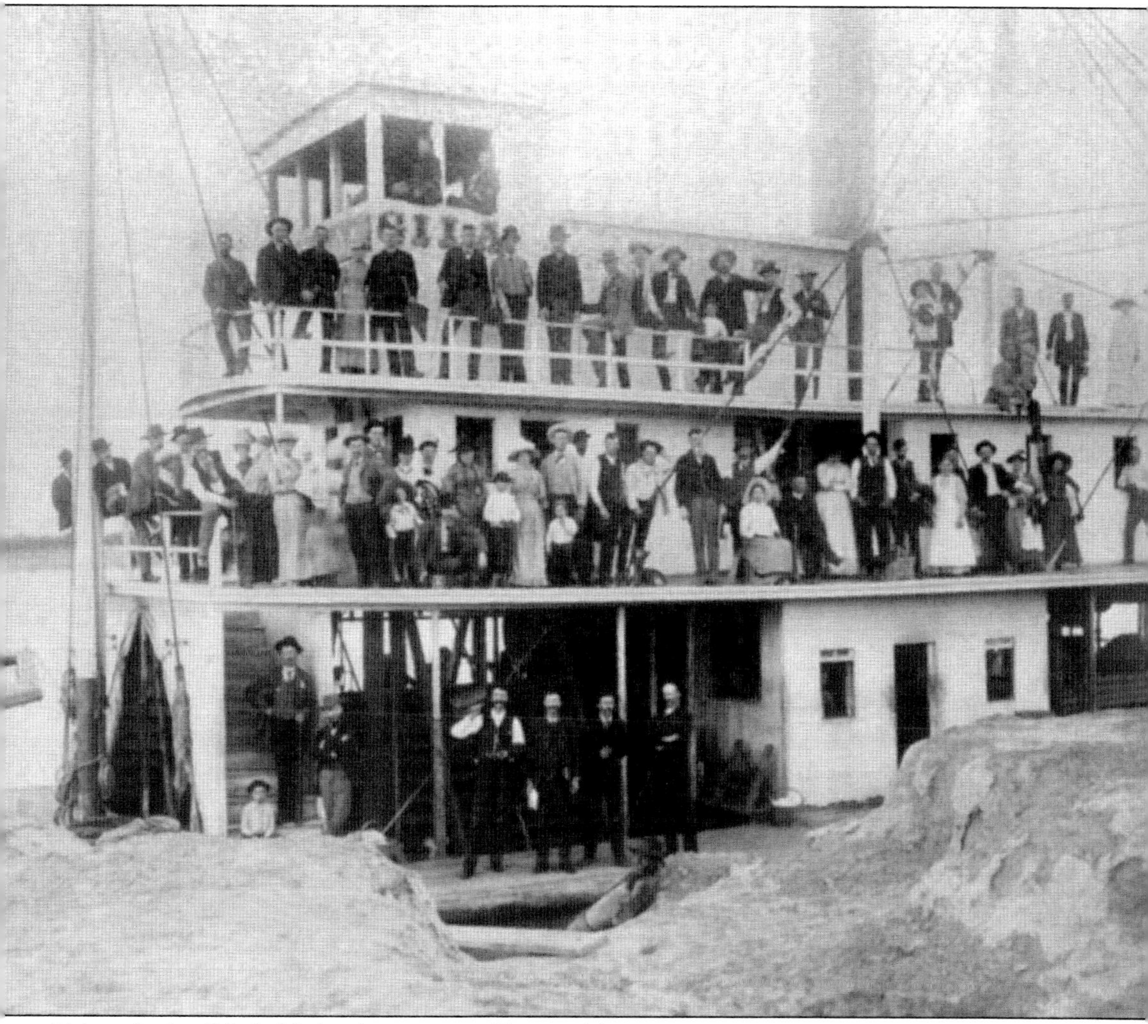

Although the *Gila* held the distinction of being able to carry more cargo tonnage than any other steamboat on the Colorado River, it was being used more and more as an excursion boat. Commanded by Capt. Jack Mellon, the *Gila* transported Martha Summerhayes from Yuma to Fort Mohave in 1874. She made the trip during September, when temperatures ranged from 107 to 122 degrees Fahrenheit. Martha bemoaned the hardships on board: "We had staterooms, but could not remain in them . . . on account of the intense heat. But that dining room was hot! The metal handles on the knives were uncomfortably warm to the touch; and even the wooden arms of the chairs felt as if they were slowly igniting." (Courtesy of NRM.)

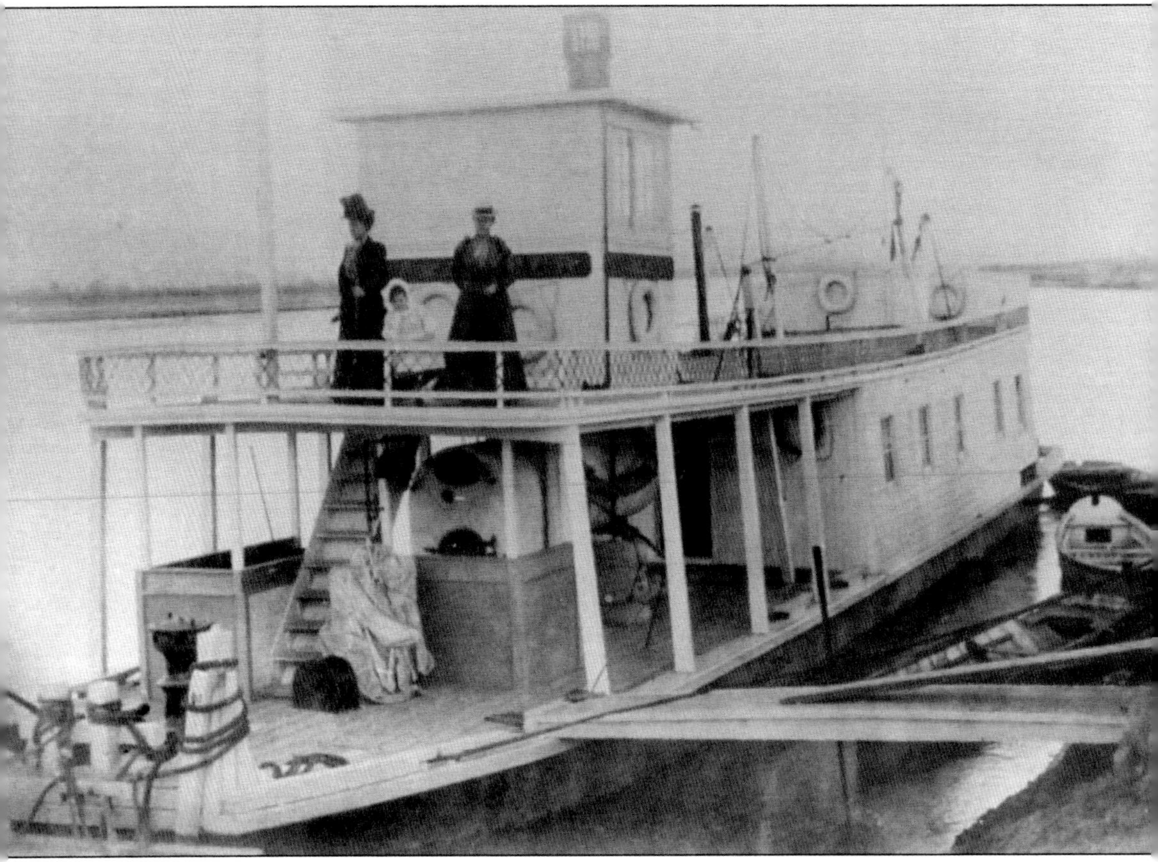

In spite of the discomforts, more people were enjoying jaunts on the river. The *St. Vallier* transports two women and a child in this 1899 photograph. (Courtesy of NRM.)

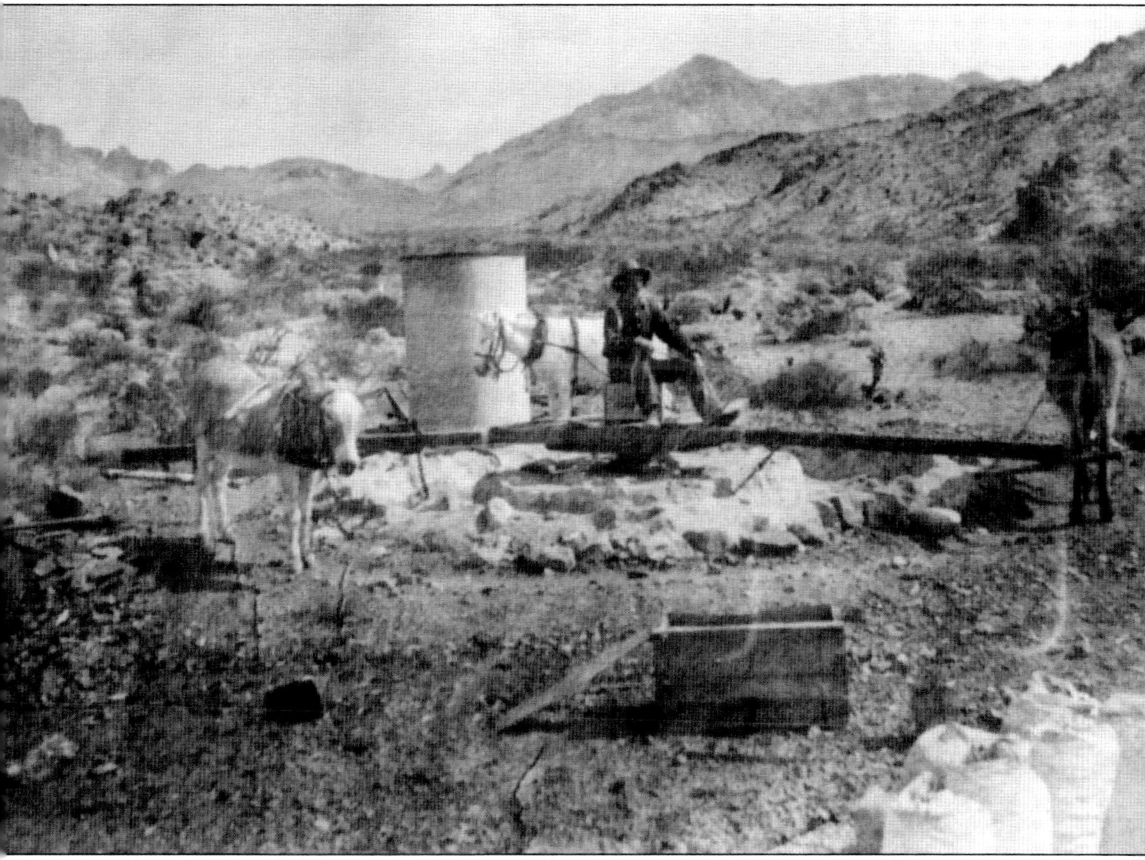

This miner uses an arrastra mill to crush his gold and silver ore. The typical arrastra would have two or more flat stones with a center post connected to a long arm, and a horse or mule would drag the stones around in a circle. Arrastras were suitable for use in small or remote mines, as they were inexpensive and could be built from local materials. (Courtesy of MMHA.)

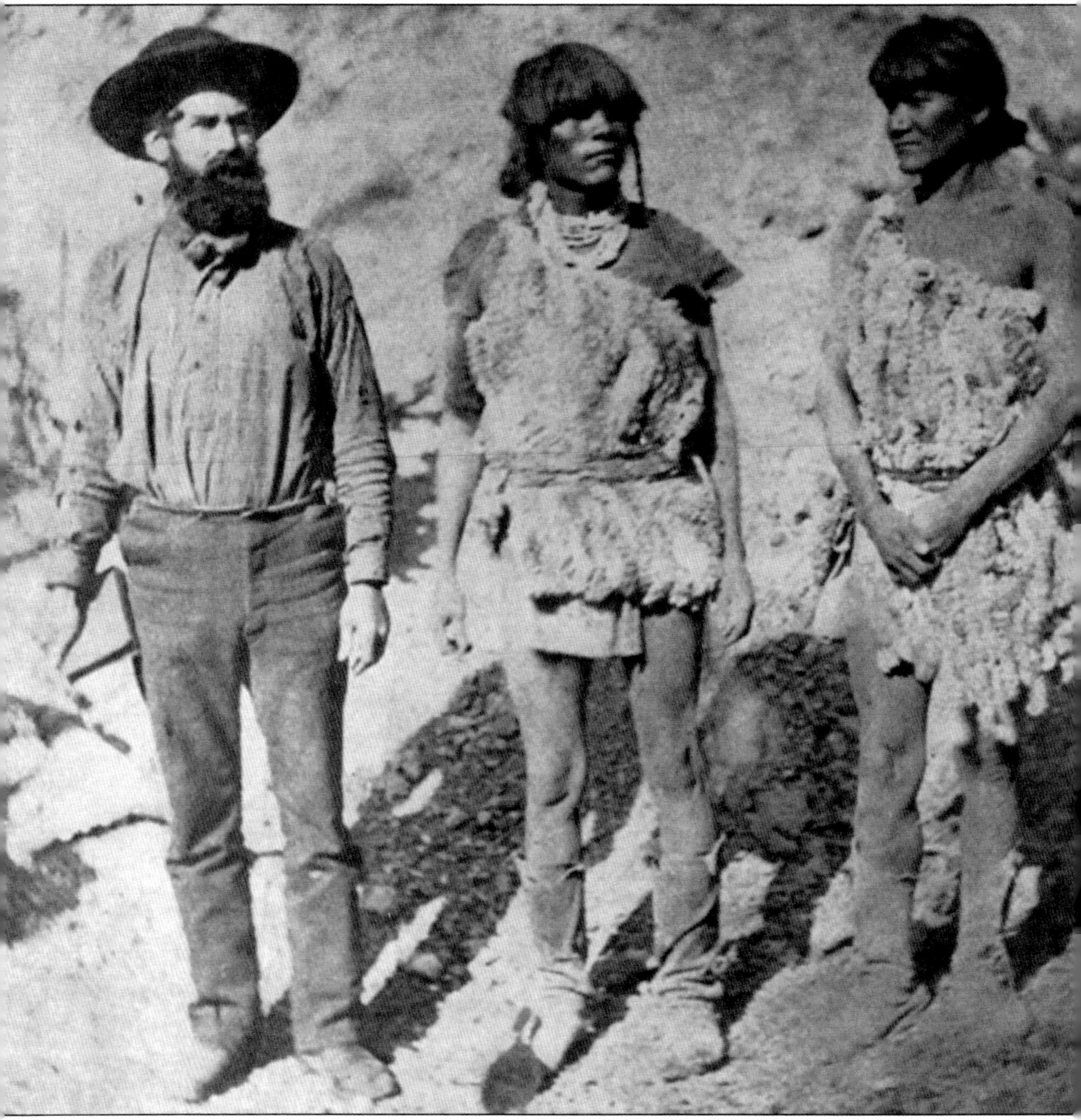

Here, a miner stands with two Indians. With their way of life rapidly changing, many Indians had found employment on the river, with the new railroad, or in the mines by the latter part of the 1800s. (Courtesy of Donna Zurcher.)

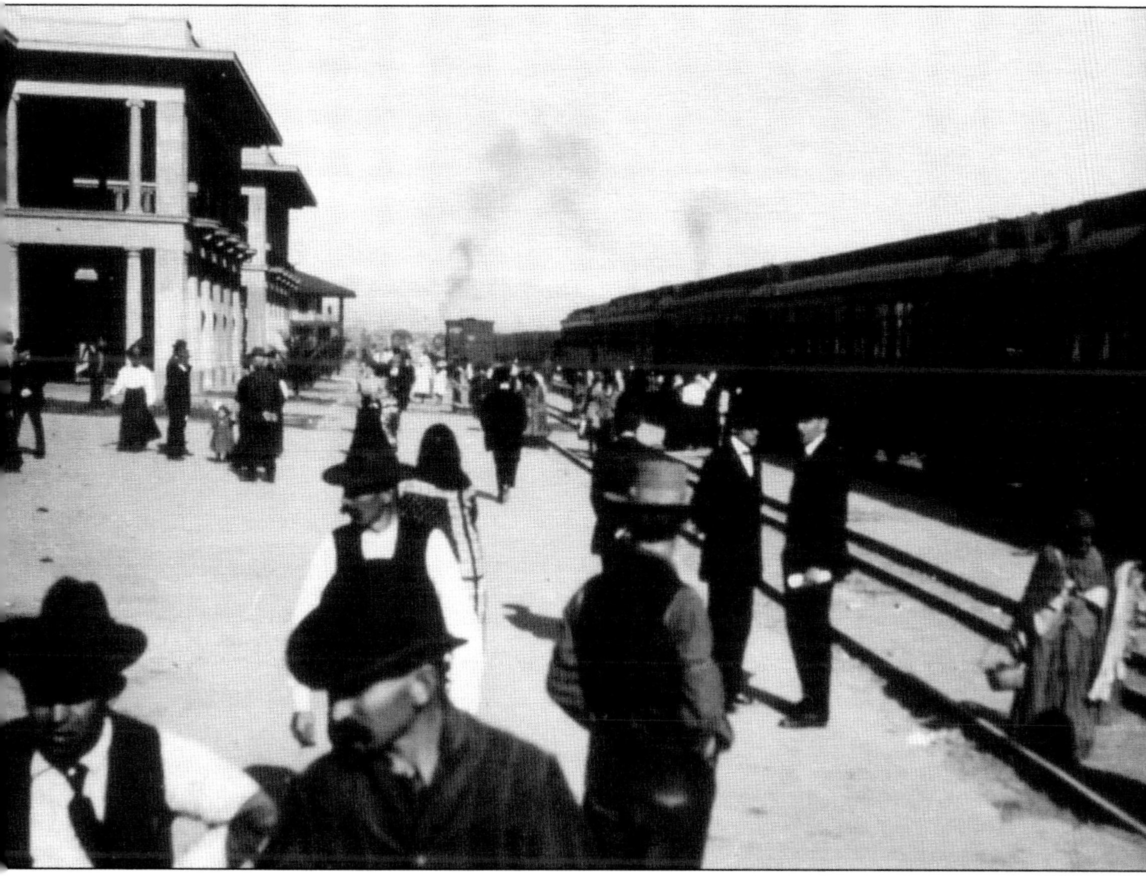

The Southern Pacific Railroad built a rail connection east from Mojave to Needles, California, where it met the Atlantic & Pacific Railroad building west from Albuquerque, New Mexico. The line opened on August 3, 1883. (Courtesy of NRM, Ron Ross Collection.)

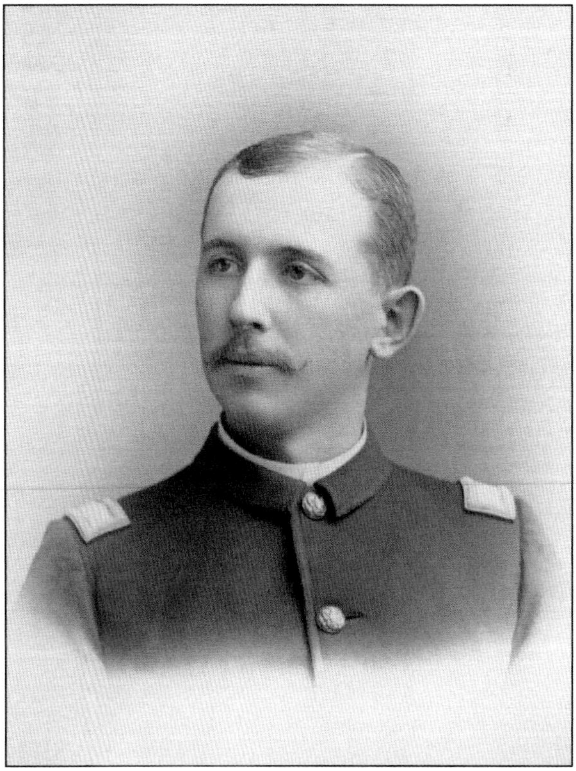

Fort Mohave's last commanding officer was 2nd Lt. Mark L. Hersey. A young lieutenant, Hersey was assigned to the 9th Infantry at the fort after graduating from the US Military Academy at West Point. (Courtesy of Jere Baker, University of Maine Special Collections.)

From left to right, Lt. Ambrose I. Moriarty, an unidentified Mojave Indian, post surgeon Dr. Thomas B. Davis, and Lt. Mark L. Hersey pose in front of the officers' quarters of Fort Mohave on March 23, 1890. Hersey supervised the transition from army garrison to an Indian boarding school during the summer and early fall of 1890. (Photograph by Robert Brewster Stanton; courtesy of Jere Baker, National Archives.)

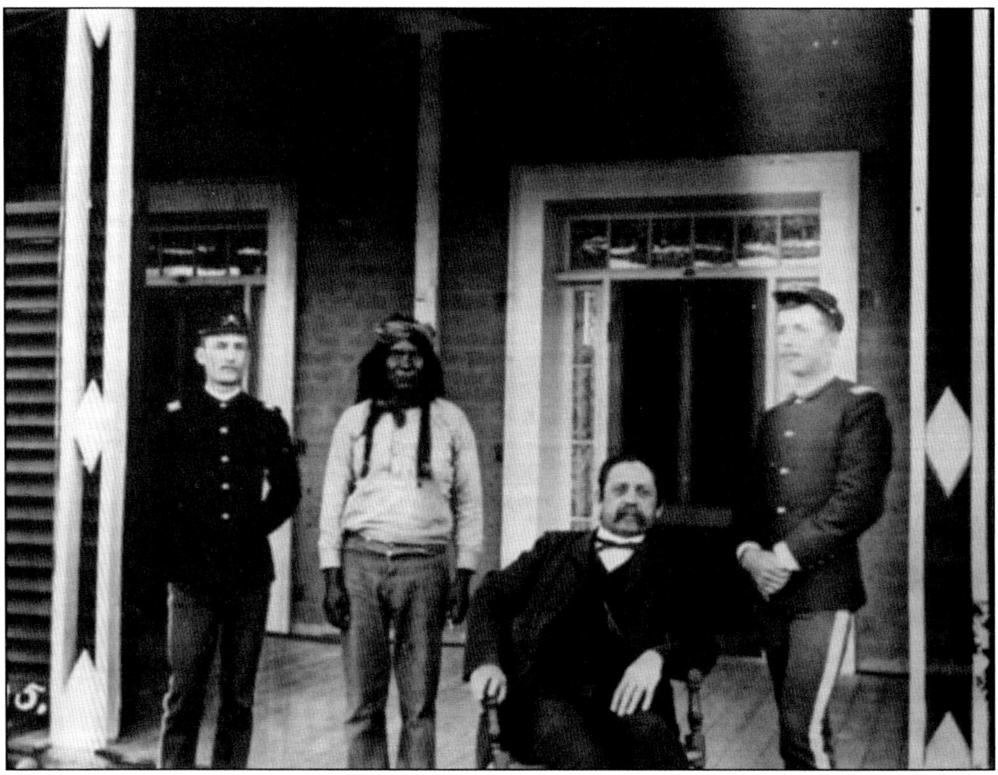

Four

Indian School
A Time of Change

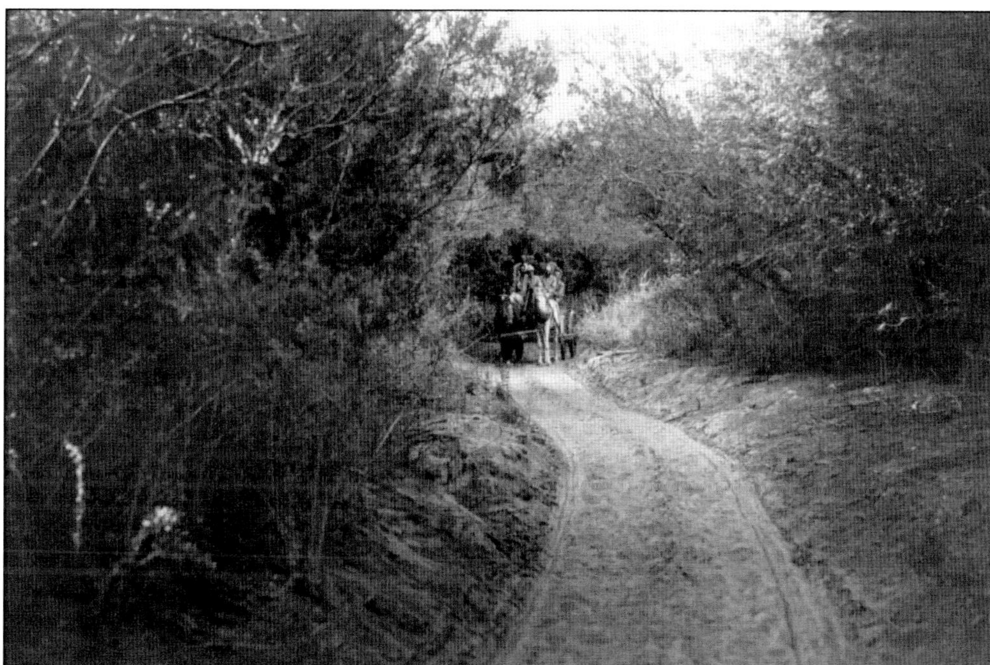

The mail road that connected Needles with the Indian school, the former Fort Mohave, passed through the Colorado River bottomland, thick with arrowweed and willow trees. (Courtesy of NRM, Ron Ross Collection.)

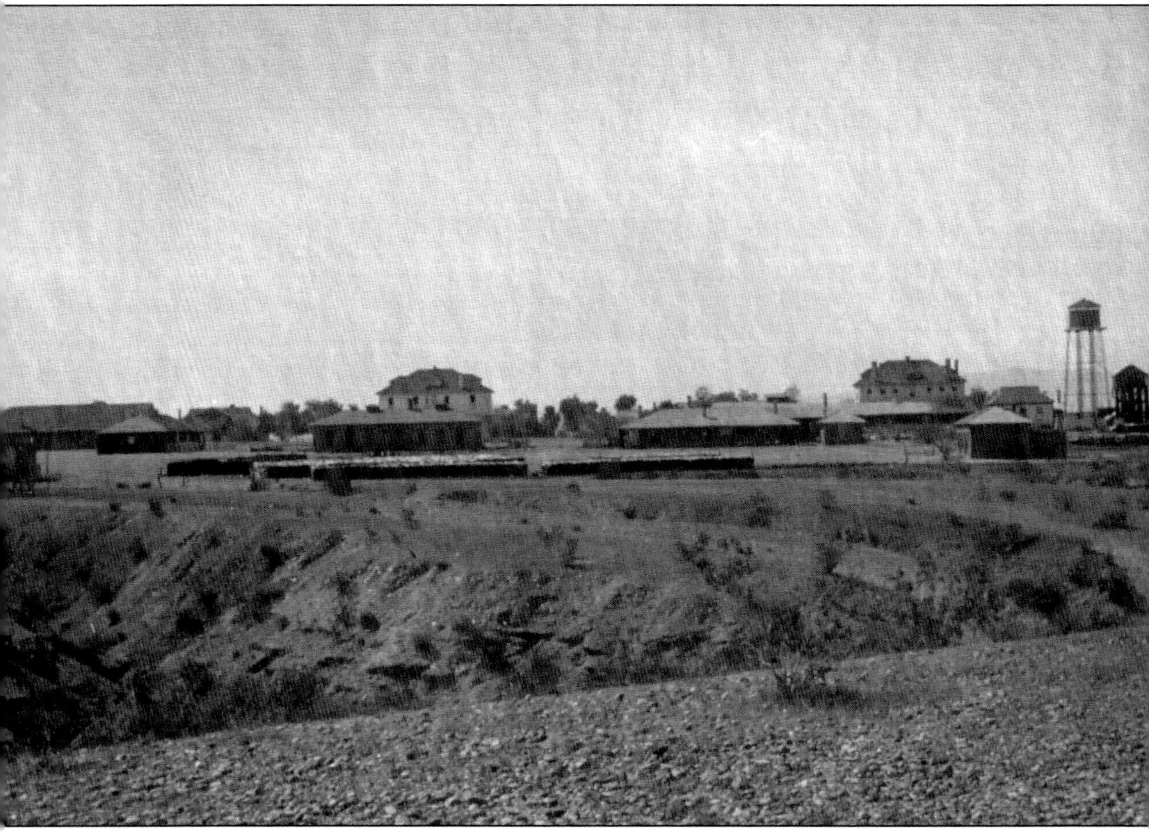

The school, as seen from a bluff, has an extensive complex of buildings. The water tower was located in the northwest corner. (Courtesy of NRM, Ron Ross Collection.)

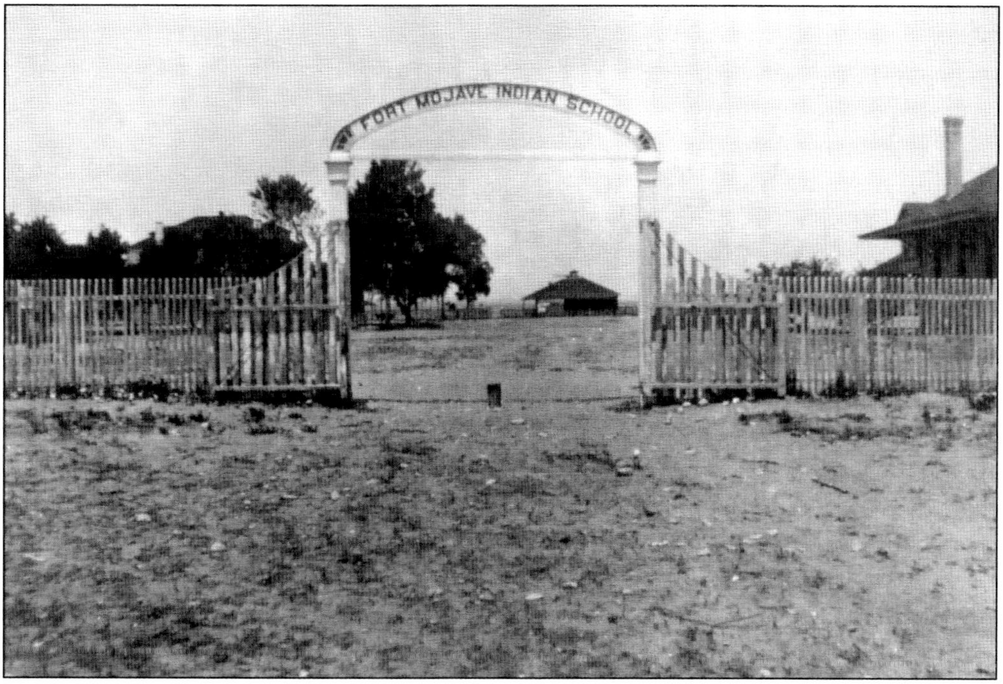

The entrance to the school opens to parade grounds and its quadrangle of buildings. Another view (below) shows the proximity of the buildings to the river. (Both, courtesy of NRM, Ron Ross Collection.)

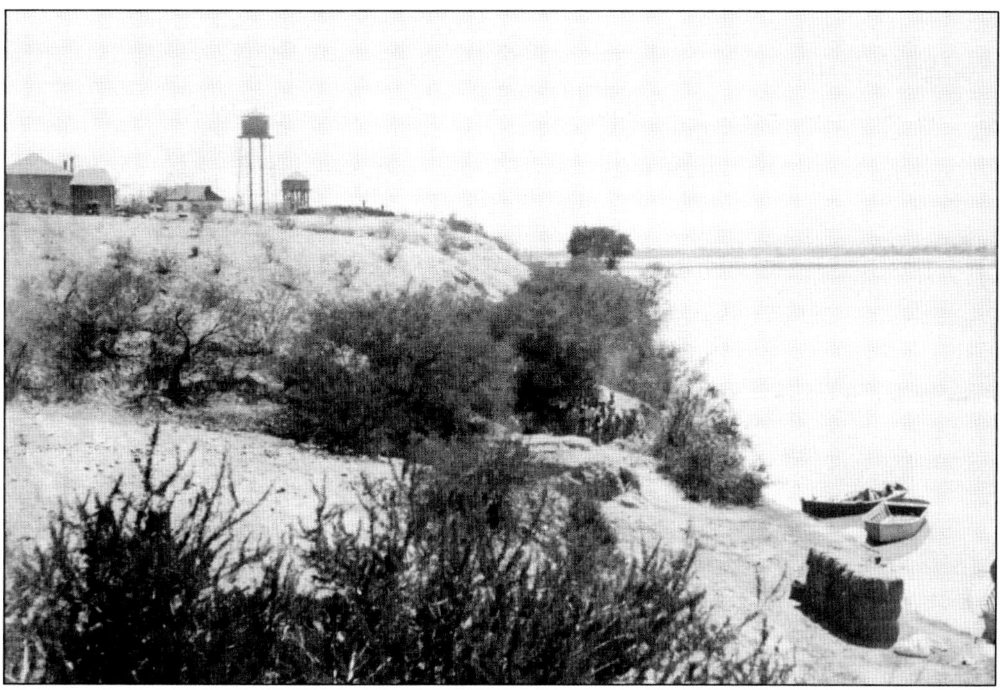

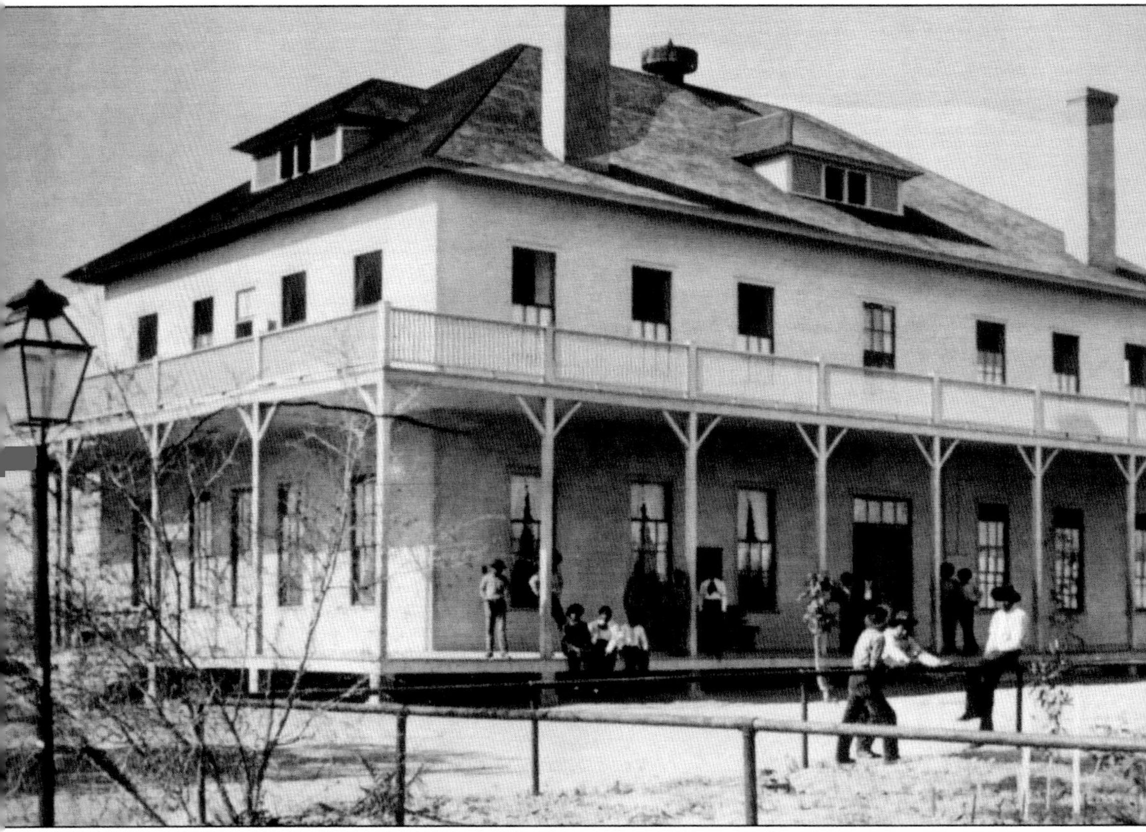

Pictured here around 1900 is the boys' dormitory, where the students could relax on the veranda and nearby grounds. The property was lit at night by gaslight, and in the heat of summer, the students would pull their beds out on the upper porch to sleep. (Courtesy of NRM, Ron Ross Collection.)

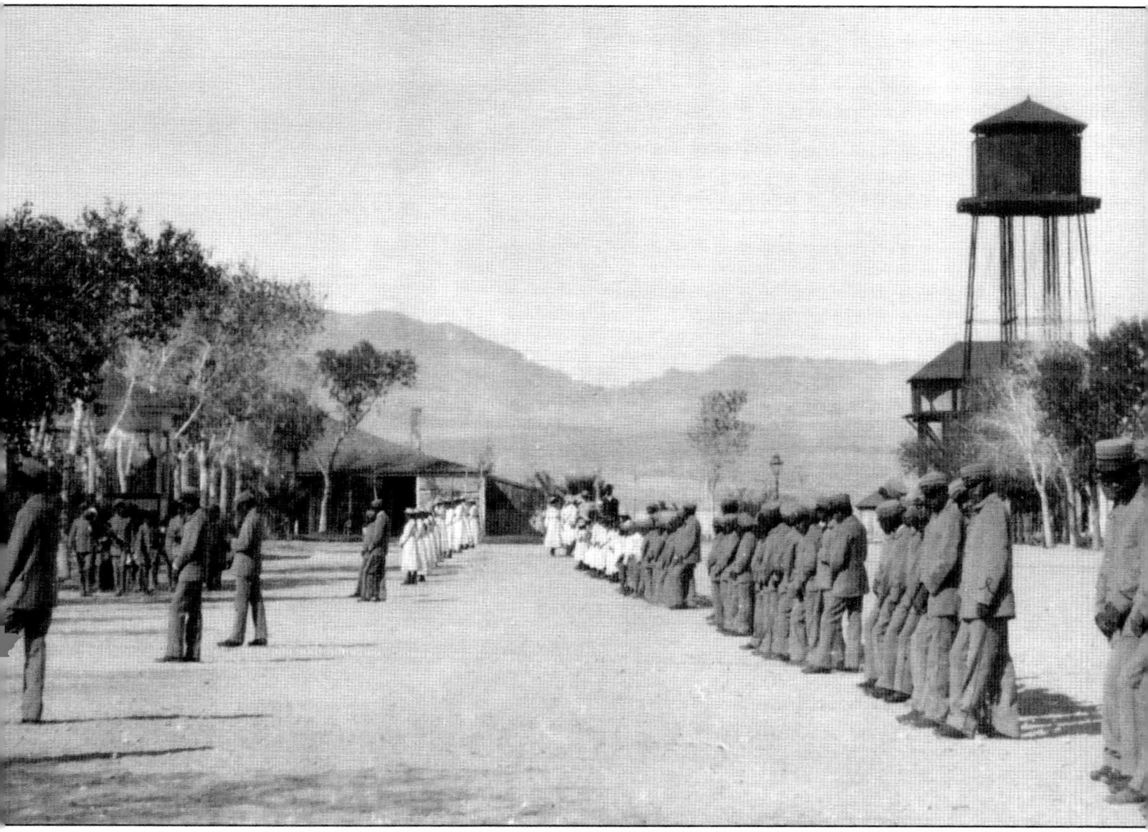

On Sunday mornings, a dress parade was held. The boys marched in their gray uniforms, the girls in their white dresses. (Courtesy of NRM, Ron Ross Collection.)

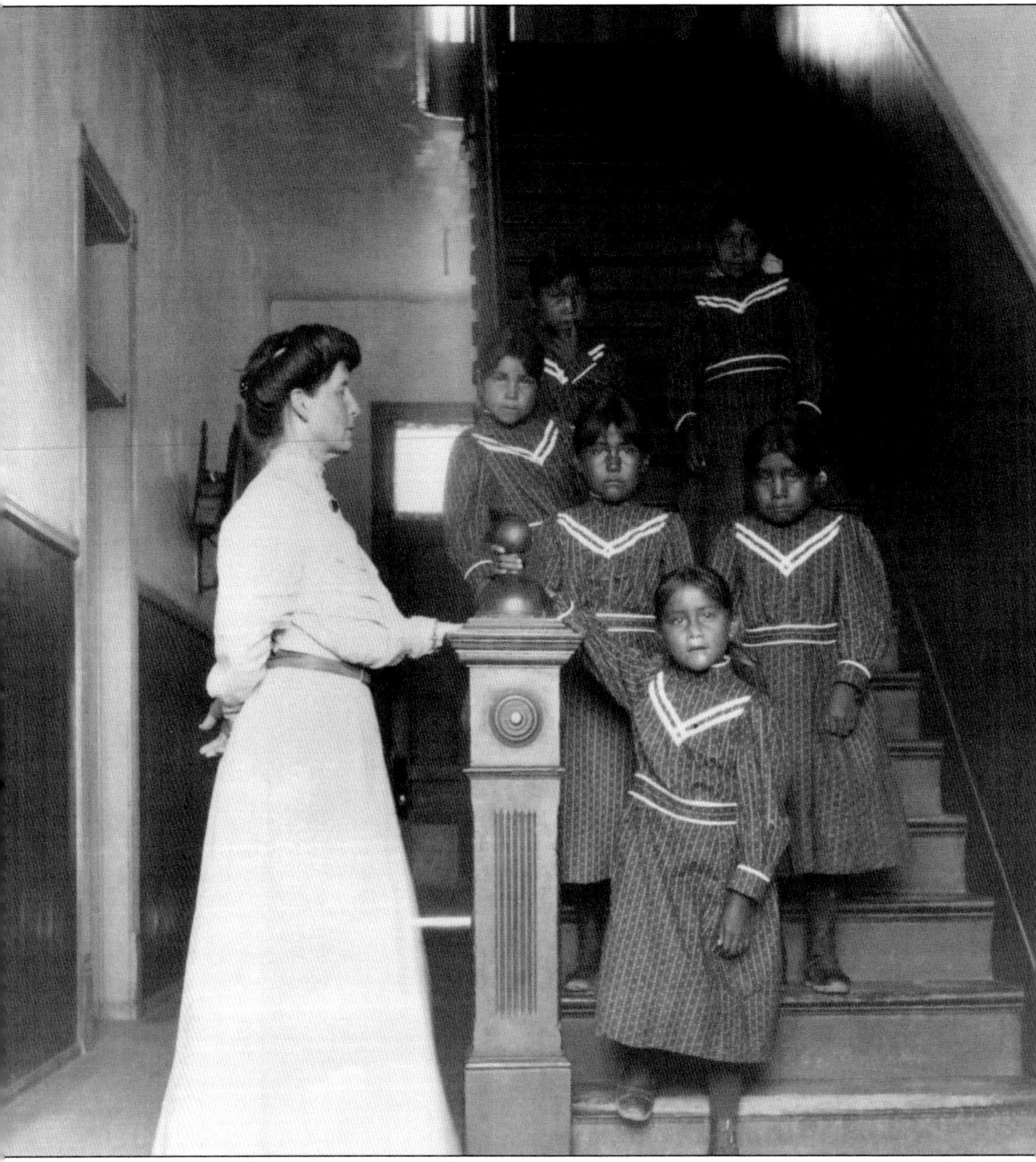

Under the watchful eye of a matron, female students line up on the stairs in the girls' dormitory. The students' uniforms were provided by the school. (Courtesy of NRM, Ron Ross Collection.)

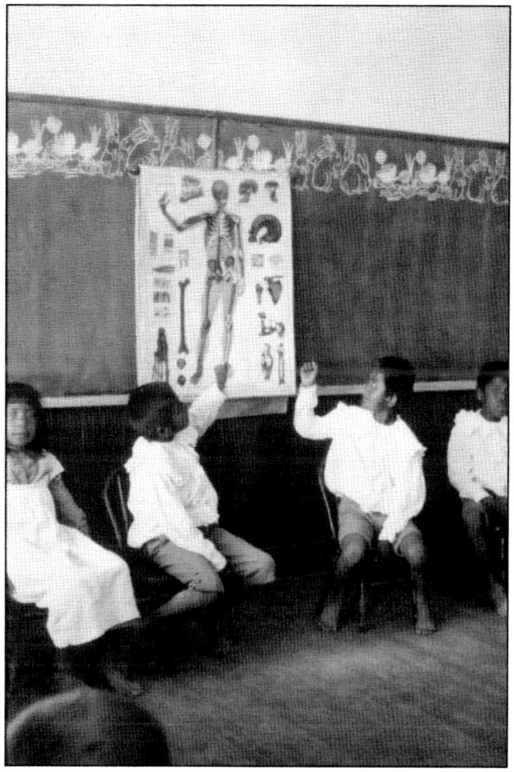

At right, Mojave boys learn about the anatomy of the human body, part of the curriculum taught to the students. There was also time for games; below, female students enjoy a round of checkers. (Both, courtesy of NRM, Ron Ross Collection.)

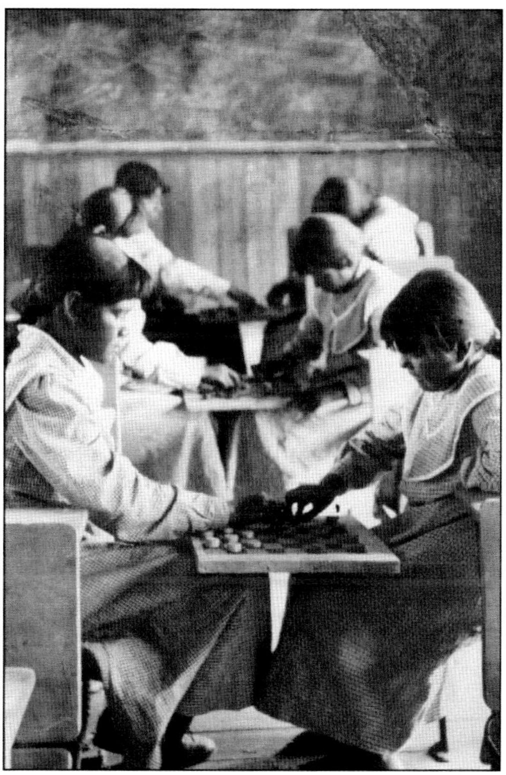

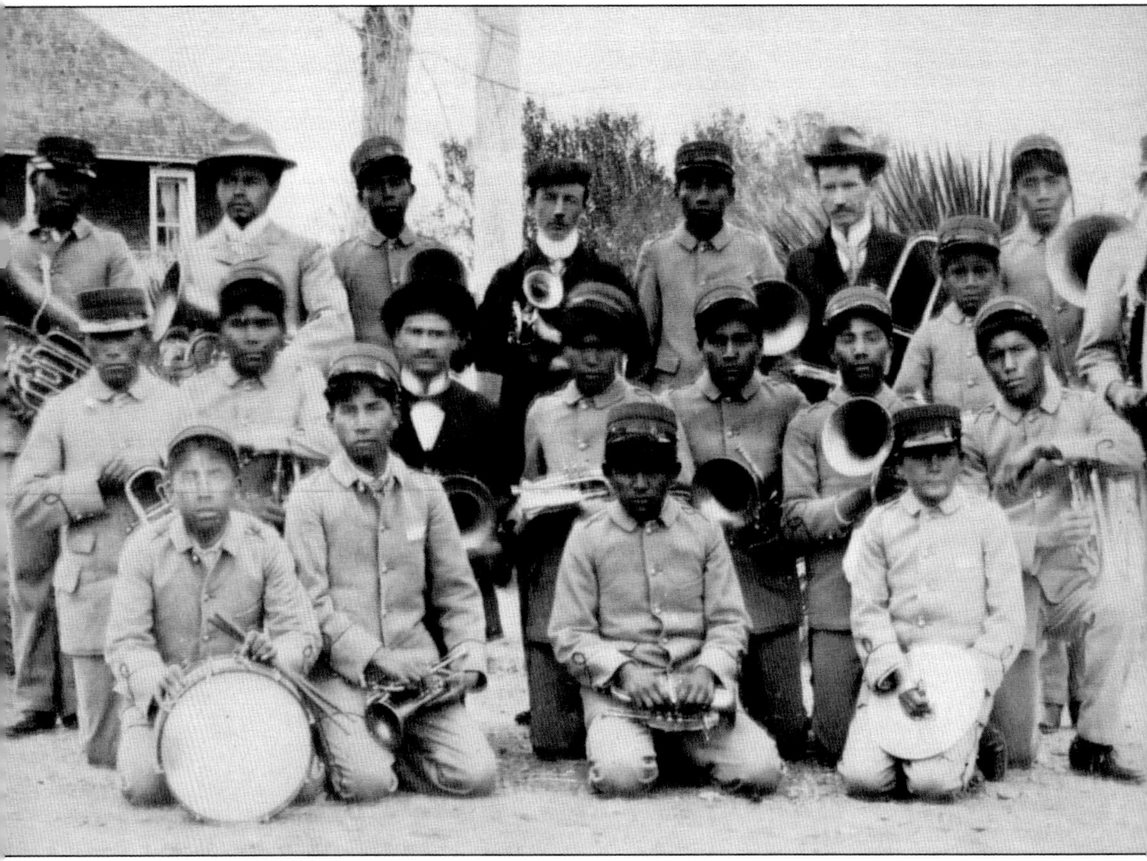

Fort Mohave School's band was directed by Albert Eller (third row, third from right), a part-time teacher at the school and an accomplished musician in his own right. Eller created the band and taught music at the school, and the tradition of the Fort Mohave band lives on today. (Courtesy of NRM, Ron Ross Collection.)

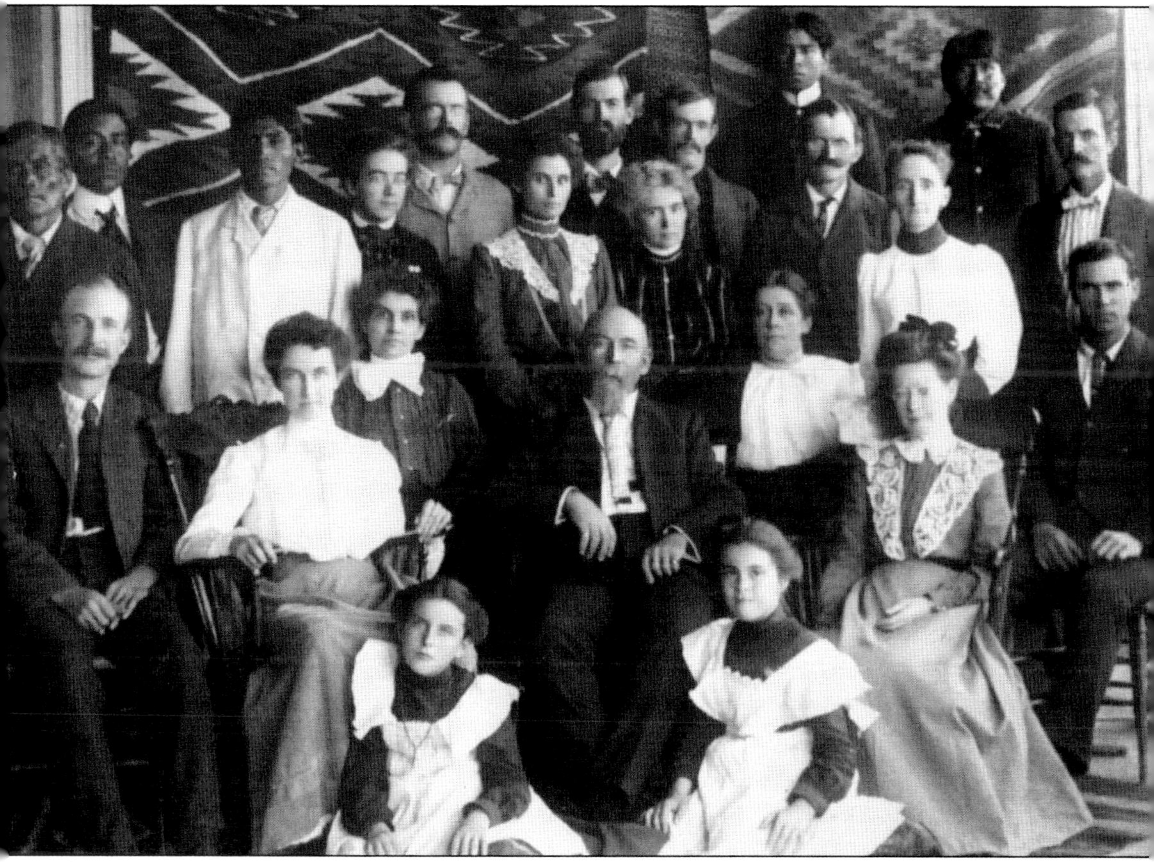

The Fort Mohave staff is assembled around Supt. John J. McKoin (seated at center) in February 1904. Those who can be identified are, from left to right, as follows: Seated in the second row are a Mr. Squires, Grace Pilcher, unidentified, John McKoin, a Miss Over, Minnie Braithwaite, and Robert Smith (engineer). Standing behind Mr. Squires is Bill Olean (night watchman), Jacob Irving (assistant engineer), and Jack Chowanna (gardener). Behind Minnie and Robert are Mollie Baker (seamstress) and Clarence Jenkins (farmer). In the last row, at upper right, are Indian policemen Lawrence Citaway and Waldo Obob. (Courtesy of NRM, Ron Ross Collection.)

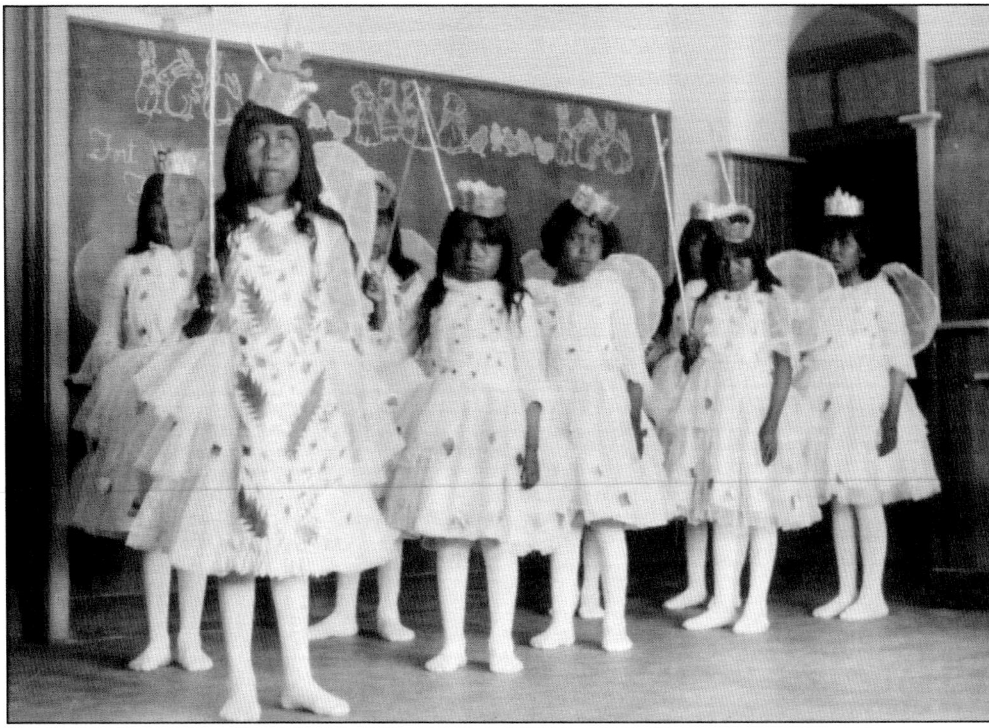

Young girls prepare to perform for a recital. Along with the standard academic subjects, the students were exposed to the arts, dancing, music, and theater. Below, students enjoy pie for dessert. (Both, courtesy of NRM, Ron Ross Collection.)

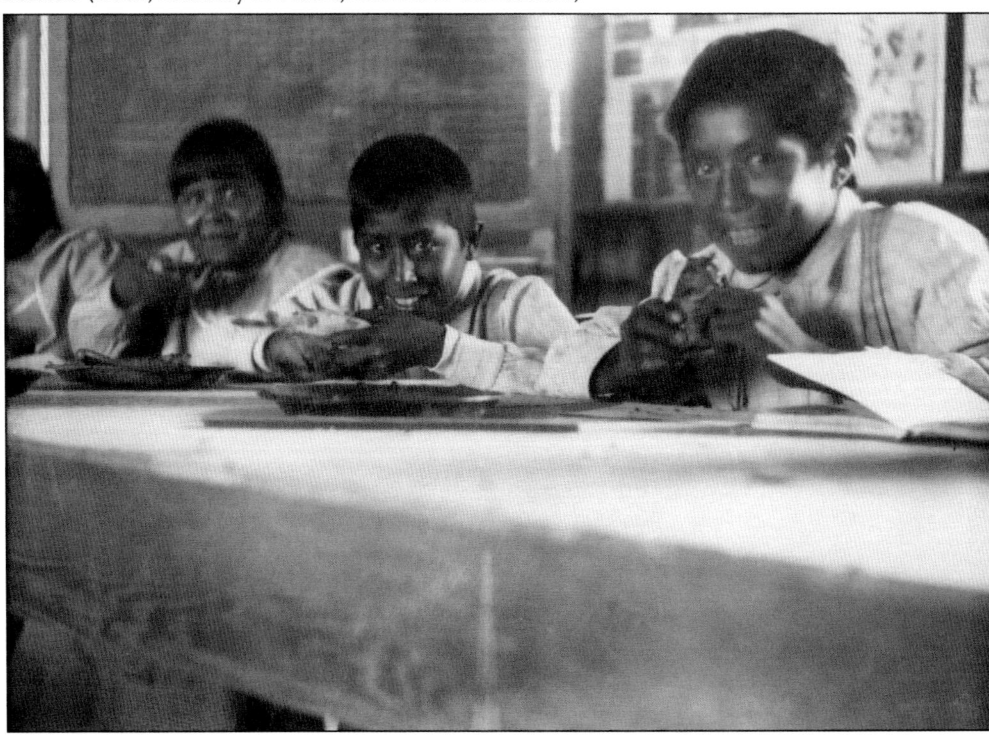

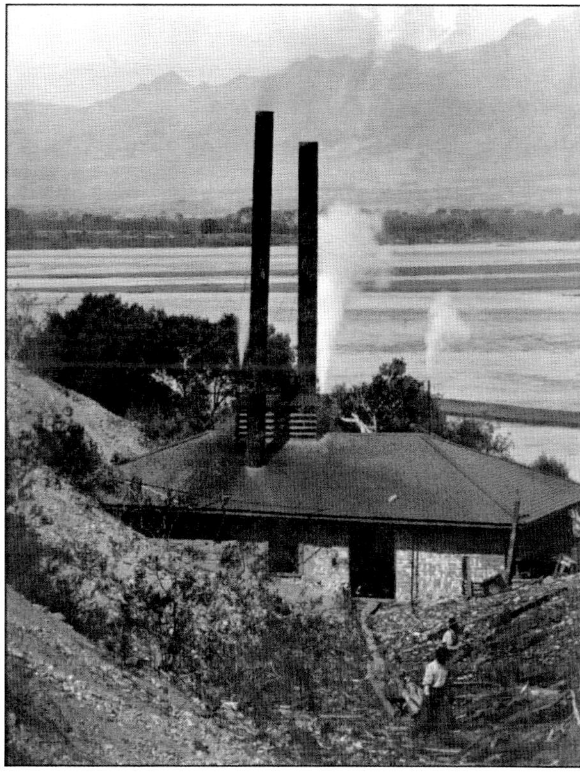

The heart of the school was the powerhouse, located at the base of the mesa. In addition to its ice machine, it pumped water and provided steam to run the school laundry. The laundry washed the clothes of more than 200 students, plus those of the teachers and other employees. The mangle in the background was used for ironing. (Both, courtesy of NRM, Ron Ross Collection.)

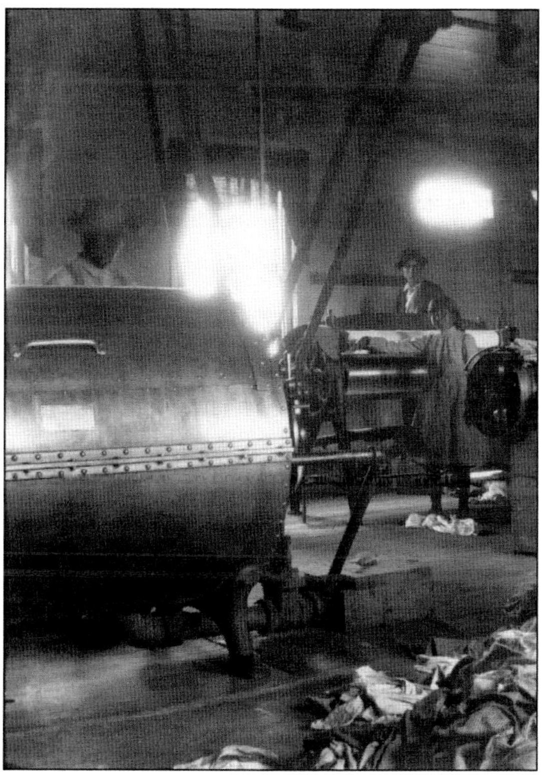

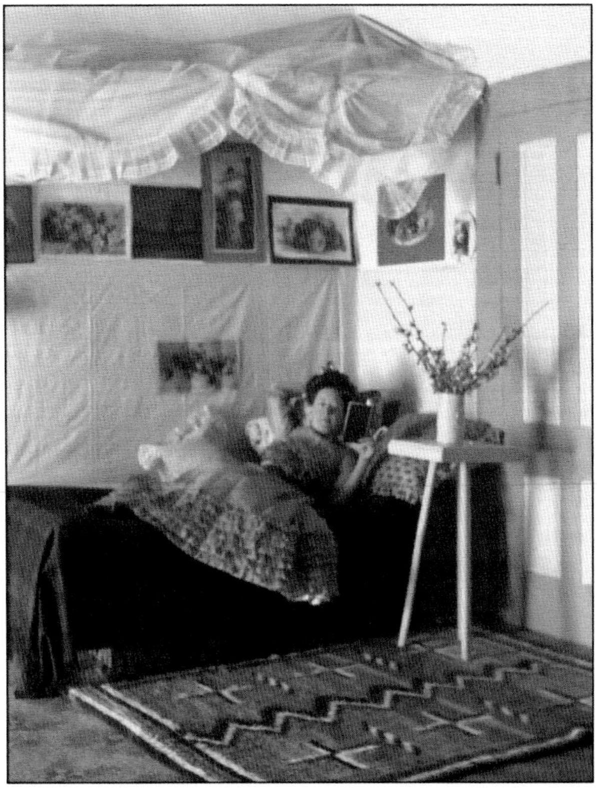

Teacher Minnie Braithwaite relaxes in her bedroom. Minnie, who was a headstrong and independent young woman, came from a prominent Virginia family. She entered into the Indian Service at the turn of the century and arrived at Fort Mohave in 1902 after teaching Navajo and Hopi children in northern Arizona. (Courtesy of NRM, Ron Ross Collection.)

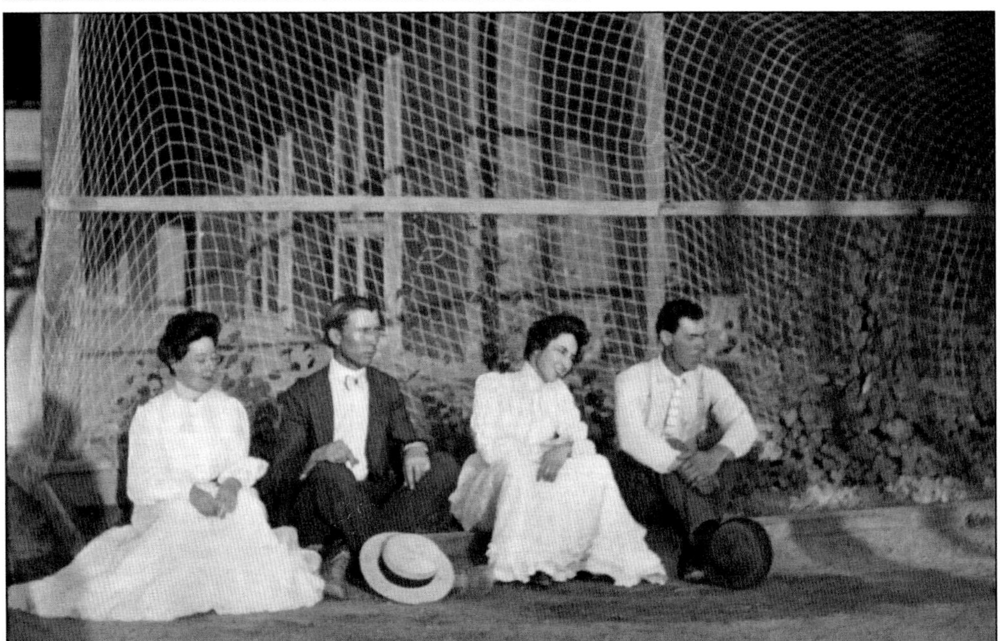

Minnie (left) is pictured here with, from left to right, Claude Compton, teacher Grace Pilcher, and Robert Smith in front of the employee quarters. Compton was the owner of Fort Mohave's trading post, and Smith was the school's engineer. (Courtesy of NRM, Ron Ross Collection.)

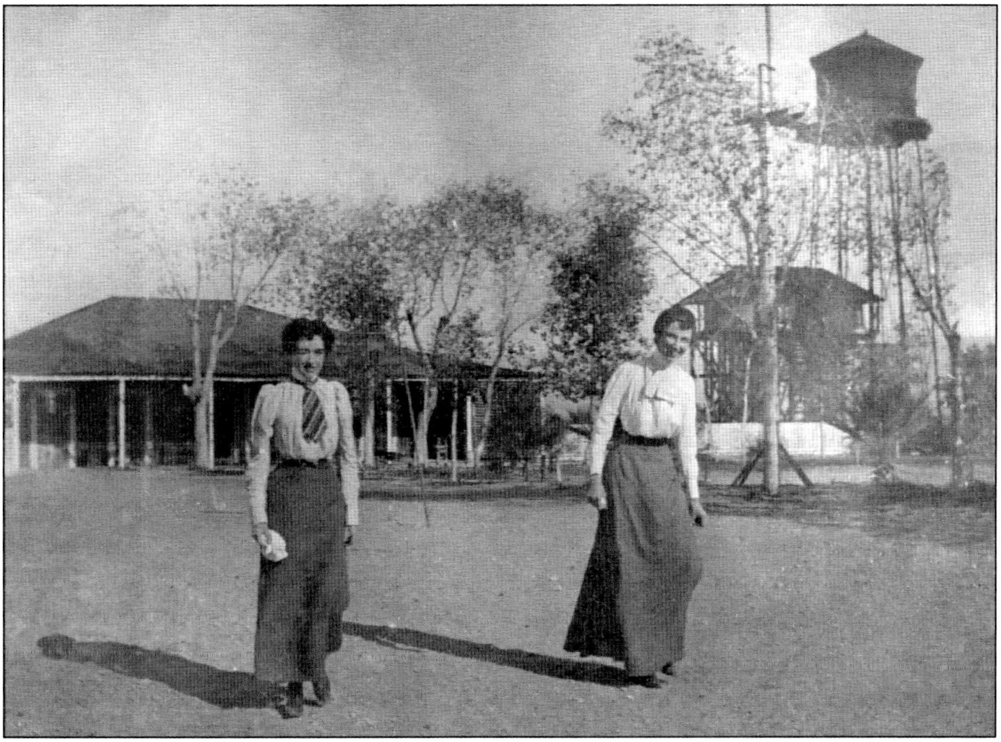

Grace Pilcher (right) and another unidentified teacher are seen here crossing the parade grounds. Both teachers and students had ample time for leisure and sports. The campus had a tennis court, and the school had its own baseball team, pictured below. (Both, courtesy of NRM, Ron Ross Collection.)

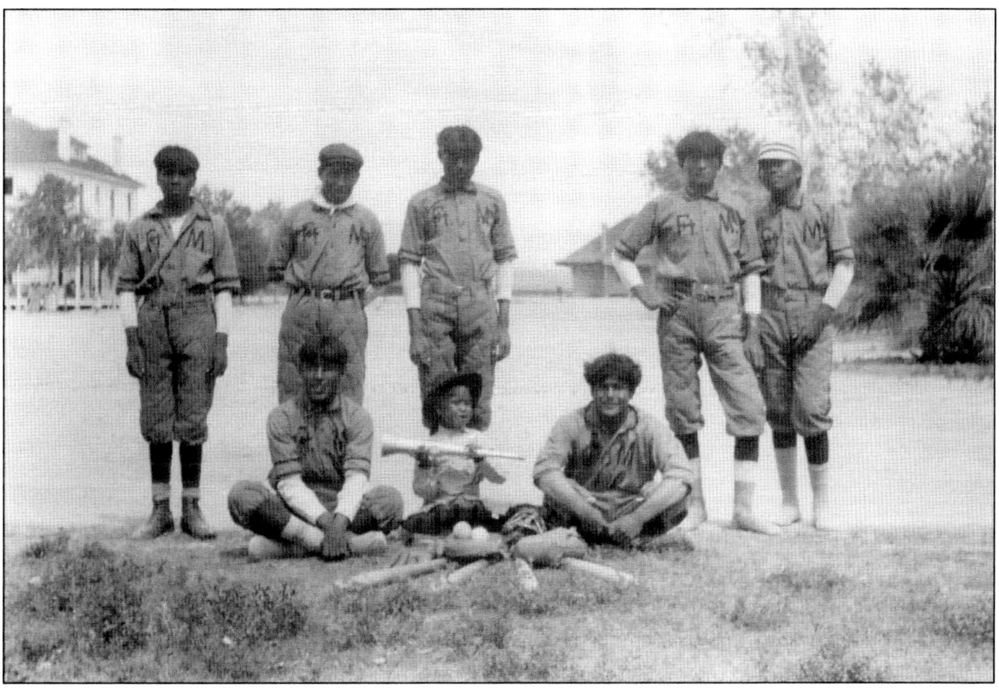

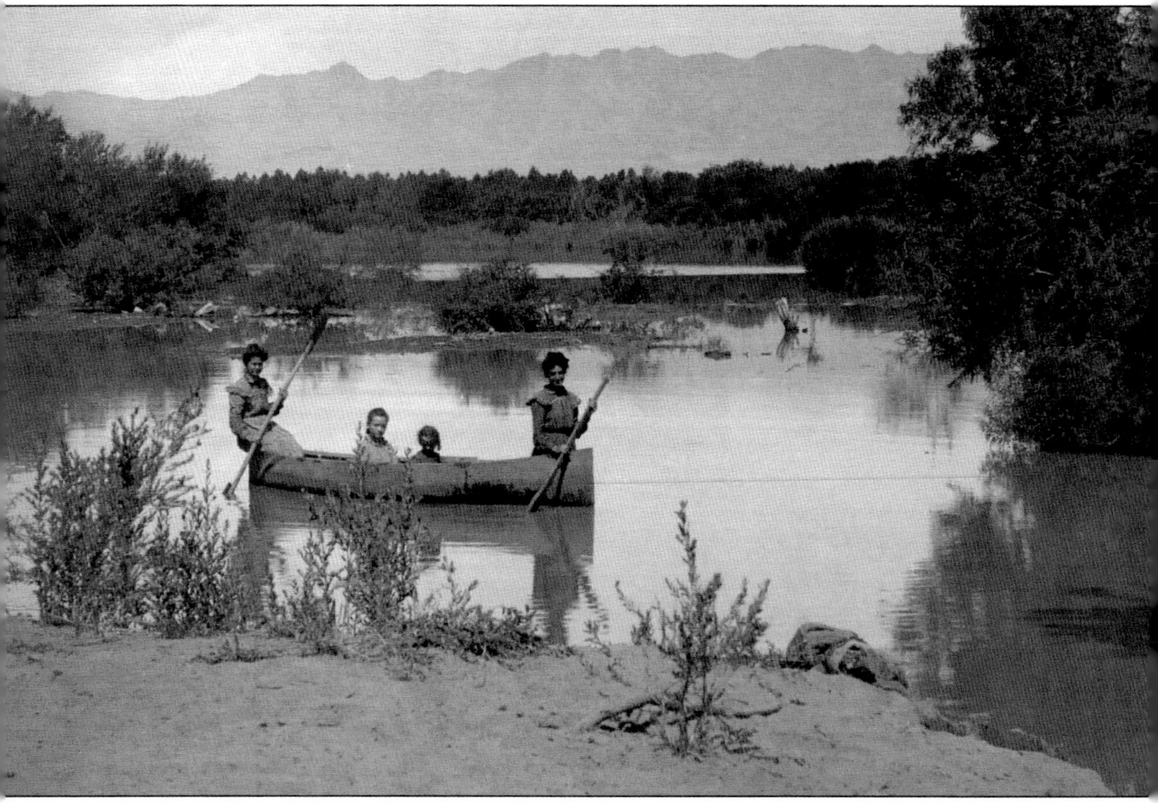

Teachers and students boat during an outing to Spatterbone Lake, five miles below Fort Mohave. The bottomland lake, named for Mojave chief Samuel Spatterbone, had once been part of the main channel of the Colorado River. The lake is no longer in existence. (Courtesy of NRM, Ron Ross Collection.)

Five

Dawn of the 20th Century

Transformation

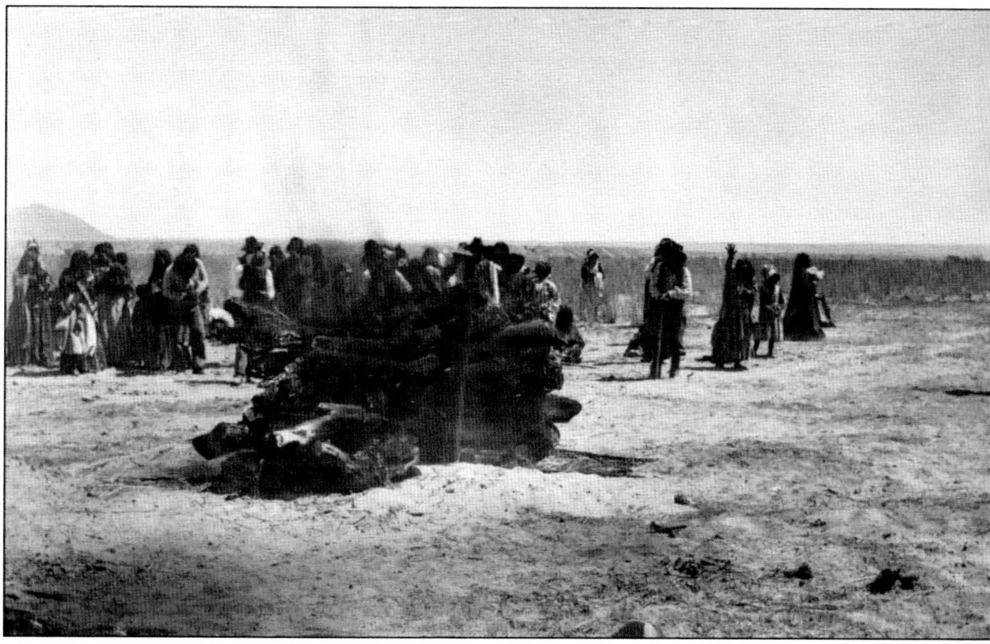

The Mojave cremation ceremony, the Big Cry, serves to assist the soul of the departed through the Indian maze and into the great beyond. Upon the death of a member of the tribe, the body, along with all of the deceased's earthly belongings, is placed upon a pyre and burned while relatives and friends gather to cry and chant prayers for the departed soul. After the ceremony, the name of the deceased is never to be mentioned again. It is said that when the great Chief Iretaba died, the tribe not only slaughtered and burned his horses but also burned down the whole village. In later years, a wily merchant would write out a check for $500 to the deceased, then place it upon the burning pyre. He was well liked for that gesture. This c. 1902 image of the funeral pyre of Chief Sistuma was taken by photographer C.C. Pierce. (Courtesy of NRM.)

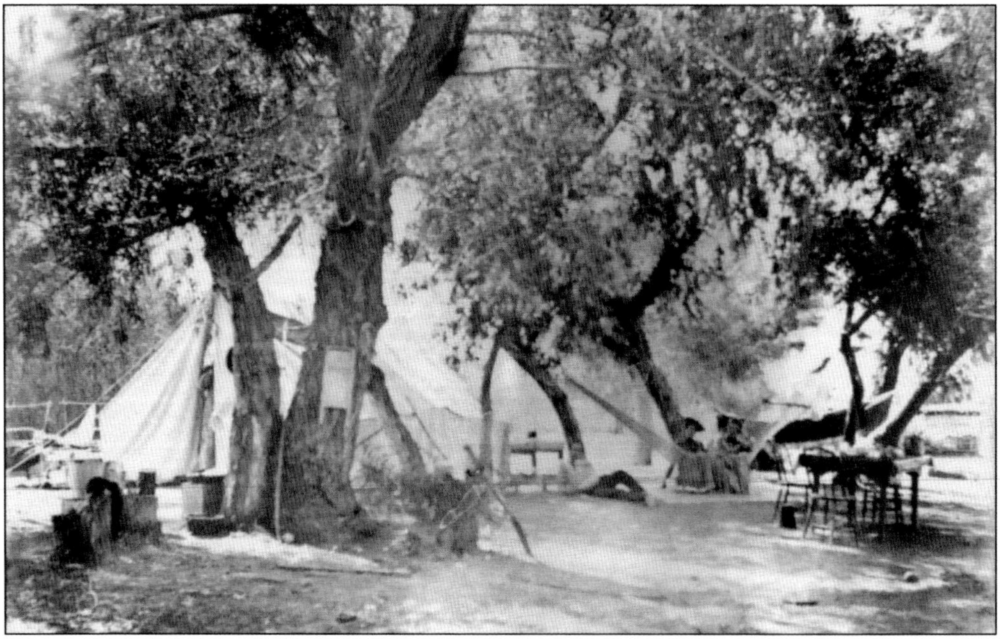

A government topographic survey party set up camp in the Mohave Valley in October 1902. Earlier that year, Congress had passed the Reclamation Act, enacted to provide federal funds for irrigation projects on public lands. Pres. Theodore Roosevelt was eager to see the vast and arid lands of the West cultivated, so teams of topographic surveyors were sent out to measure rivers and streams and survey the land. (Courtesy of NRM, Ron Ross Collection.)

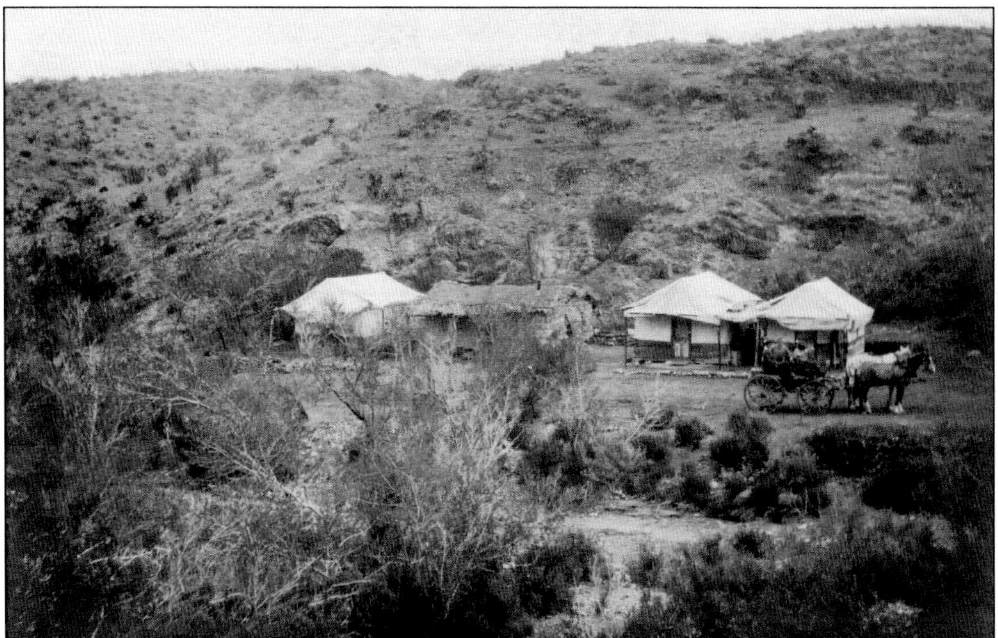

In 1903, a makeshift mining camp for the California Moss Gold Mining Company was set up southeast of what is now Bullhead City. The miners discovered what they believed to be the rich lost vein of the Moss Mine. (Courtesy of NRM, Ron Ross Collection.)

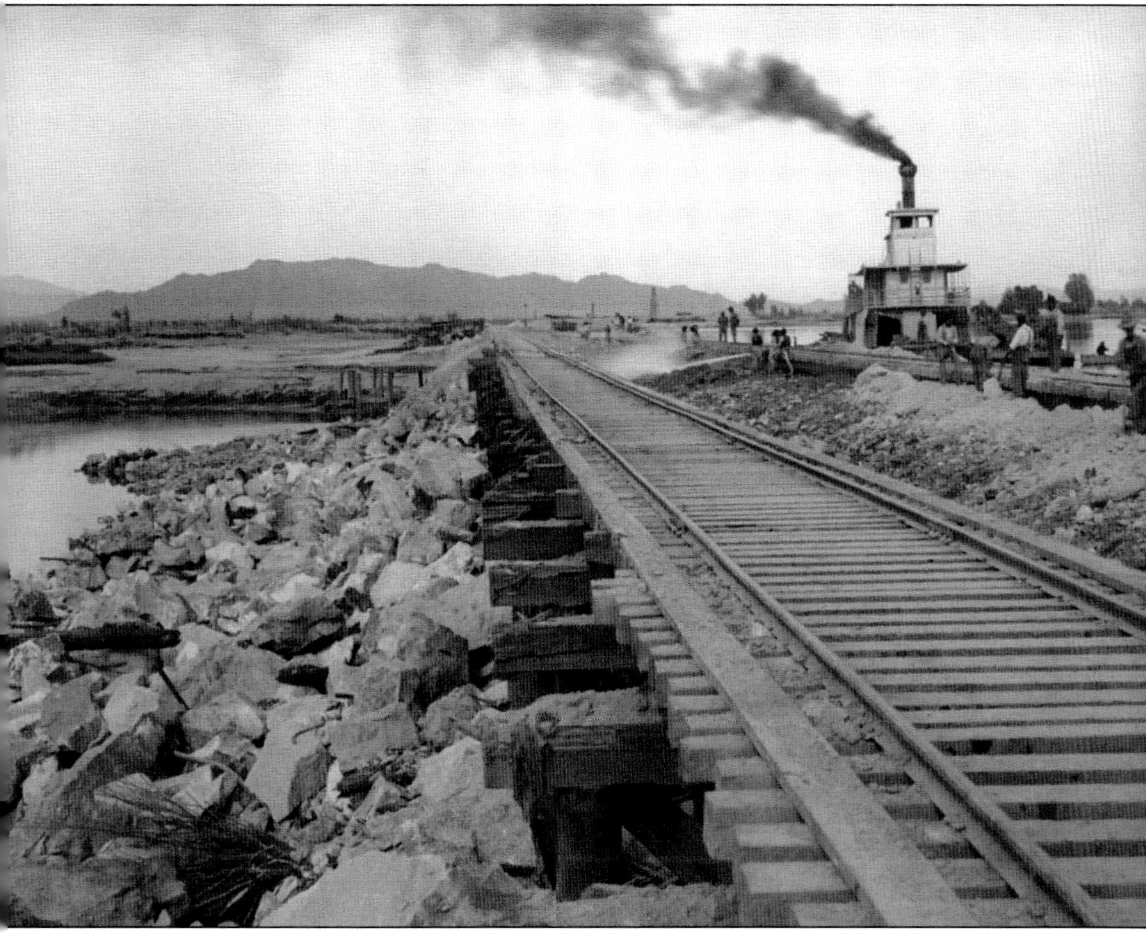

Steamboats monopolized the Arizona freight business until the arrival of the railroad. The *Searchlight*, moored here next to the railroad tracks, was perhaps the last steamship to run on the Colorado River. Launched in 1902, it was lost on the river in 1916. (Courtesy of NRM.)

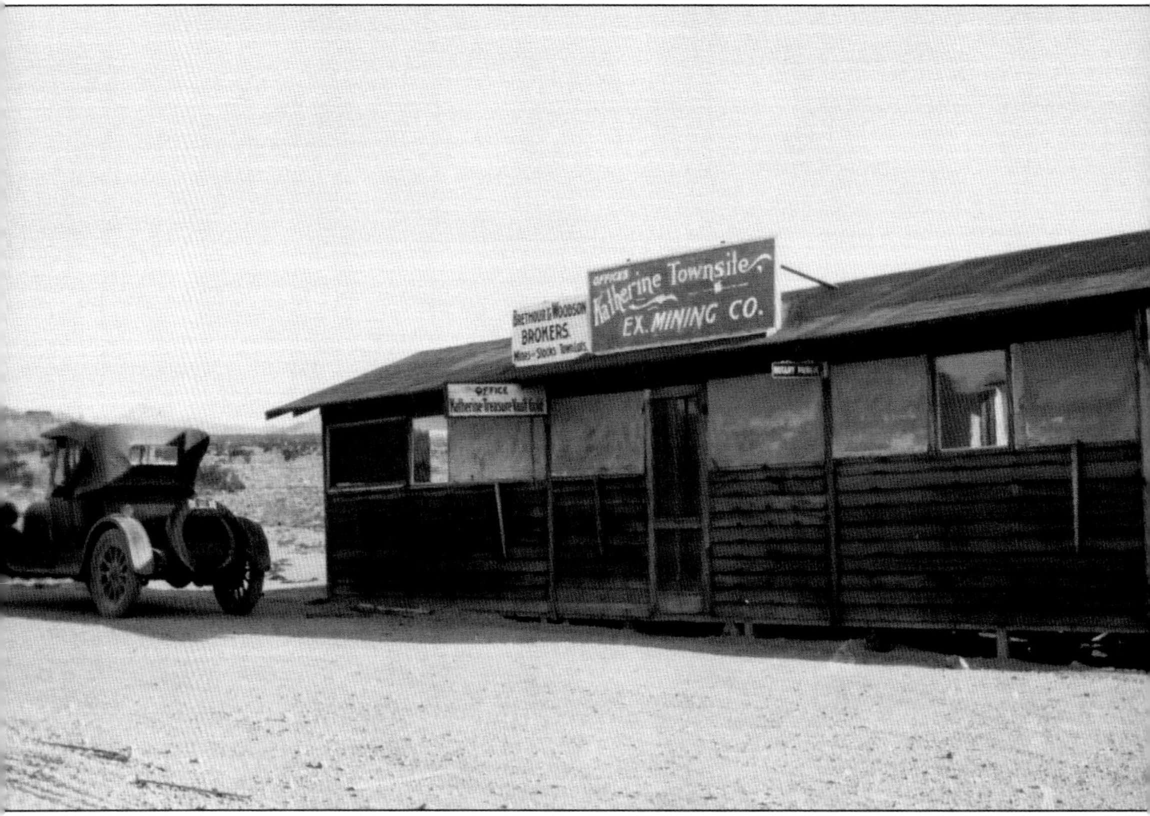

The New Comstock Mining Company developed the Katherine Mine, which S.C. Baggs had discovered about five miles northeast of the present-day Davis Dam in 1900. The Arizona-Pyramid Gold Mining Company took over the mine in 1904. Little profit was made, however, and operations were suspended in 1906. (Courtesy of CRHS.)

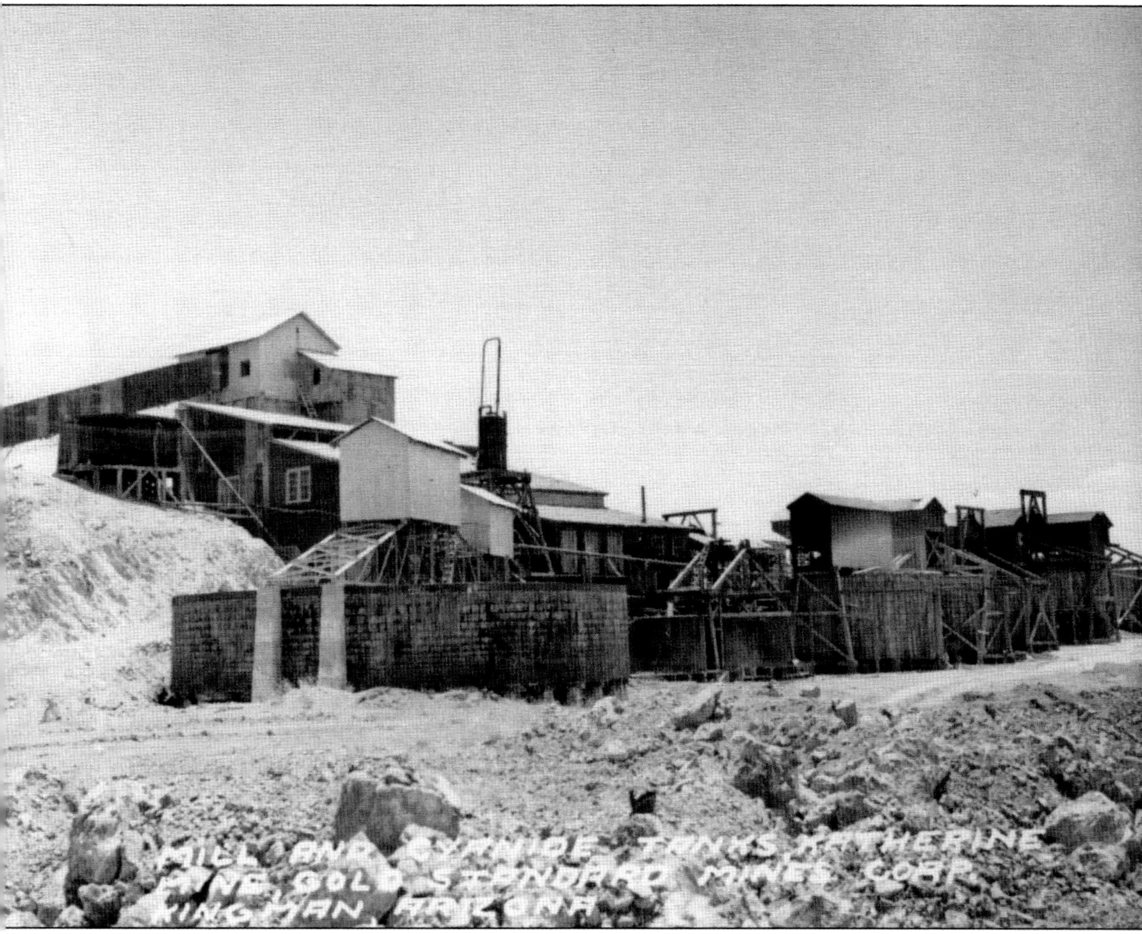

The Katherine Gold Mining Company took over the mine in 1919. A new shaft was sunk and a 150-ton cyanide mill was installed to reduce the cost of processing ore. (Courtesy of CRHS.)

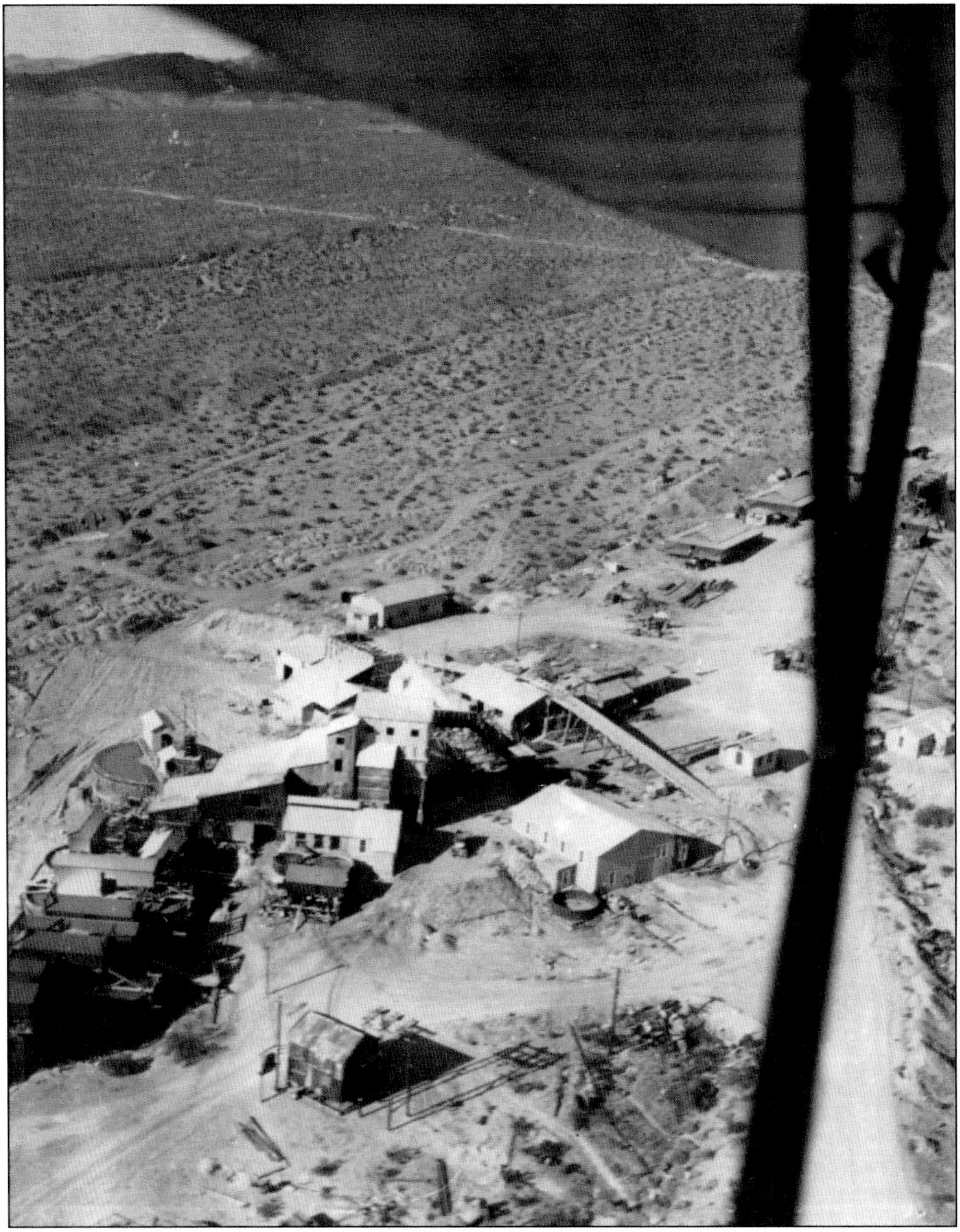

The Katherine Mine mill and camp was developing into one of the larger working mine operations in the area. The Gold Standard Gold Mining Company acquired the title to the Katherine Mine in 1935. (Courtesy of CRHS.)

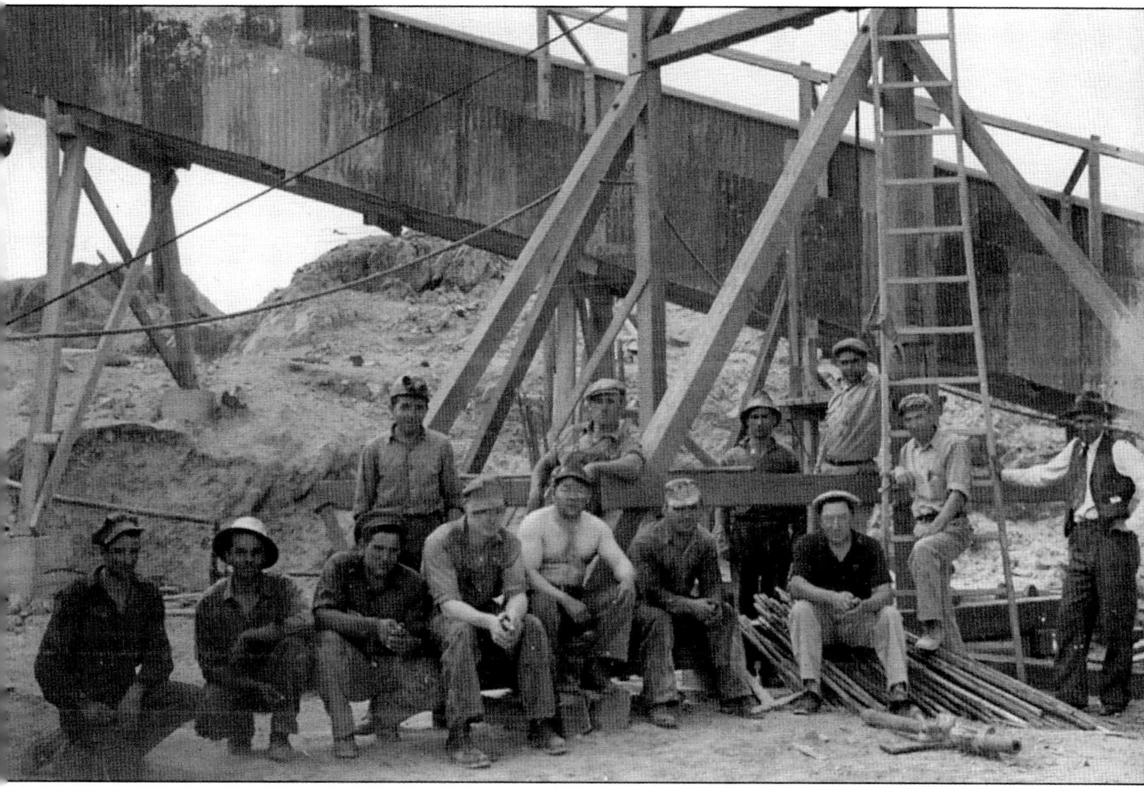

A crew works to retimber 900 feet of burned mine shaft from a fire that severely damaged the structure in 1934. Once the mine had been rehabilitated, with all the fire damage repaired, the mill would resume operation by November 1934, processing ore from the local mines. (Courtesy of CRHS.)

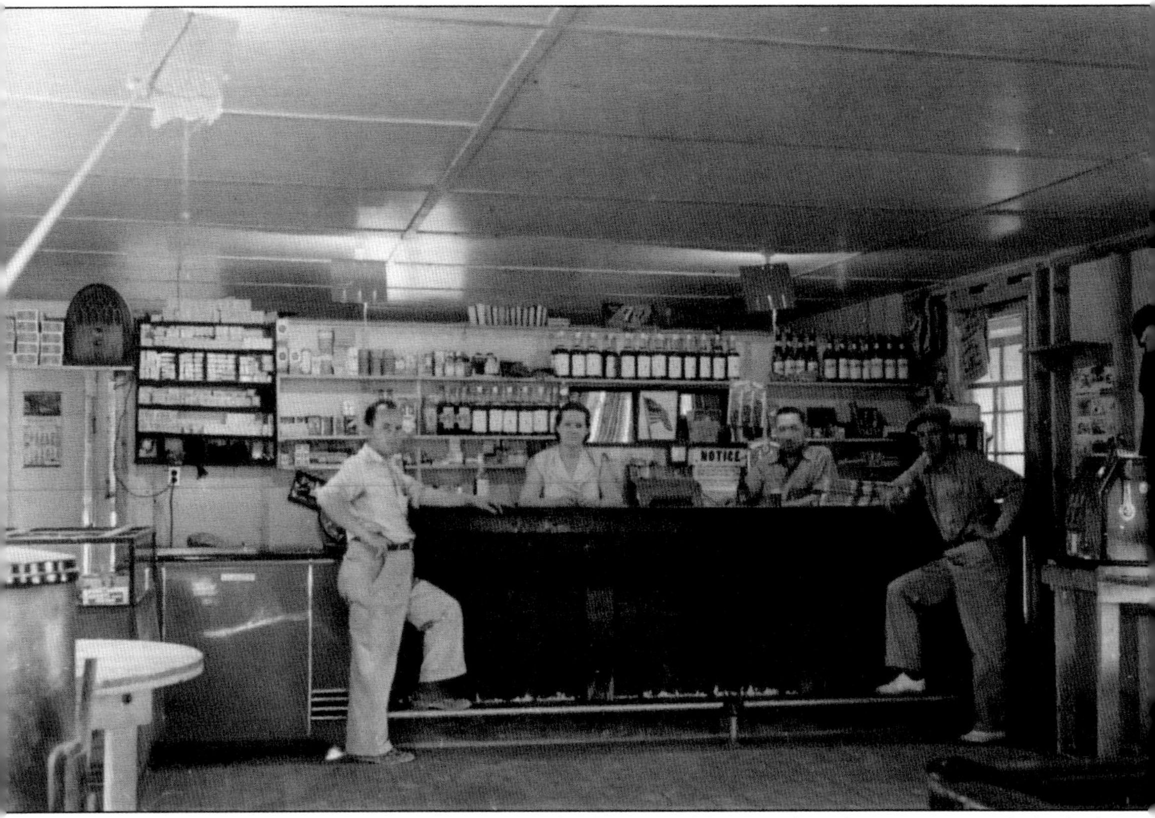

The commissary at Katherine Mine served a large workforce. After the mine was refurbished and the fire damage repaired, the Katherine Mine was in production from 1937 to 1940. The associated mill ran continuously until April 15, 1943, when it was closed by the War Production Board. (Courtesy of CRHS.)

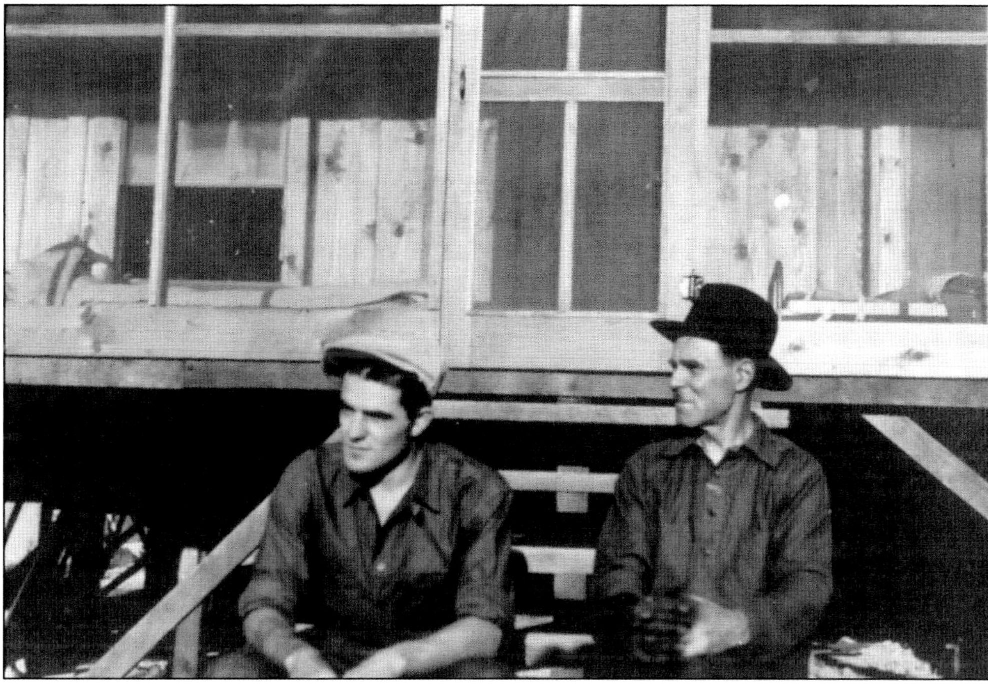

Known by his pen name, a young Louis L'Amour and his father, L.C. LaMoore, are pictured on the steps of the barracks at Katherine Mine around 1926. Louis returned from a world tour on a steamer and worked the mine when he was 18 years old. His experiences in the West no doubt influenced the body of work he would produce. He primarily wrote Western novels (which he referred to as "Frontier novels"), including *Mojave Crossing.* During his nearly 40-year-long career, L'Amour wrote 89 novels, 14 short story collections, and two nonfiction books. L'Amour also boxed professionally during the time he was employed at Katherine Mine, fighting under the names "Duke La Moore" and "Michael Mickey Moore" and winning 51 out of 59 heavyweight fights. (Both, courtesy of CRHS.)

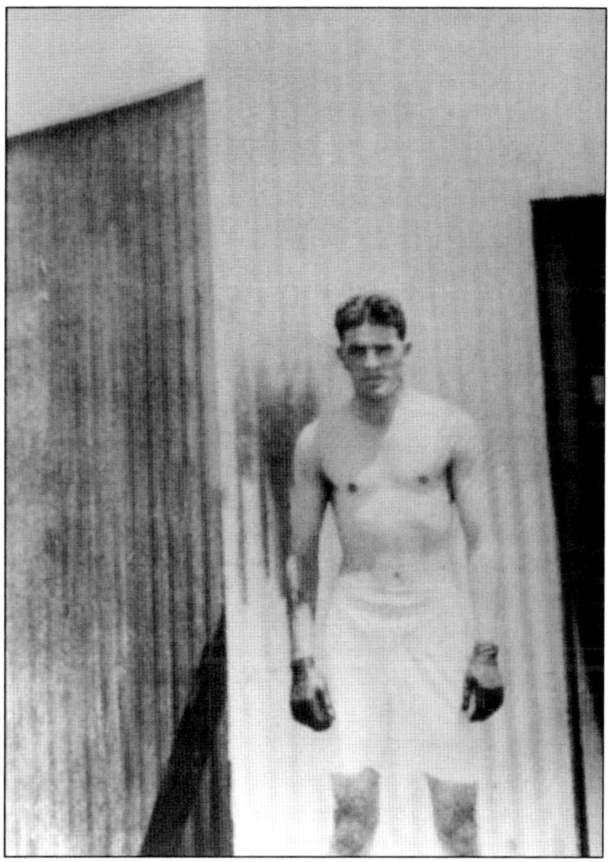

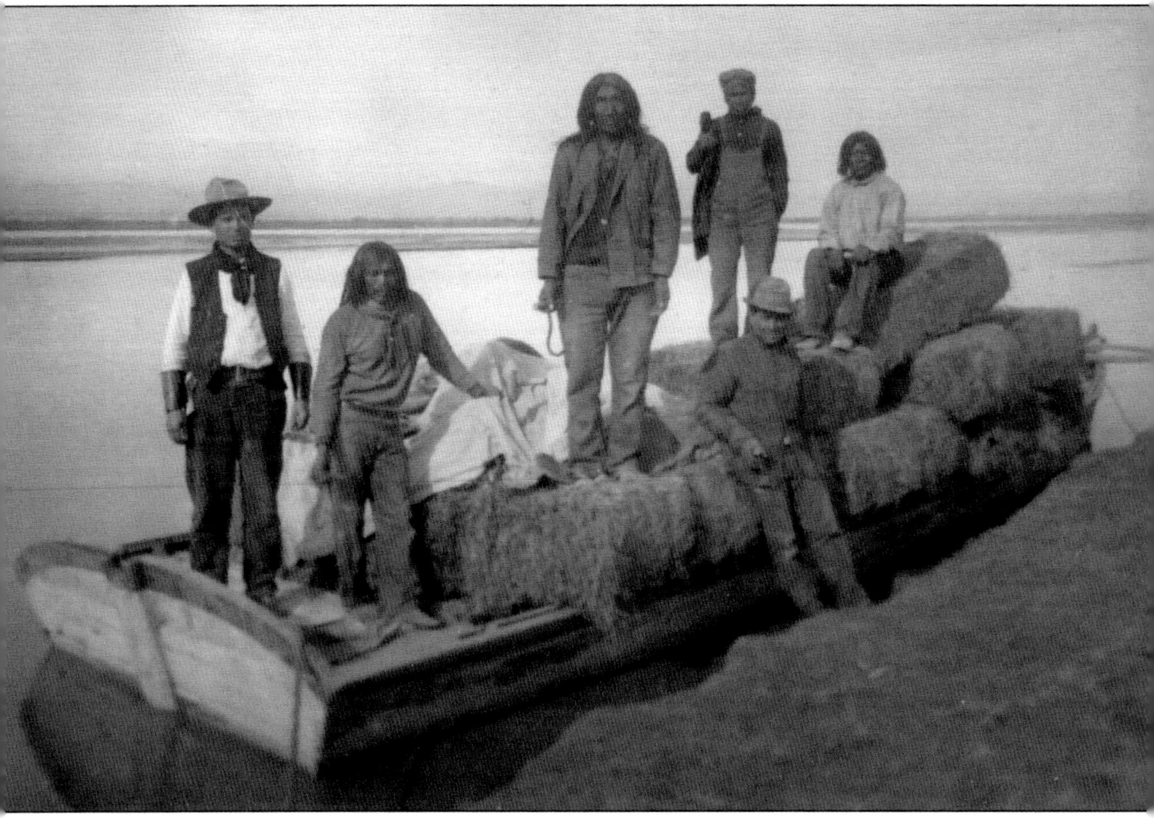

Many things were changing in the early days of the new century. Here, a ferry transports hay for the ranches that were dotting the valley during the short-lived era of the cowboy in the Mohave Valley. Only one element remained constant—the Colorado River. And that, too, was about to change. (Courtesy of MMHA.)

Six

World War II
Training the Troops

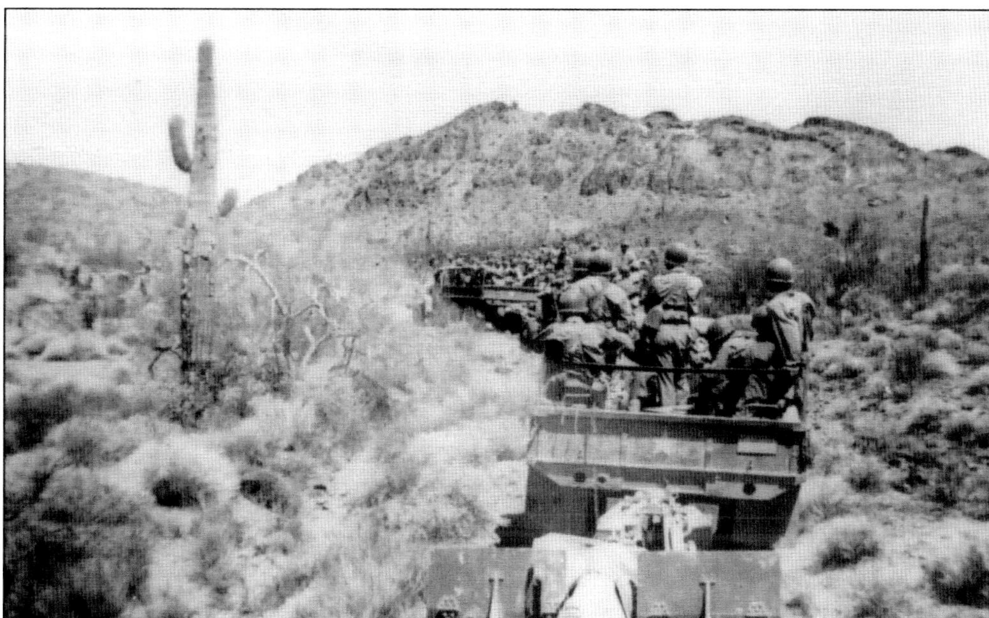

When the United States was thrust into World War II, the government created the Desert Training Center in the Mojave Desert for combat exercises. The troops trained there to fight the German Afrika Korps in the North African desert. (Courtesy of BLM.)

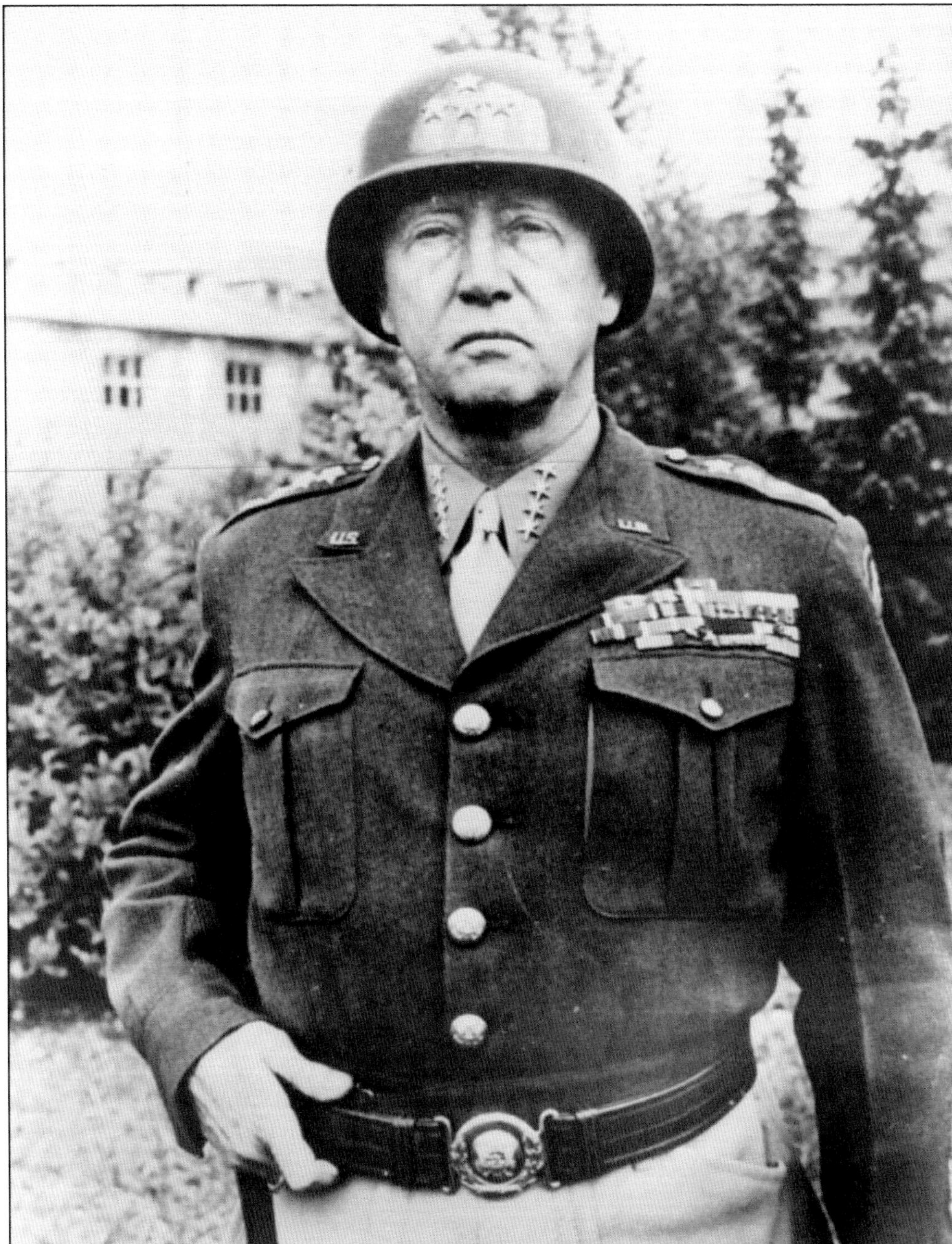

When Maj. Gen. George S. Patton came to the Desert Training Center at Camp Young (now Chiriaco Summit), his first orders as commanding general were to select other areas in the desert that would be suitable for large-scale maneuvers. It would become the world's largest military training facility, with 18,000 square miles of desert land divided into 10 divisional camps under the direction of Camp Young. (Courtesy of BLM.)

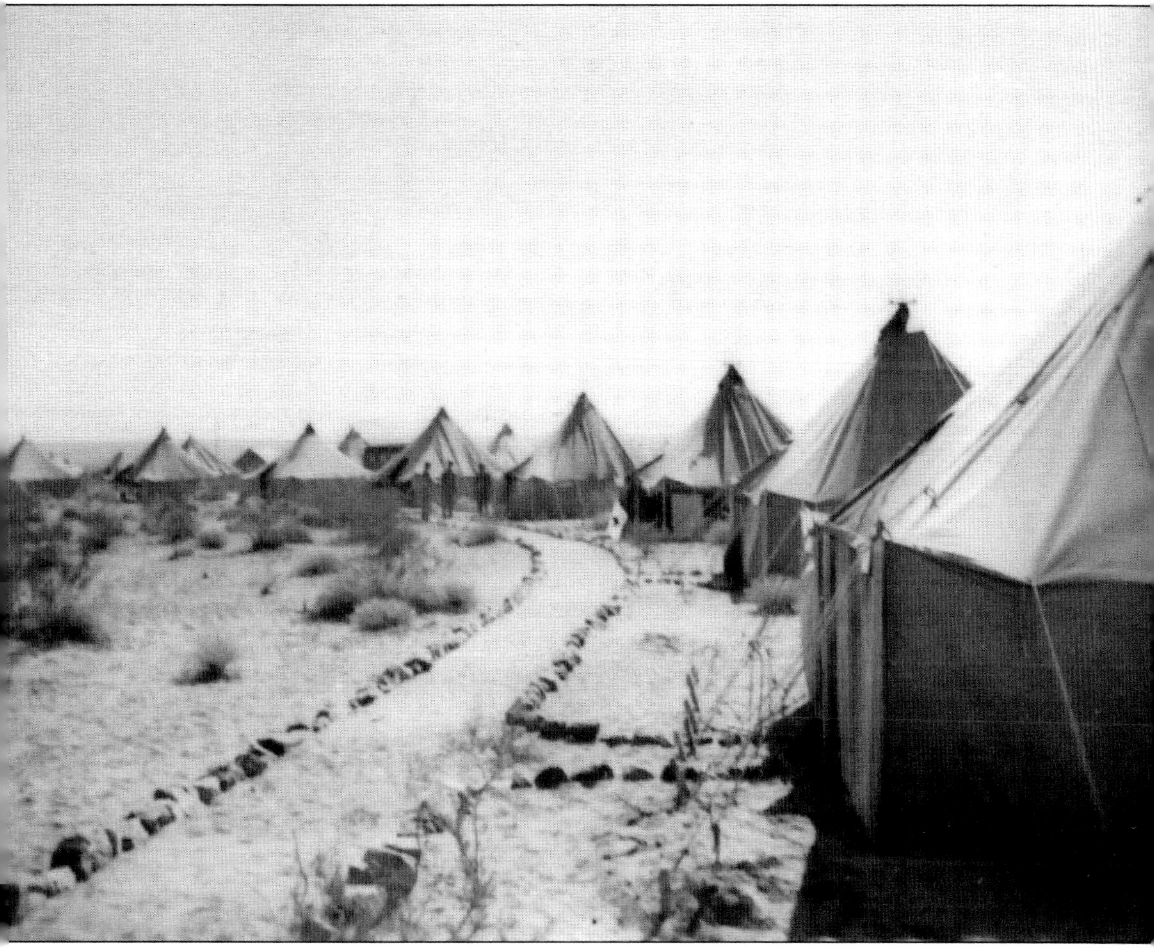

Camp Ibis was located southwest of Bullhead City, on the California side of the Colorado River. The 4th Air Division was stationed at the airfield under the command of Patton. They practiced air strikes on armored tanks by dropping sacks of flour to simulate bombs. (Courtesy of BLM.)

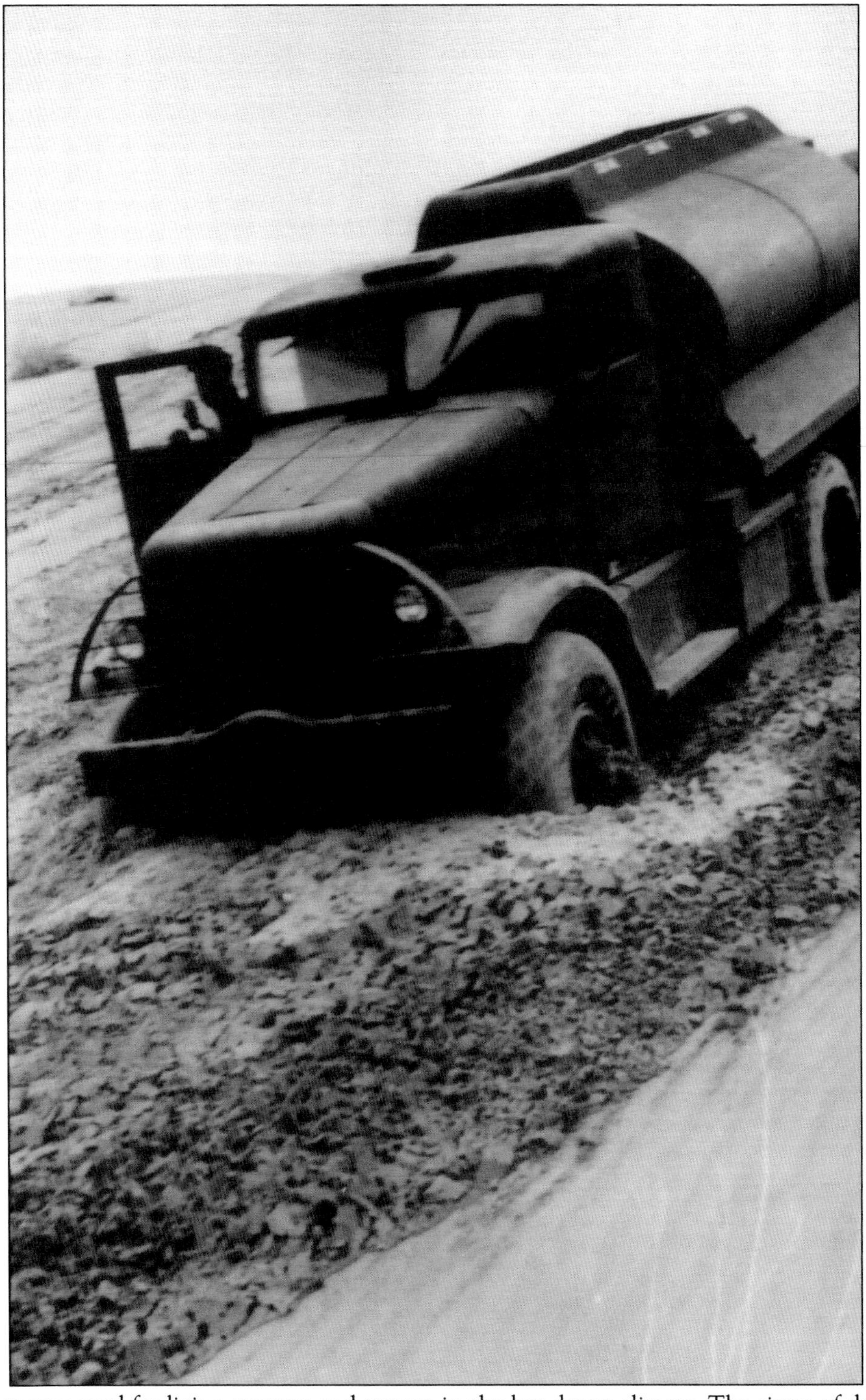

Tents were used for living quarters and storage in the hot desert climate. The rigors of desert training often included mishaps such as this military supply truck stuck in a sand dune. (Courtesy of BLM.)

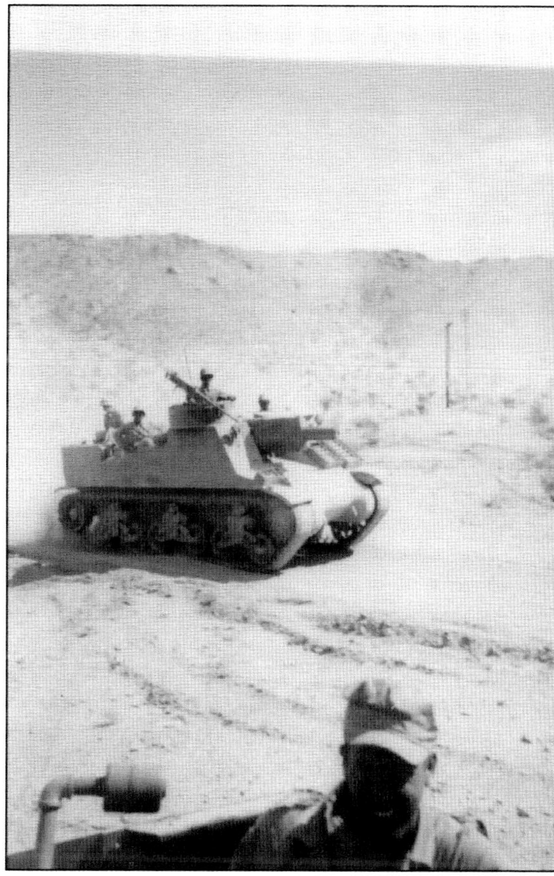

Participation in armored vehicle tactics, known as Tank Destroyer School, prepared the troops for combat on desert terrain. The 4th, 9th, and later, the 11th Armored Division took part in these maneuvers. (Both, courtesy of BLM.)

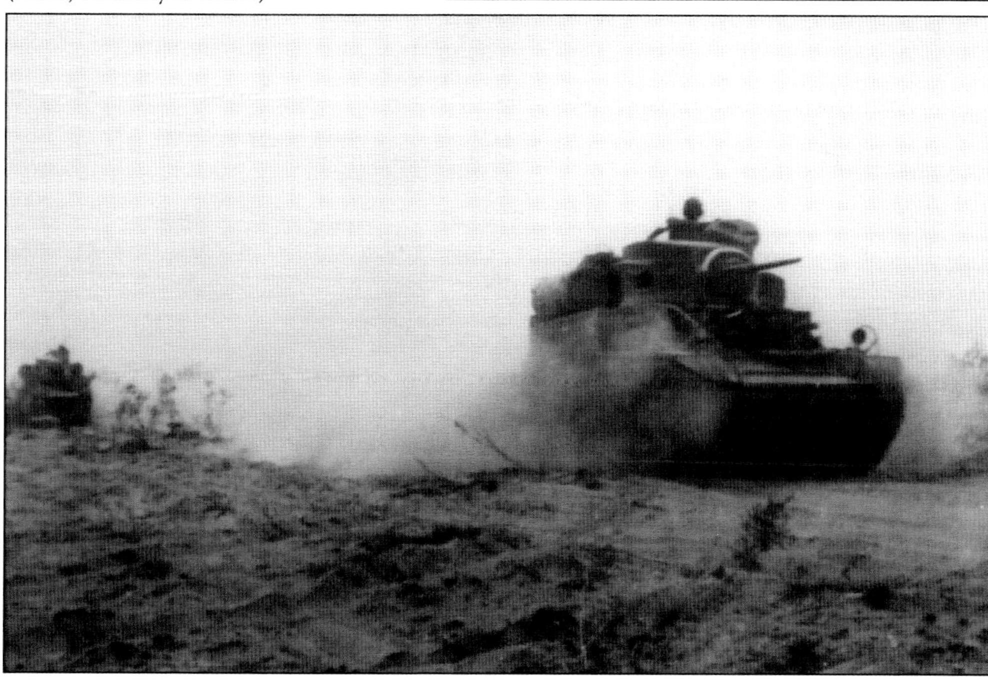

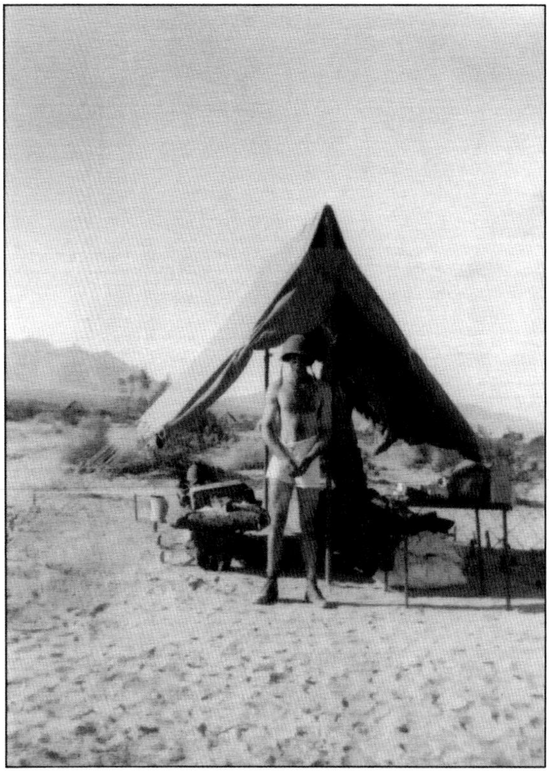

Many of the young soldiers who trained at Camp Ibis would join General Patton on the battlefield. The rigorous training the troops received at the camp fully equipped them to handle combat overseas. (Both, courtesy of BLM.)

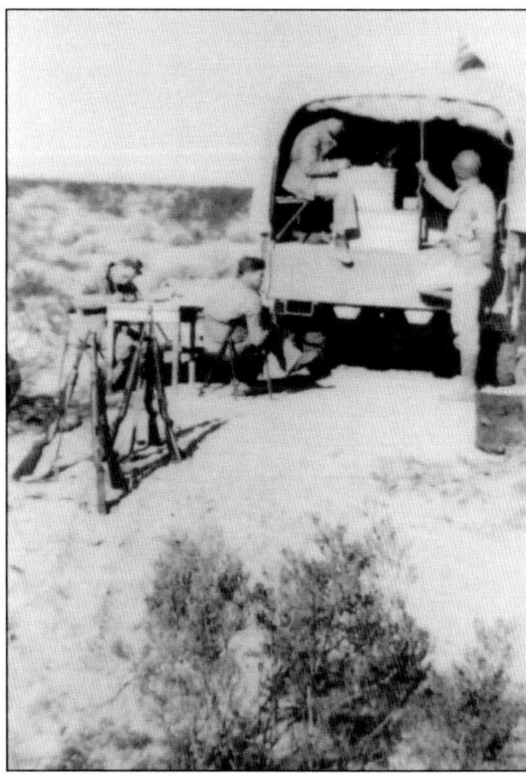

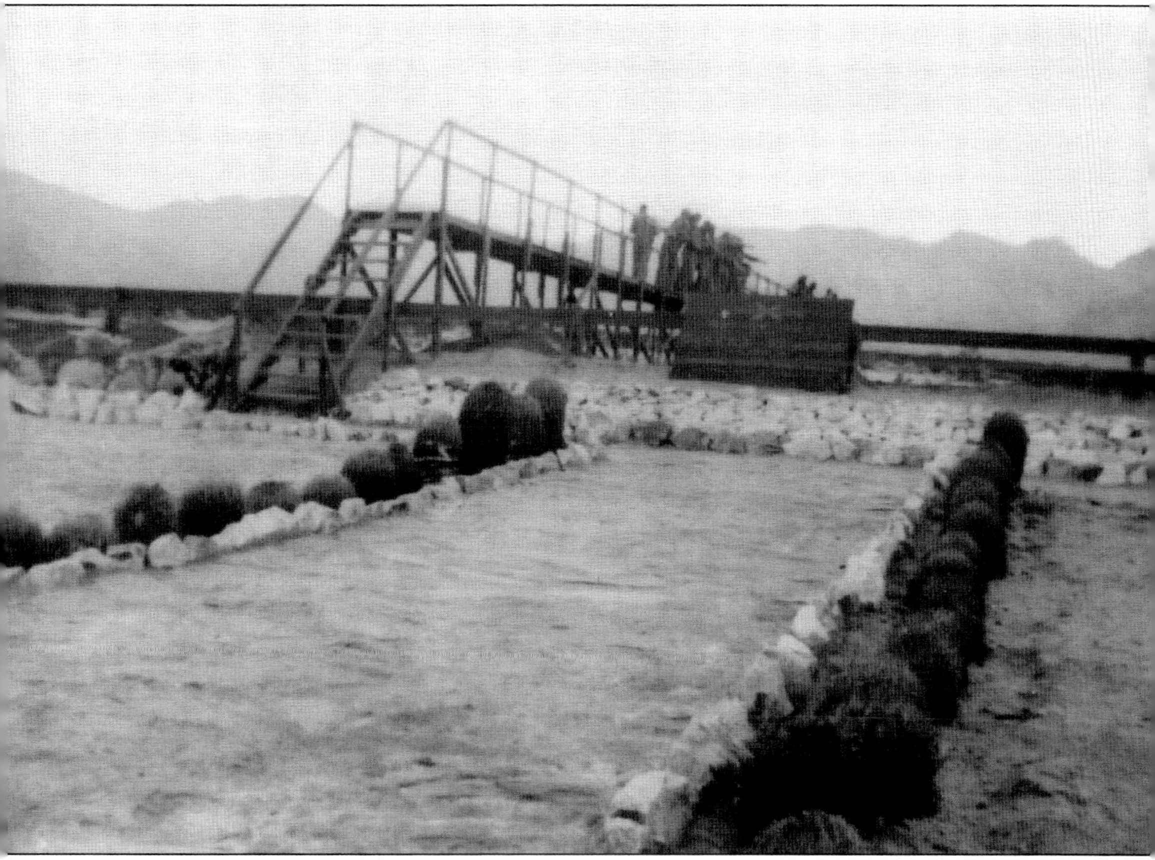

Patton devised an ingenious "war board" upon the desert floor. A bridge of sorts was built over the area where maneuvers and strategies were mapped out, creating an optimal viewing platform for all the participants. (Courtesy of BLM.)

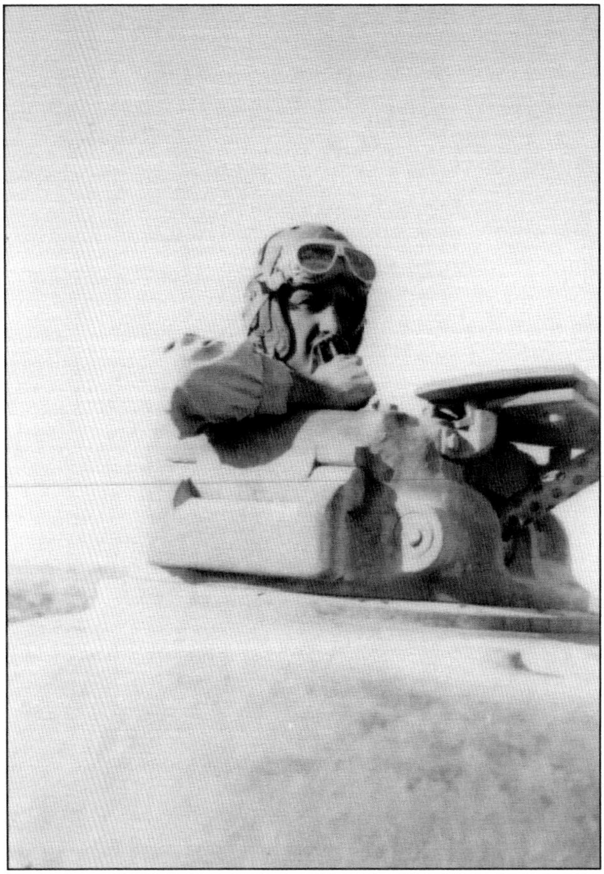

The United States will always be indebted to its military, particularly the (mostly young) men who fought in World War II. It was a highly mechanized war for a lot of youths who had never before driven an automobile, yet in combat training, they were operating enormous weapons of war. (Both, courtesy of BLM.)

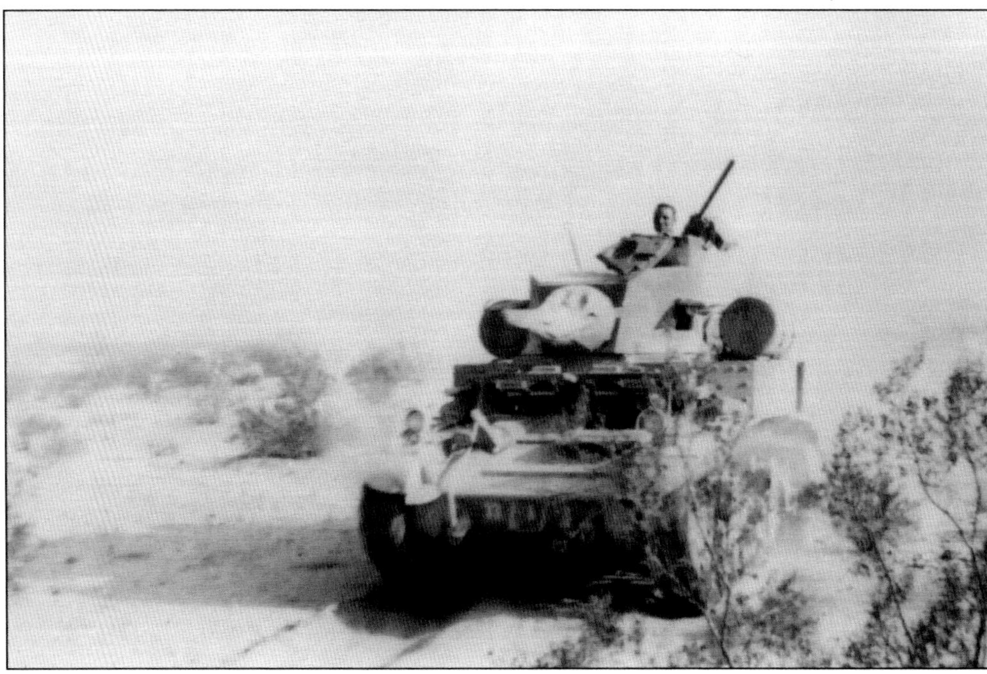

Seven

Davis Dam
Harnessing the River

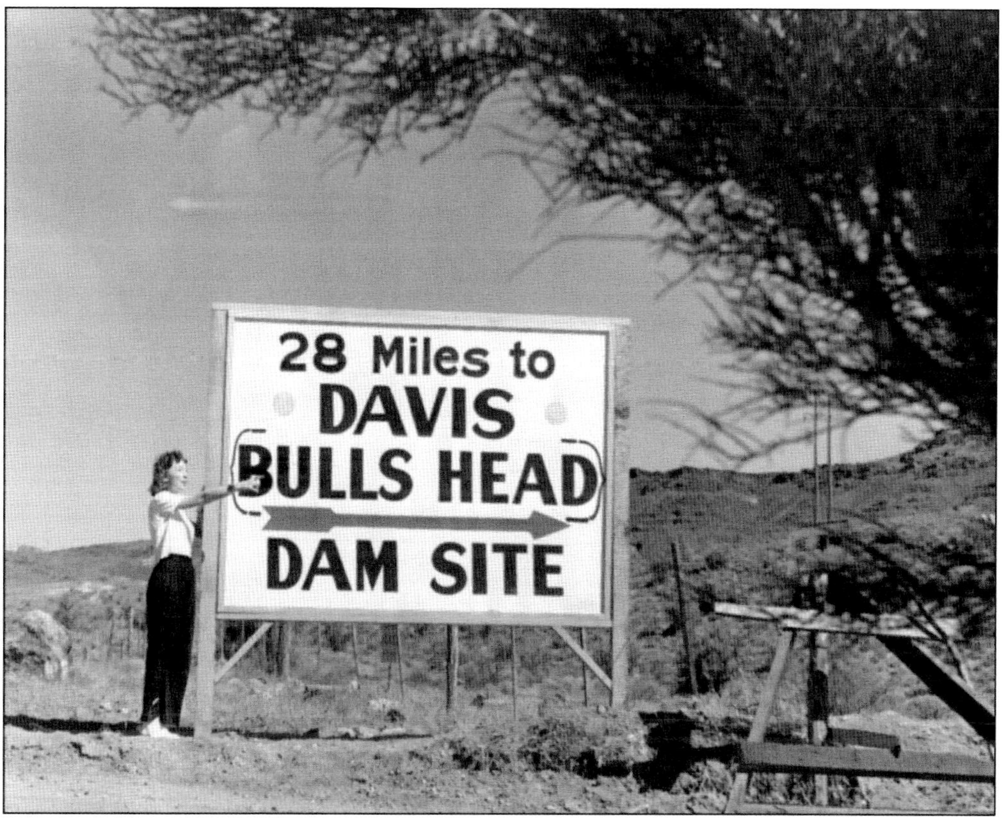

Without Davis Dam, Bullhead City as we know it today would not exist. Named for the iconic "Bull's Head Rock" that was a navigational aid on the river long before the white man arrived, Bullhead City went from a sleepy, seasonal fishing village on the Colorado River to a bustling "micropolitan" in modern times. (Courtesy of CRHS.)

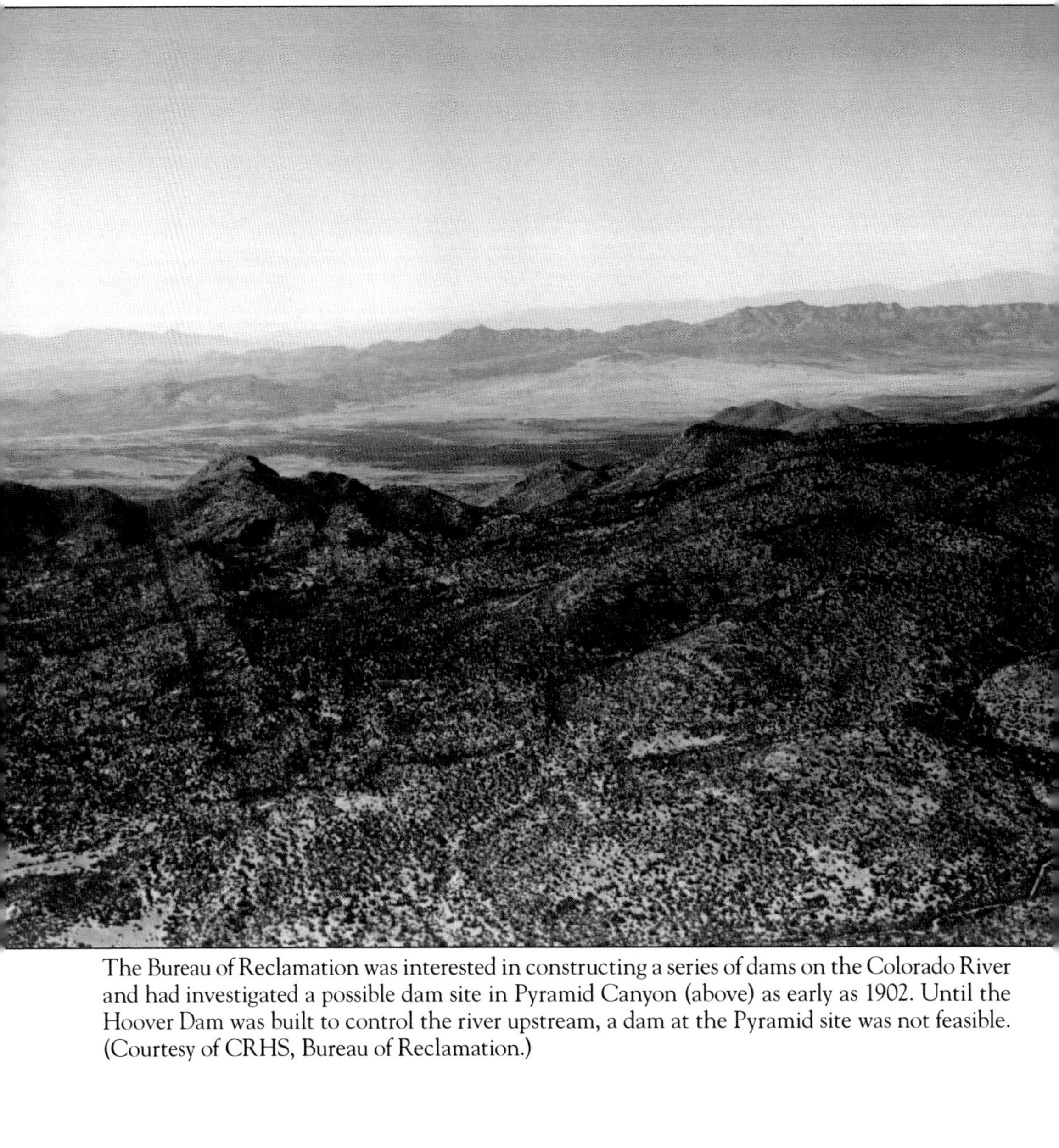

The Bureau of Reclamation was interested in constructing a series of dams on the Colorado River and had investigated a possible dam site in Pyramid Canyon (above) as early as 1902. Until the Hoover Dam was built to control the river upstream, a dam at the Pyramid site was not feasible. (Courtesy of CRHS, Bureau of Reclamation.)

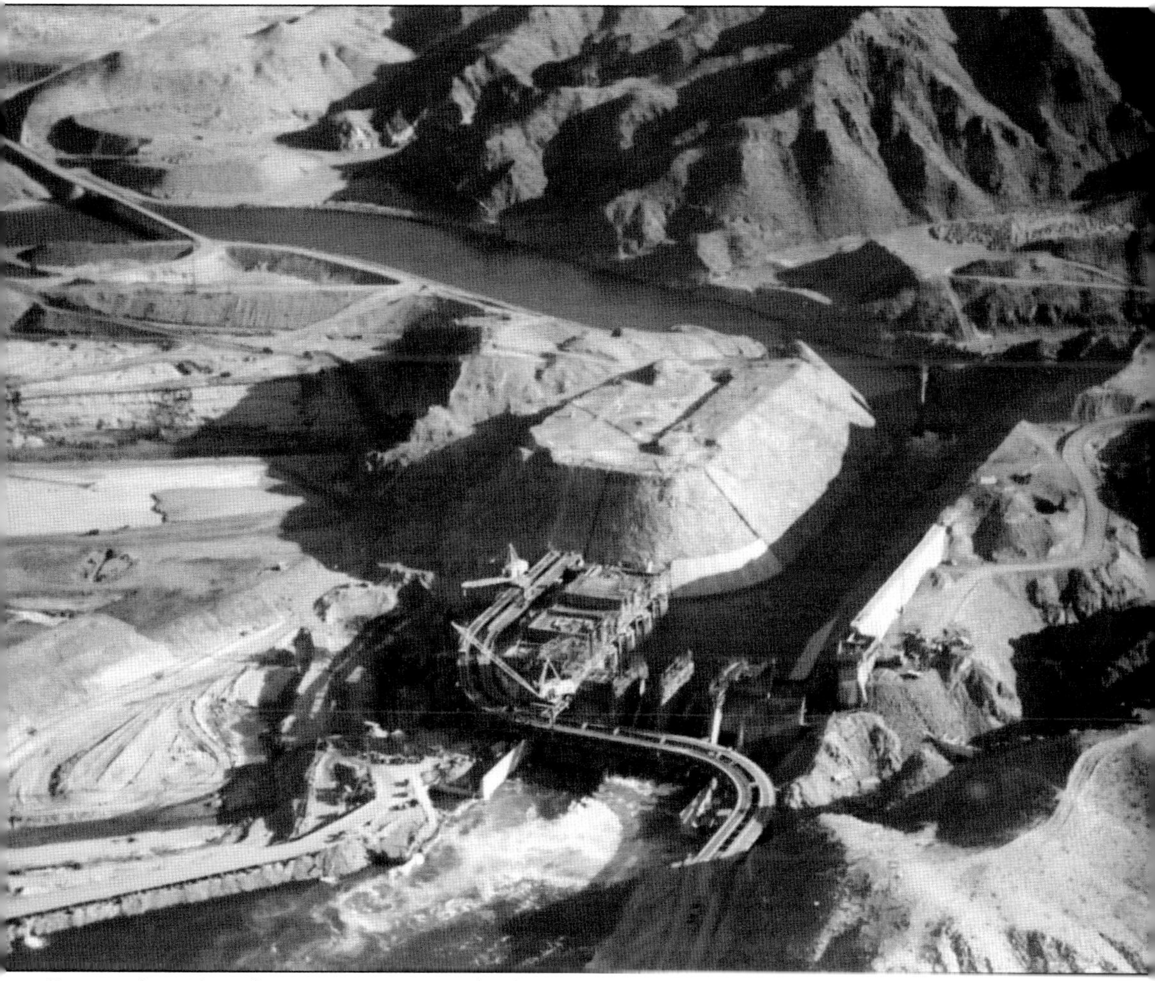

During the 1930s, the Hoover Dam south of Las Vegas, Nevada, and the Parker Dam north of Yuma at Parker, Arizona, were completed. Davis Dam's construction was authorized in 1941 and work began, but ended abruptly in December of 1942 at the start of World War II. The dam was named in honor of Arthur Powell Davis, director of reclamation from 1914 to 1932. (Courtesy of CRHS, Bureau of Reclamation.)

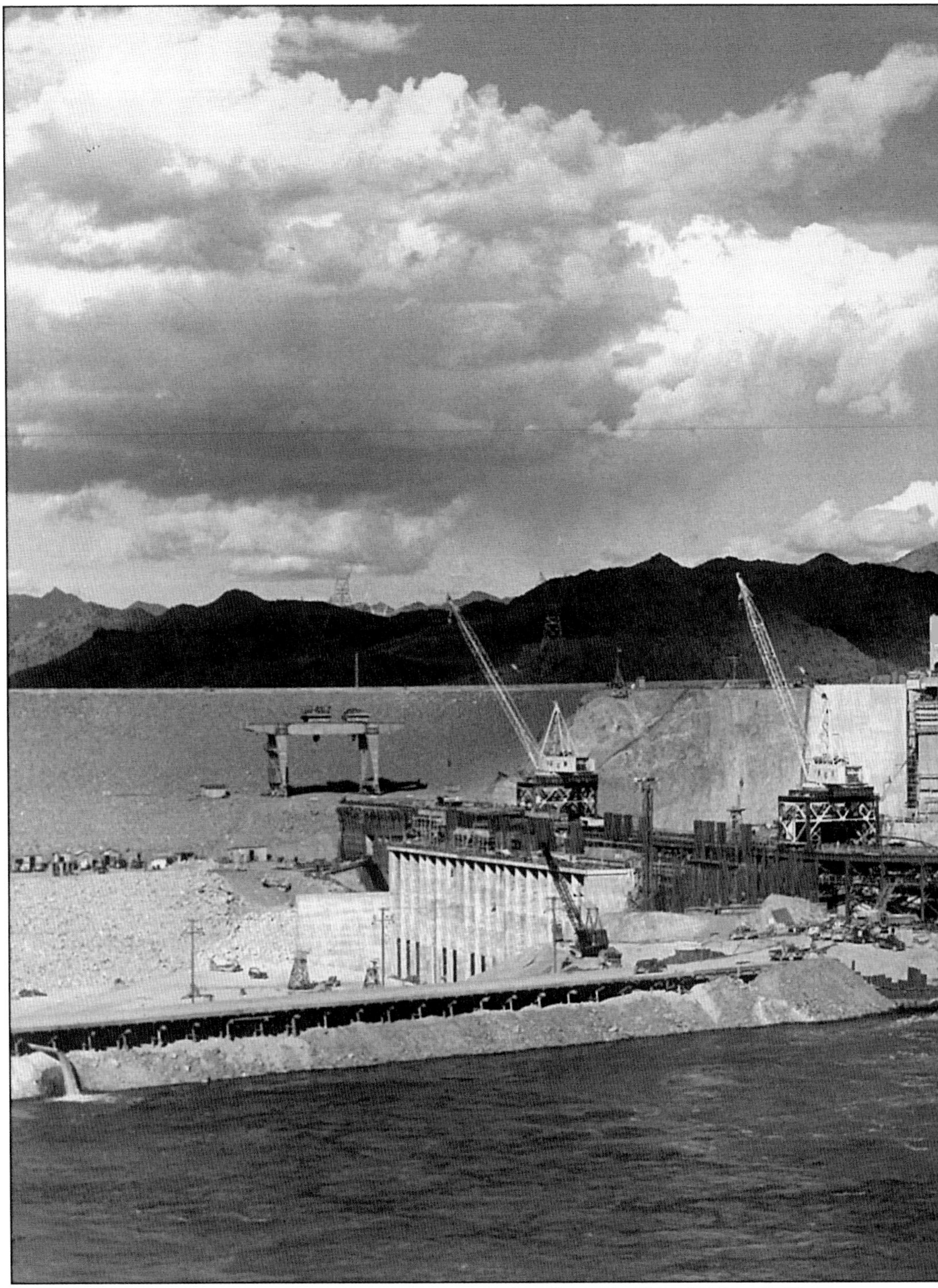

Work on Davis Dam finally resumed in 1946, a year after the end of World War II. The primary purpose of the dam is to reregulate Hoover Dam releases to meet downstream needs, including the annual delivery of 1.5 million acre-feet of water to Mexico, in accordance with a 1944 water treaty. Two work camps, or towns, were created during construction of the dam: Davis Camp on

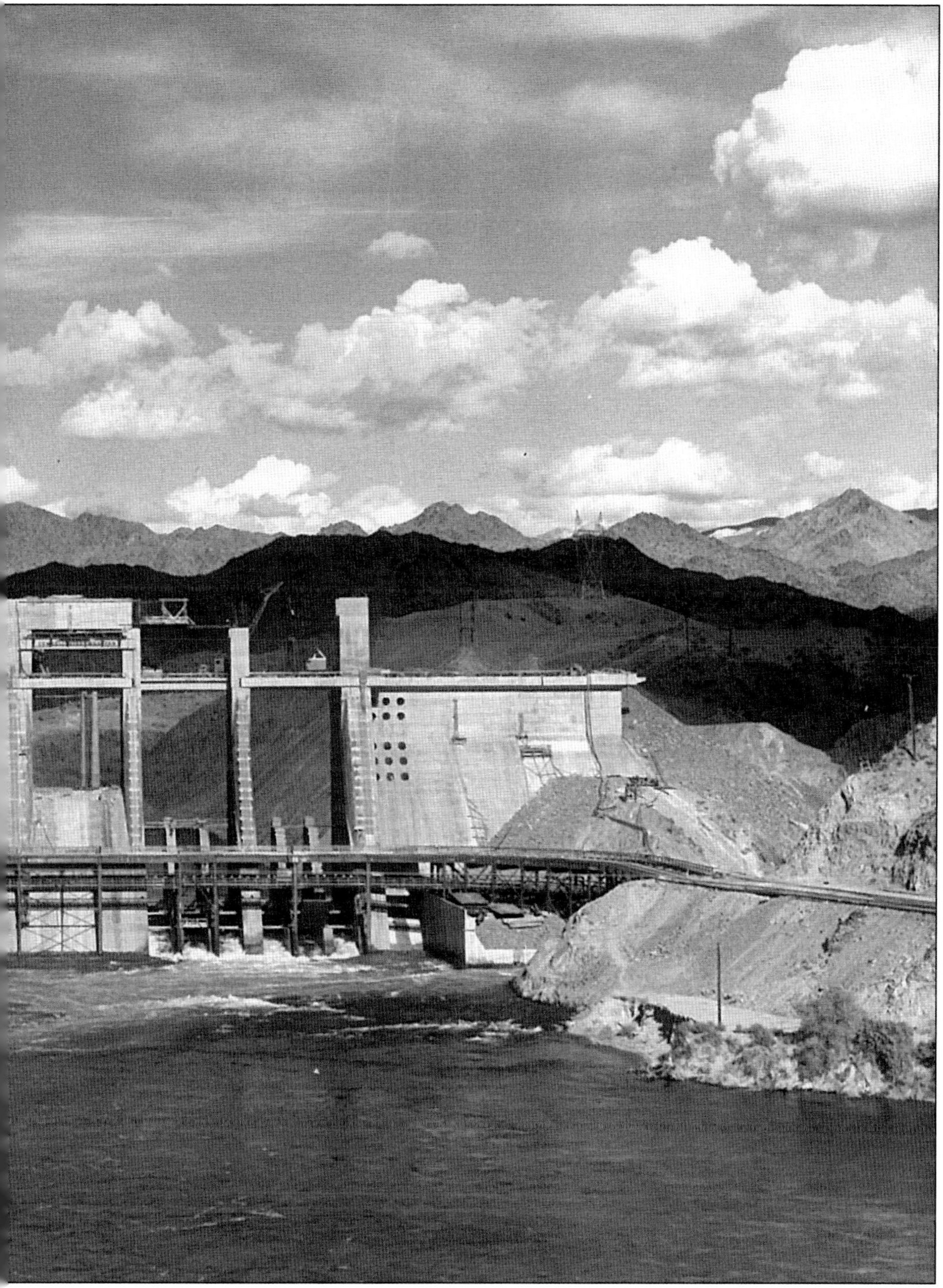

the Arizona side of the Colorado River and Union Camp on the Nevada side of the river. This northward view shows the downstream side of the spillway and outlet structure. (Courtesy of CRHS, Bureau of Reclamation.)

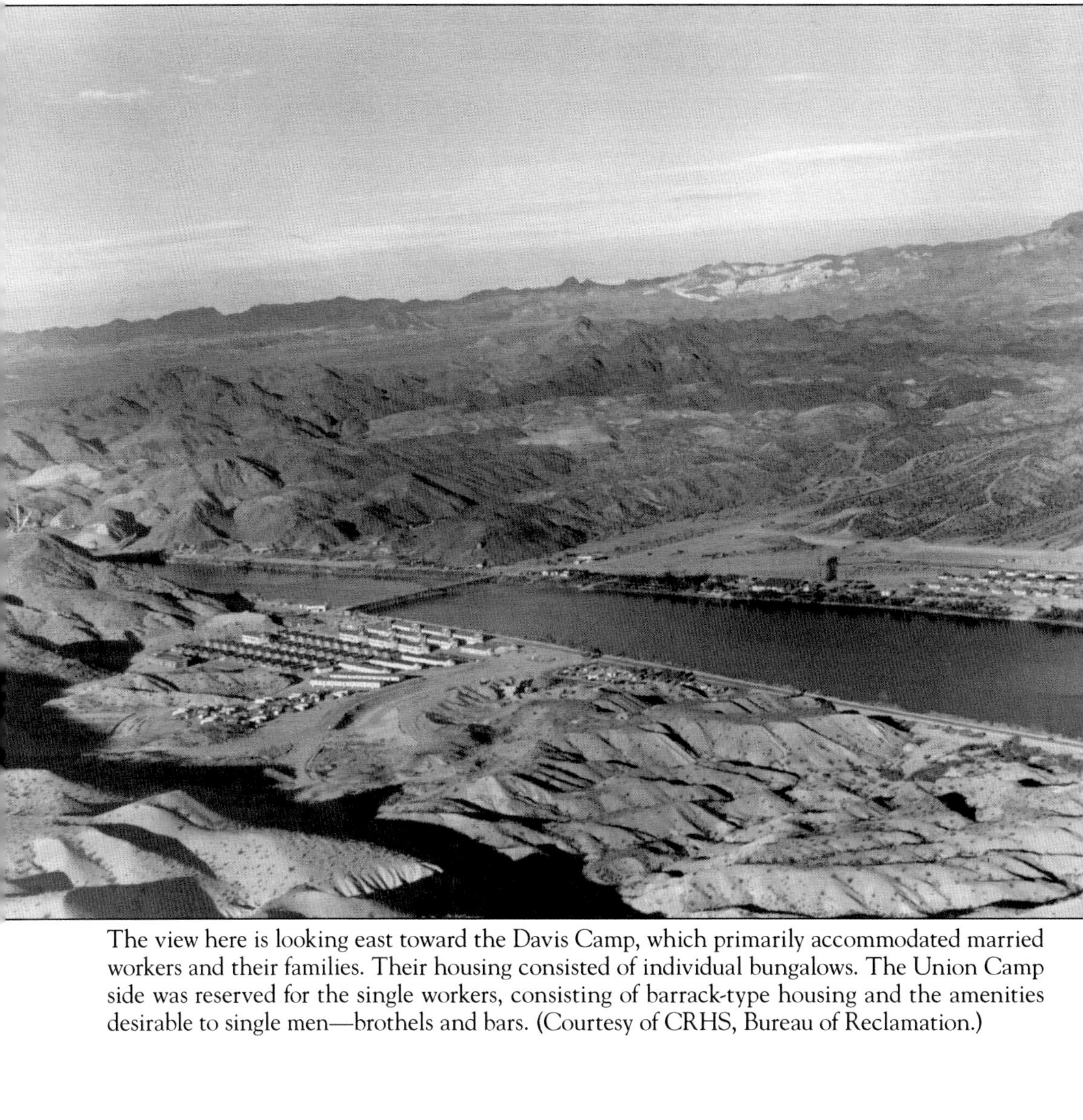

The view here is looking east toward the Davis Camp, which primarily accommodated married workers and their families. Their housing consisted of individual bungalows. The Union Camp side was reserved for the single workers, consisting of barrack-type housing and the amenities desirable to single men—brothels and bars. (Courtesy of CRHS, Bureau of Reclamation.)

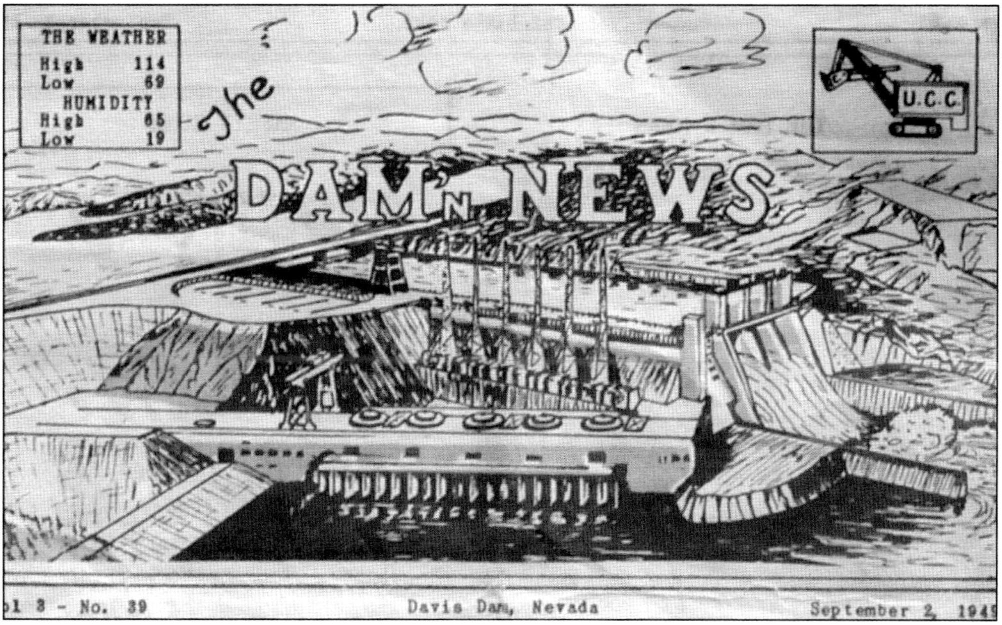

The dam workers had their own newspaper, the *Dam'n News*, shown above. Note the temperature and humidity for September 2, 1949. Another view of Davis Camp, seen below in the late 1940s, shows a row of tents, possibly temporary living quarters. (Both, courtesy of CRHS.)

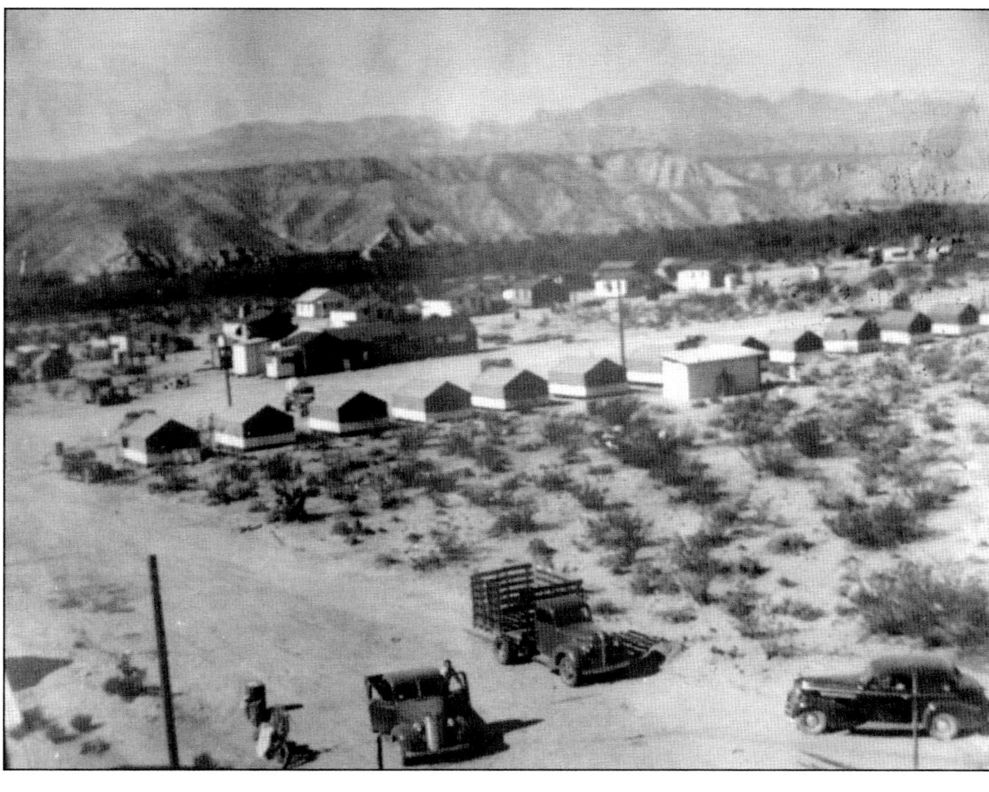

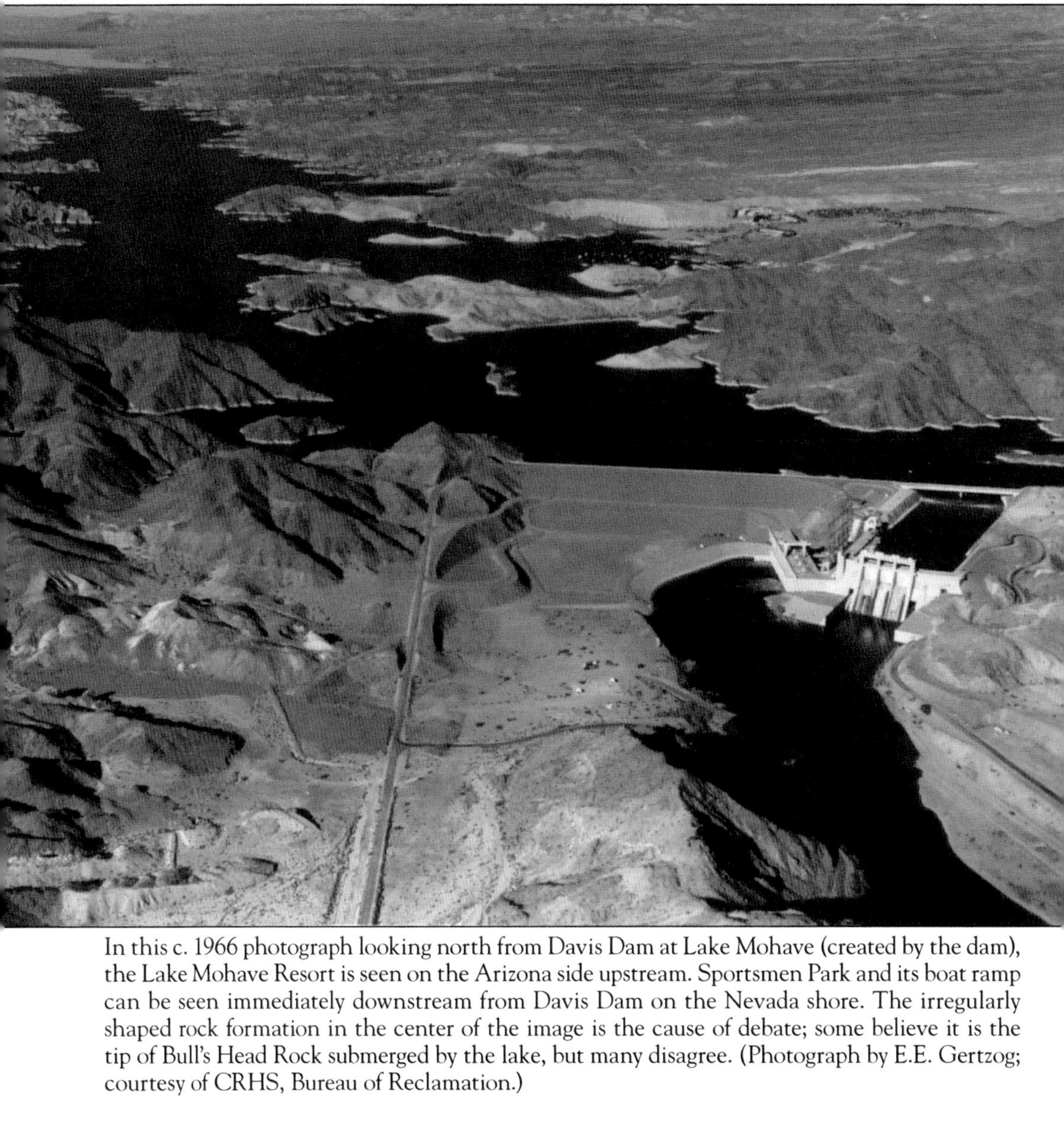

In this c. 1966 photograph looking north from Davis Dam at Lake Mohave (created by the dam), the Lake Mohave Resort is seen on the Arizona side upstream. Sportsmen Park and its boat ramp can be seen immediately downstream from Davis Dam on the Nevada shore. The irregularly shaped rock formation in the center of the image is the cause of debate; some believe it is the tip of Bull's Head Rock submerged by the lake, but many disagree. (Photograph by E.E. Gertzog; courtesy of CRHS, Bureau of Reclamation.)

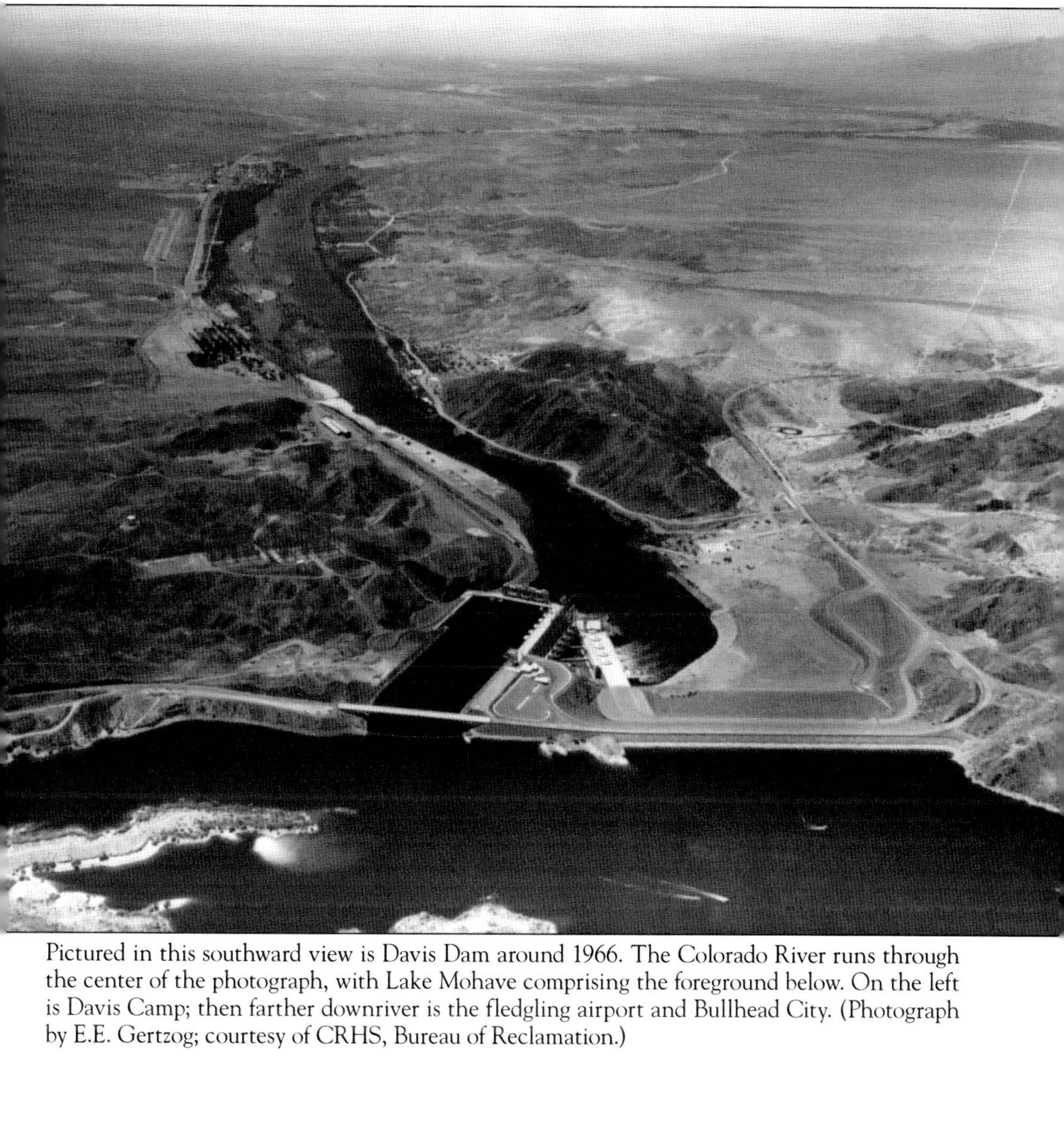

Pictured in this southward view is Davis Dam around 1966. The Colorado River runs through the center of the photograph, with Lake Mohave comprising the foreground below. On the left is Davis Camp; then farther downriver is the fledgling airport and Bullhead City. (Photograph by E.E. Gertzog; courtesy of CRHS, Bureau of Reclamation.)

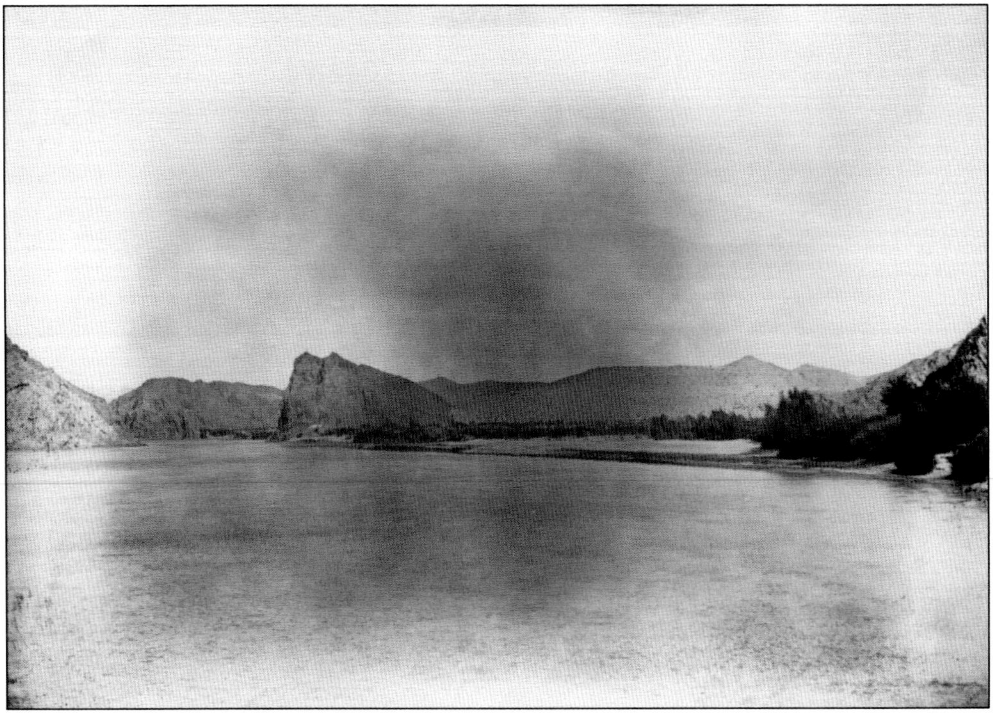

Bull's Head Rock was a well-known navigational landmark for the Indians and early explorers. Two photographs of the rock are shown here, both taken from roughly the same angle. The US Geographical Survey shot the above view around 1908, probably by their agent W.T. Lee. The image below was taken in the late 1940s or early 1950s, before the rock was submerged. The top of the rock is indented, lending itself to the shape of a bull's head. (Above, courtesy of Dennis Casebier; below, courtesy of MMHA.)

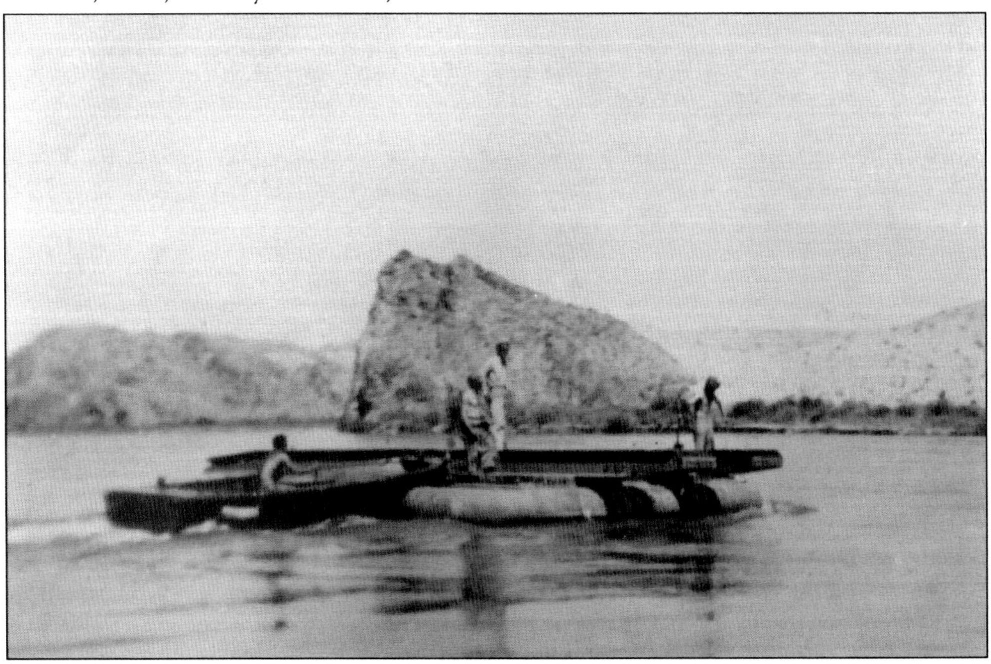

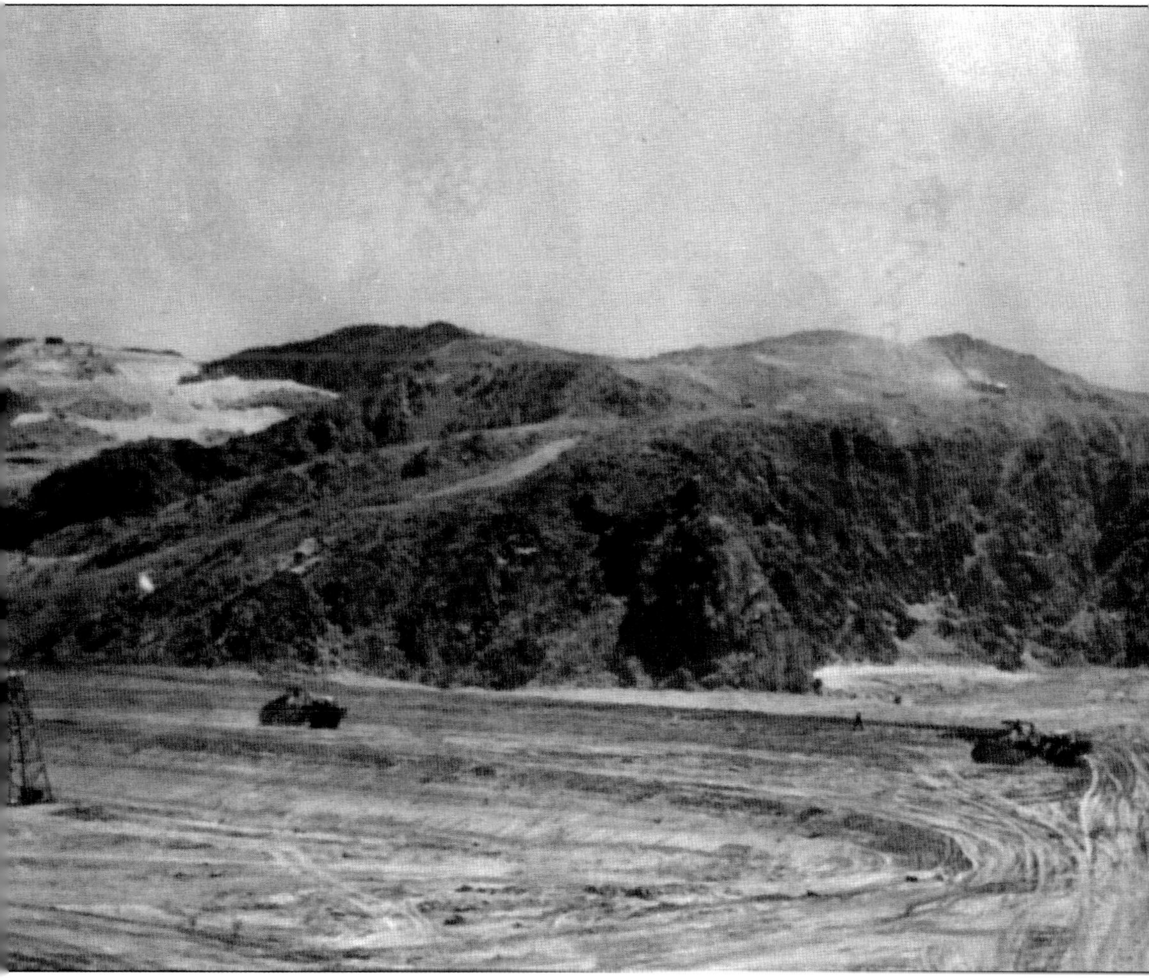

This image of Bull's Head Rock depicts a different angle, photographed during construction of Davis Dam. The sheer size of the rock dwarfs the men and heavy equipment on the dry riverbed. The play of light and shadow on the hills behind the rock make it appear as though it has horns. Perhaps that imagery is what the early inhabitants saw when they gave it the name "Bull's Head Rock." (Courtesy of Tom Brady.)

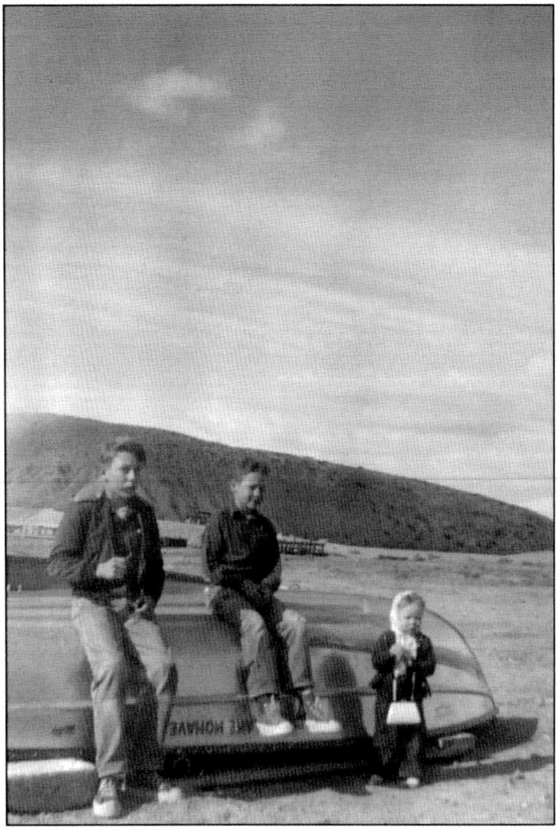

After the dam was completed in 1953, Lake Mohave quickly became a vacation destination, as seen by the unidentified children at left. Fred Favor, with friend and general manager Hamm Pratt, developed Katherine Landing at the Lake Mohave Resort. With 237 miles of shoreline, the lake boasted swimming, water-skiing, scuba diving, boating, and fishing. Favor later added other amenities to Katherine Landing's small dock and single building seen below. Soon, there were more boat slips and docks, a café, and lodging accommodations, including a motel, RV park, and eventually, houseboats for hire. (Both, courtesy of Donna Zurcher.)

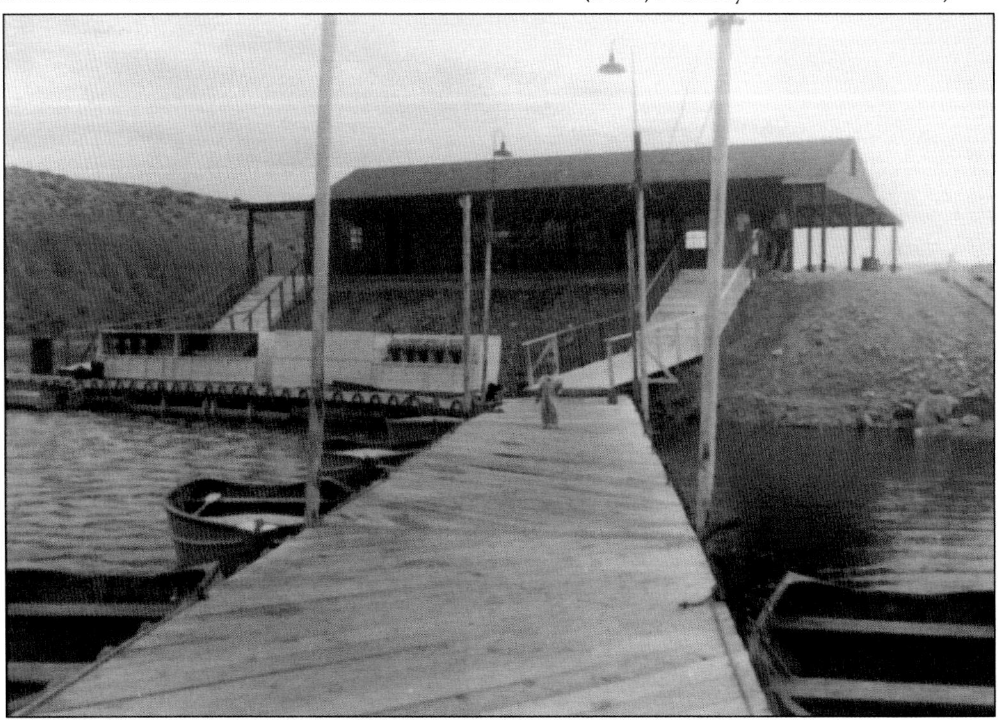

Eight

Bullhead City
Tourist Destination

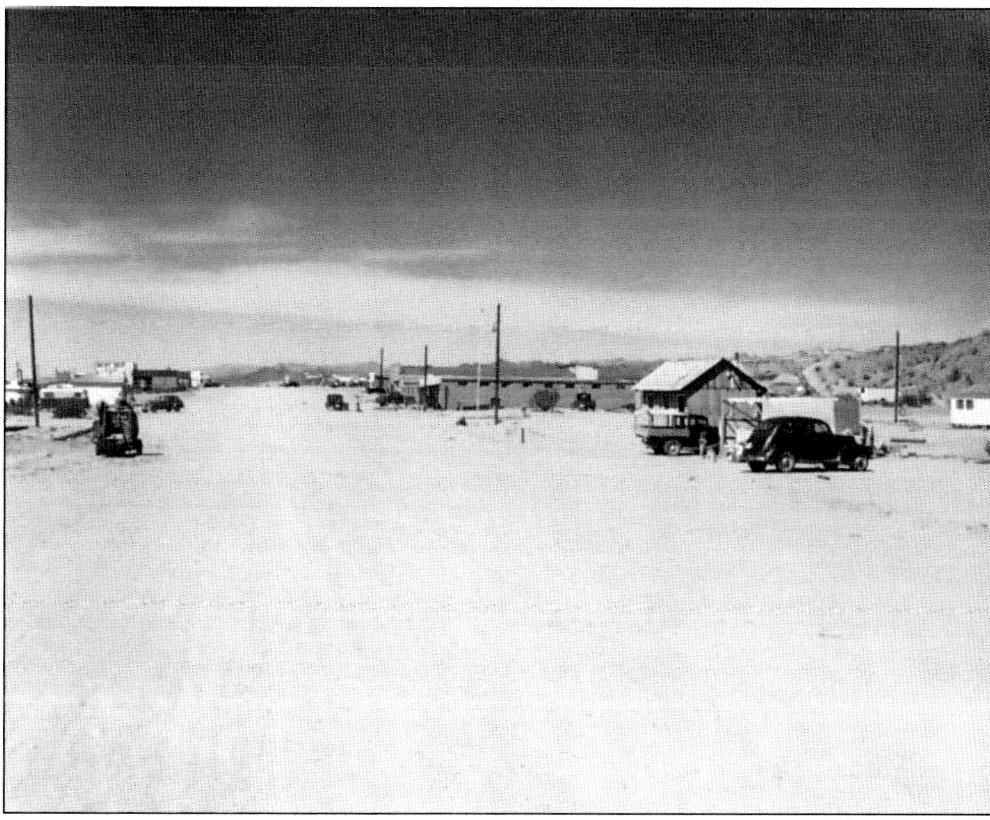

After the completion of Davis Dam in 1953, the concept of a town named Bull's Head started to become a reality, as many workers from the dam project remained with their families and put down roots. The name was soon changed to Bullhead City. (Courtesy of CRHS.)

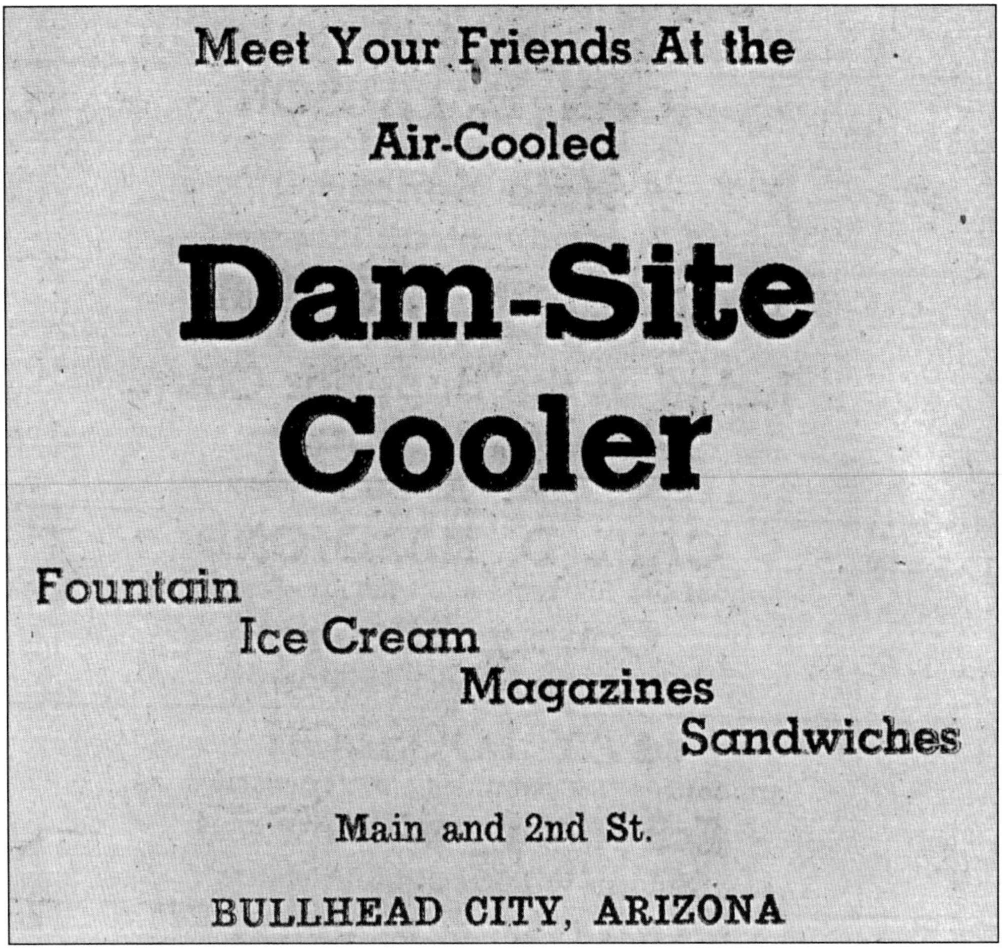

Bullhead City has some of the hottest weather in the world; temperatures can reach 128 degrees Fahrenheit or higher. Without the modern invention of air-conditioning, it is highly unlikely that Bullhead City would have developed as a place for year-round residency. The name of the first eatery in Bullhead City, the Dam-Site Cooler, is evidence of that. (Both, courtesy of MMHA.)

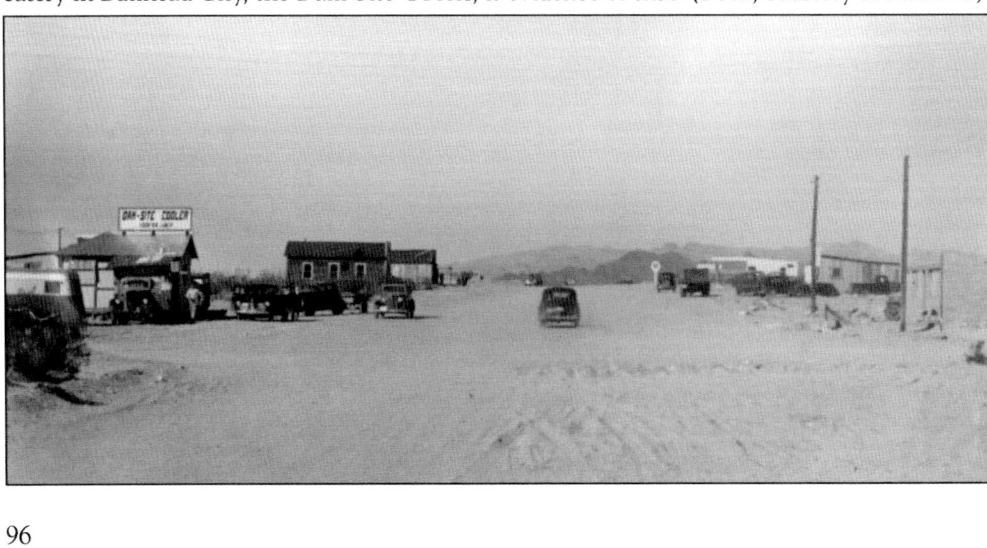

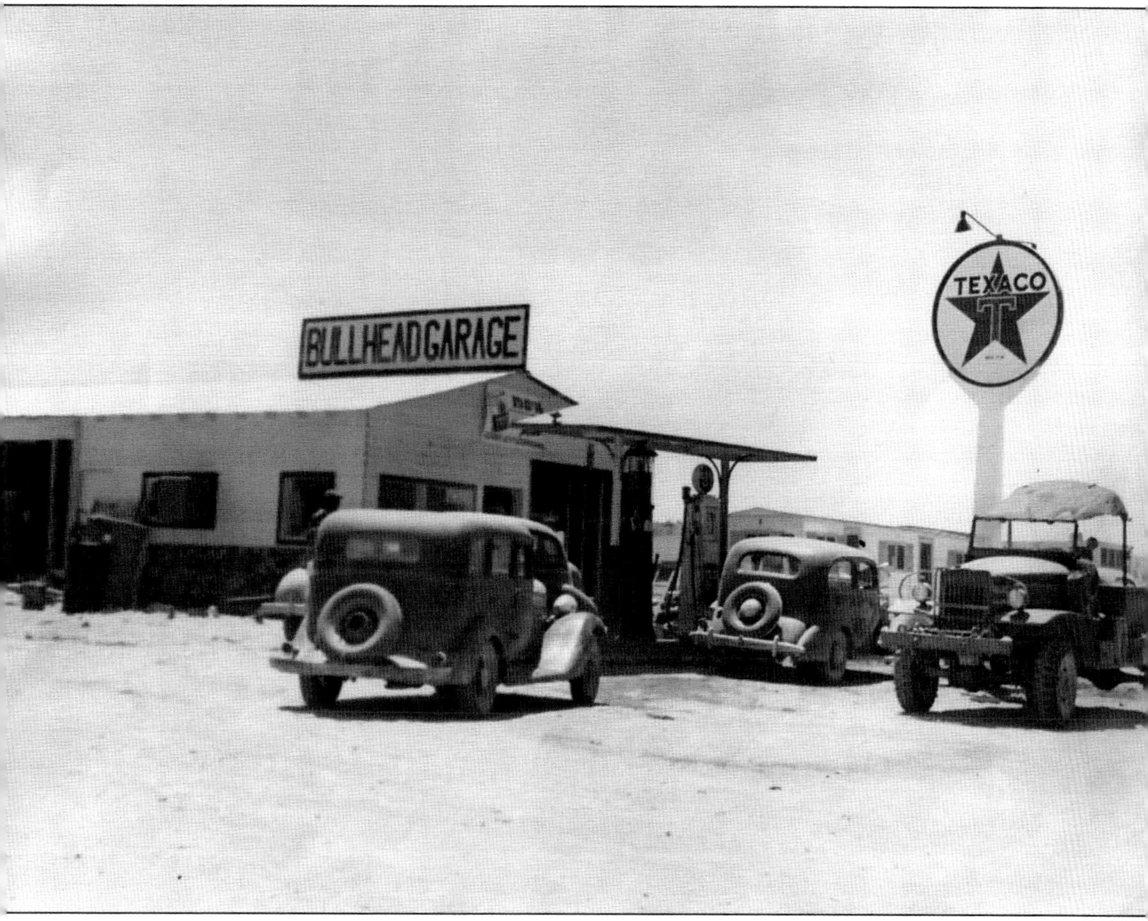

O.C. Buck owned the first gas station in the new city. Automobiles were instrumental in the development of this isolated desert town, and Buck was one of the early entrepreneurs who helped grow Bullhead City. (Courtesy of MMHA.)

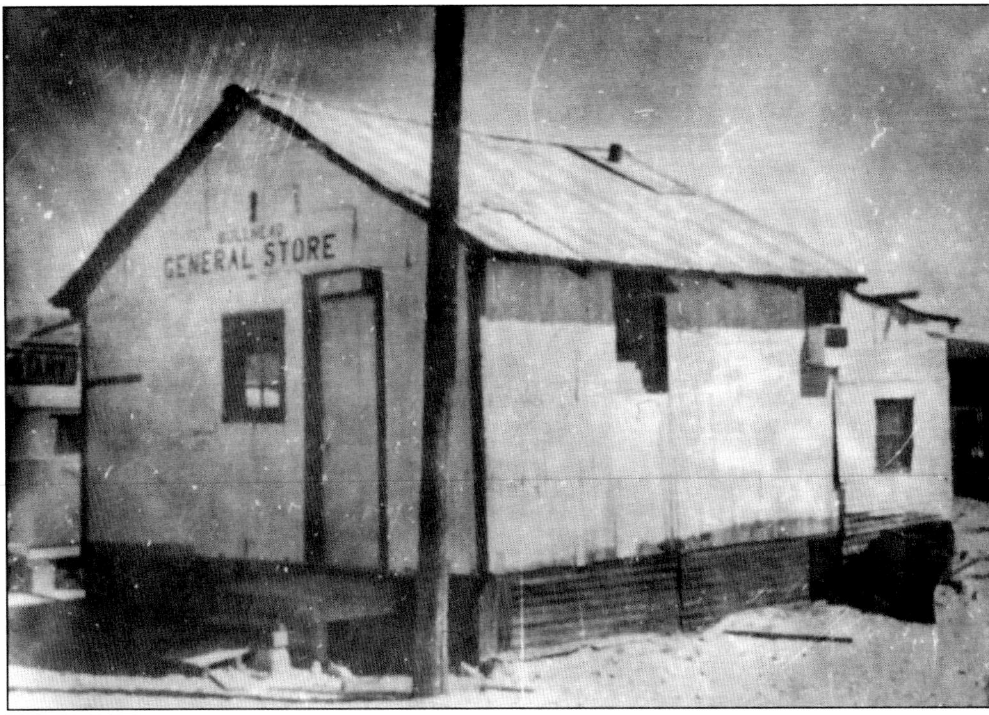

The first general store was located on the then unpaved Main Street, which in time would become Highway 95. The general store was later replaced by Valley Market, seen in the background behind a man known only as "Unk" to early residents. (Above, courtesy CRHS; below, courtesy MMHA.)

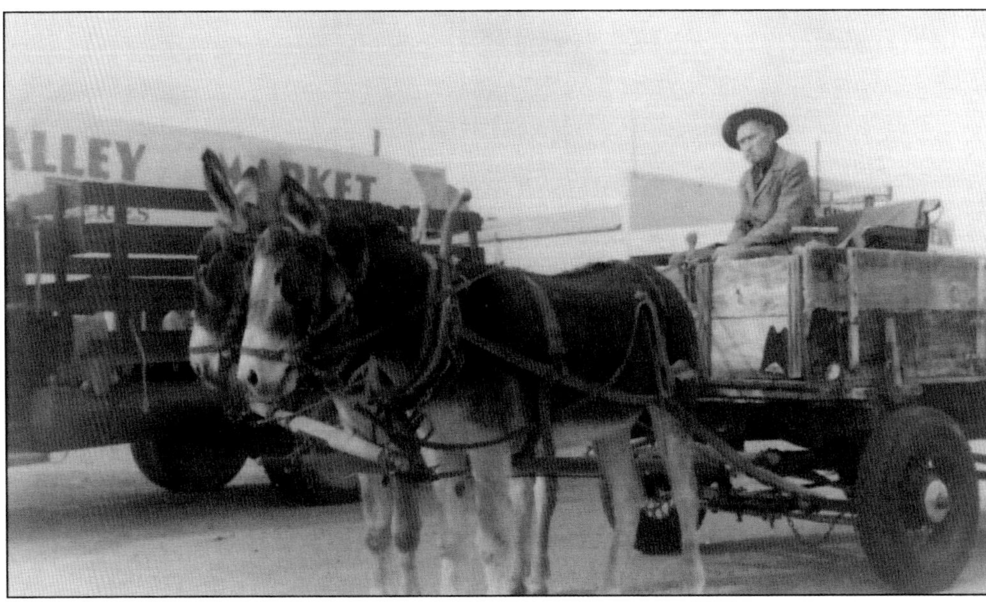

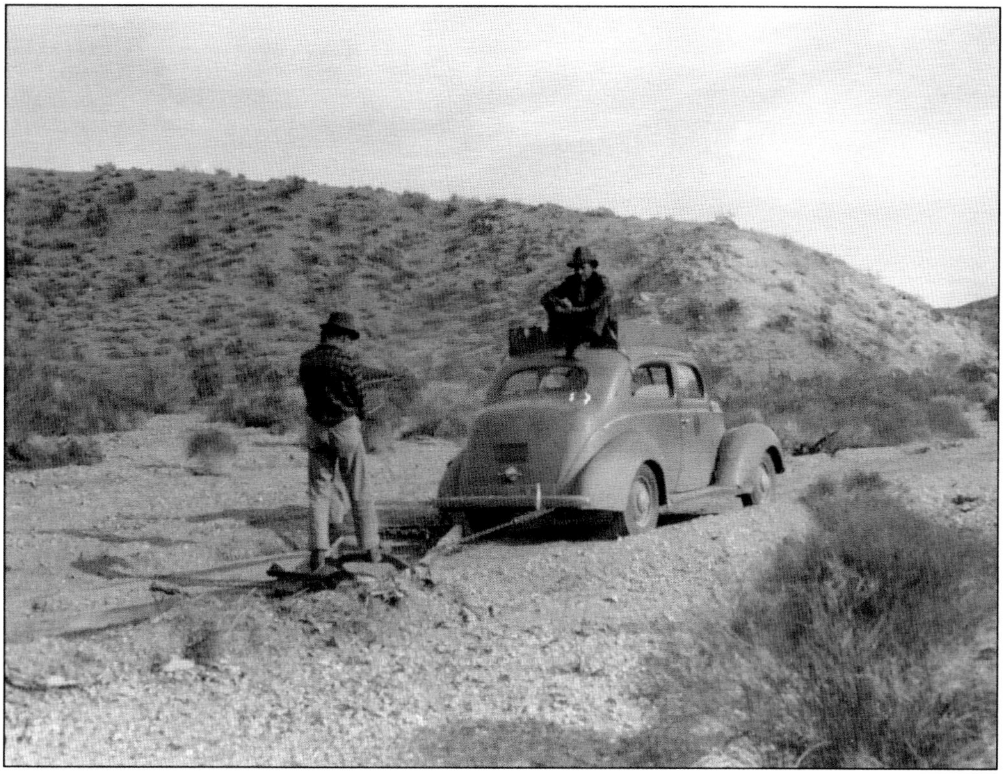

Early Bullhead residents had to use ingenuity when materials were scarce. These men appear to be attempting to grade a desert dirt road by dragging a car frame over it with one of the men as a ballast. (Both, courtesy of MMHA.)

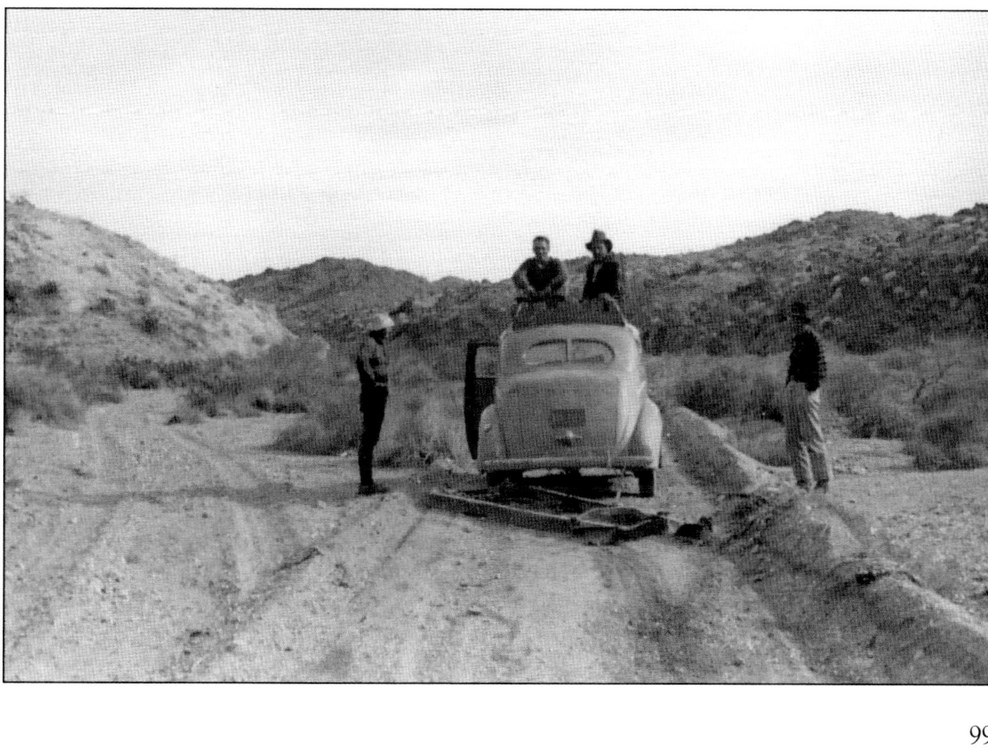

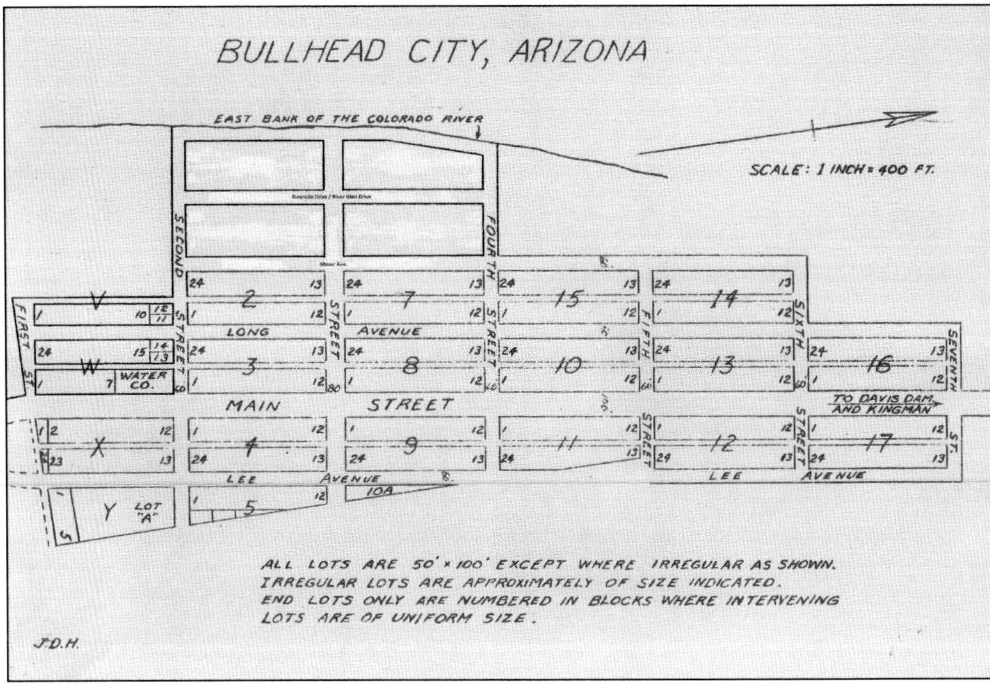

Here, the layout of the new town is beginning to take shape. The map details the area now known as Original Bullhead, from First Street north to Seventh Street. The image captures the view facing east on Second Street. From this early footprint, the city grew to 28.5 square miles in size. In the early 2000s, another 14.4 square miles was annexed to achieve its current size of 42.9 square miles. (Above, courtesy of MMHA; below, courtesy of CRHS.)

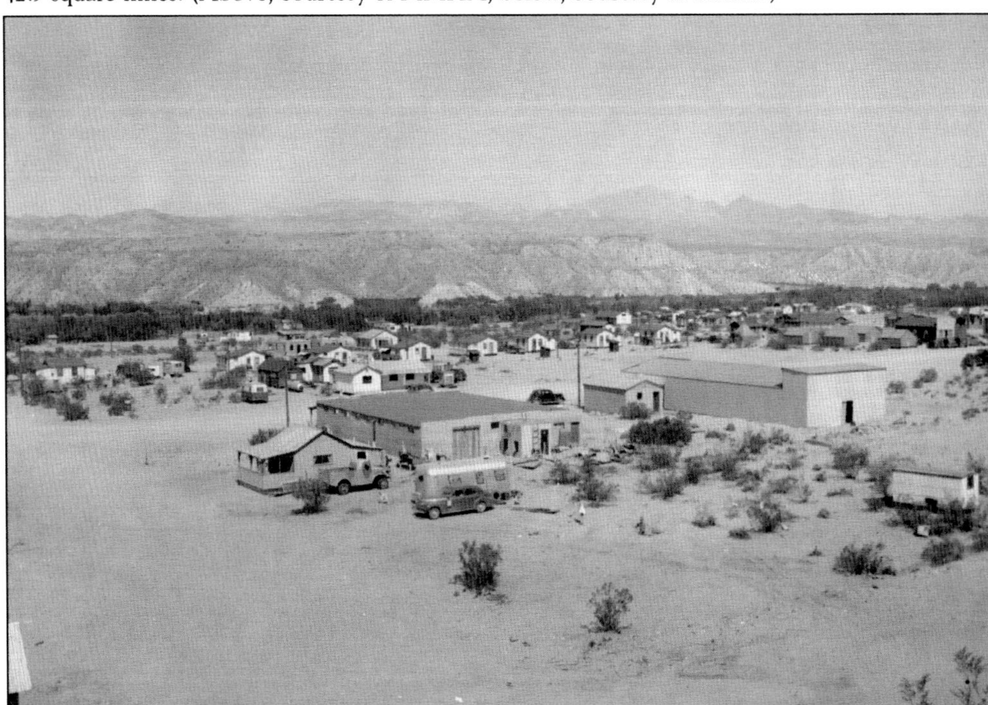

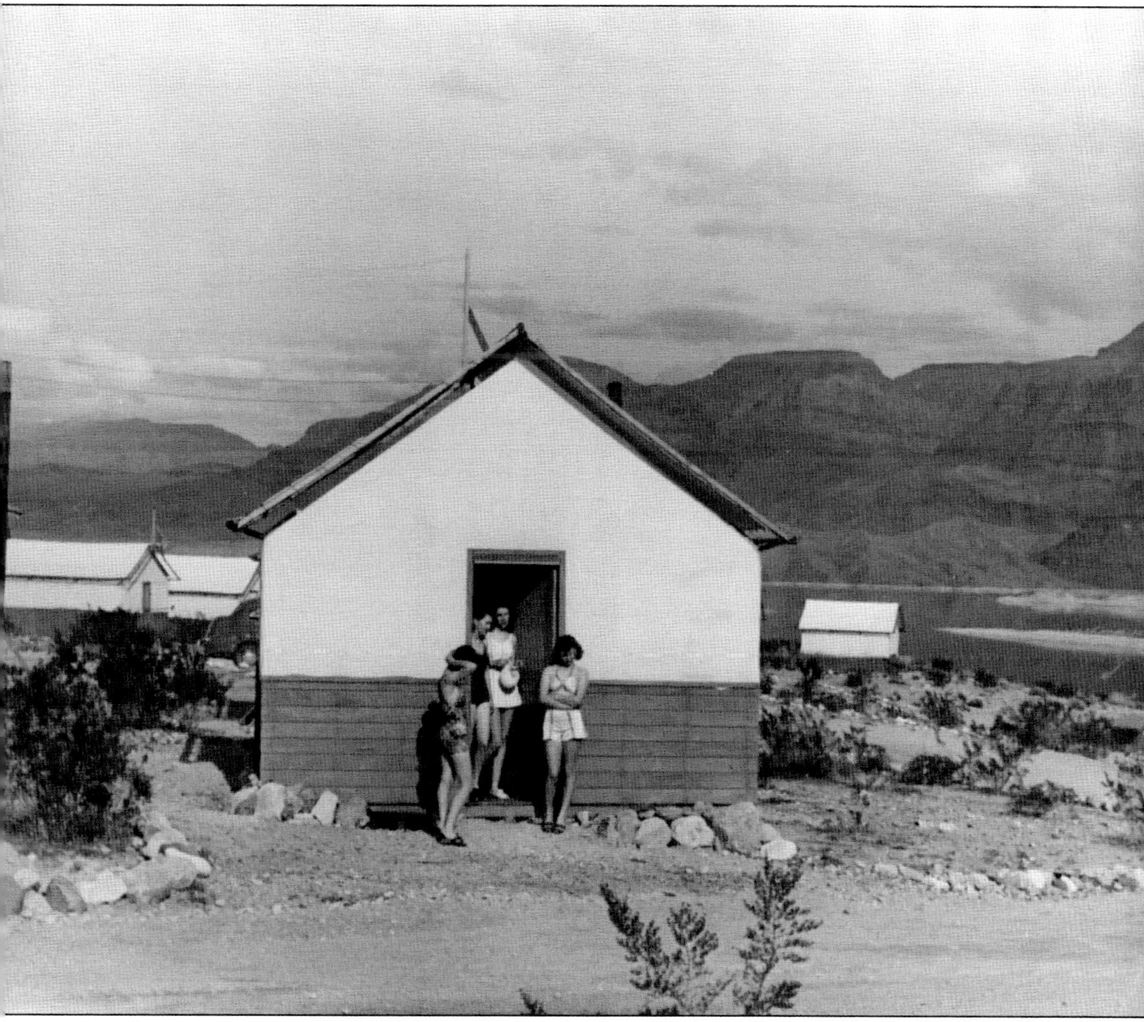

Girls in bathing suits stand outside their tented bungalow at Lake Mohave around 1949. The area was becoming popular among tourists for water sports and the dry desert air. The 67-mile lake remains one of the premier destinations in the Lake Mead National Recreation Area, located southeast of Las Vegas, Nevada. (Courtesy of MMHA.)

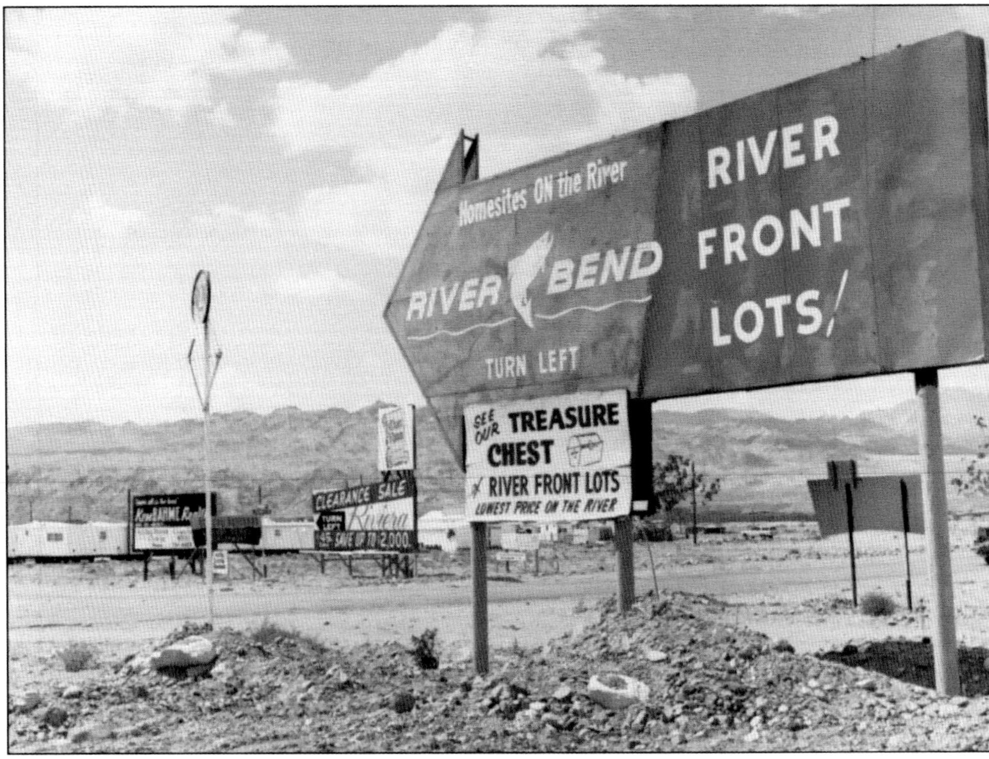

Real estate developers were soon carving up the city into lots for housing subdivisions, hoping to entice visitors to buy property in Bullhead City. One of the largest subdivisions, Riviera, was located on the big curve of the river known as River Bend. With the company's growing commercial presence and its own post office designation, the area became known as Riviera. Today, both terms—River Bend and Riviera—are used to describe this section of Bullhead City. (Both, courtesy of CRHS.)

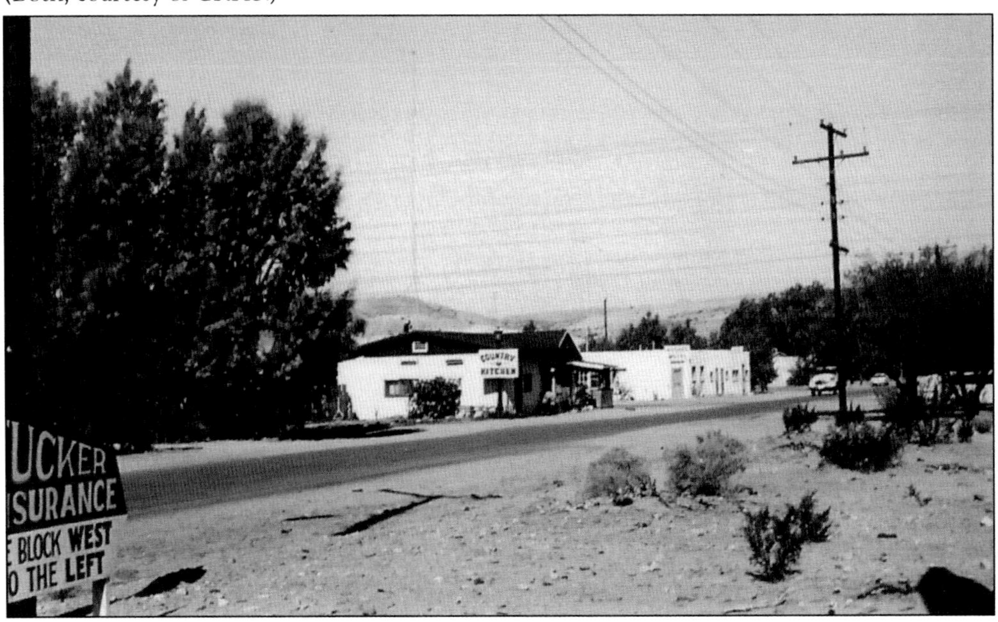

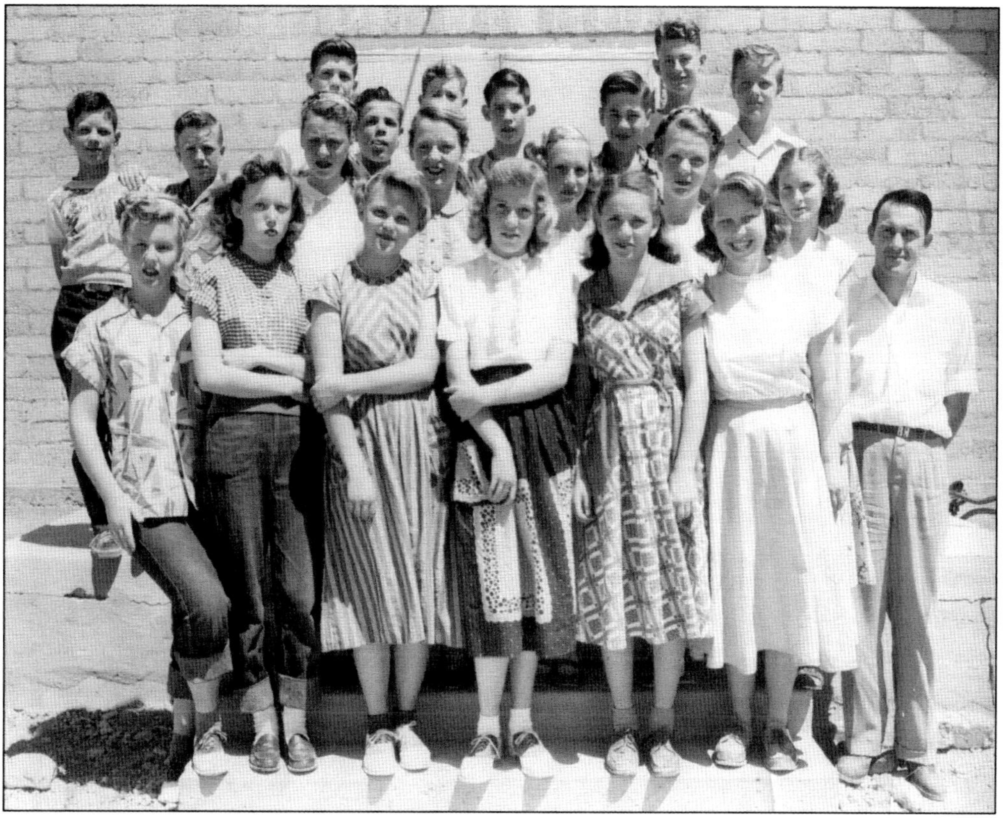

Seen here in 1953, seventh and eighth grade students pose on the steps of the Bullhead City Grammar School, founded in 1948. From left to right are (first row) Donna Olea, Carol Wood, Laura L., Laura Porter, Mary Allen, Patricia McIntyre, and principal and teacher Robert Wiley; (second row) Bill McCune, Roger Bryan, Joanne Davidson, Sharon Loose, Linda Wilkas, Linda Loose, and Rosalea Clayton; (third row) Richie McDowell, Robert Dell, Michael Morris, David VanDahalson, Rylie McDowell, Lyle Winkle, and Joe Farnum. Not pictured are David Laffoon, Dick Henson, Gerald Bryan, and Donald Graham. (Courtesy of Robert Dell.)

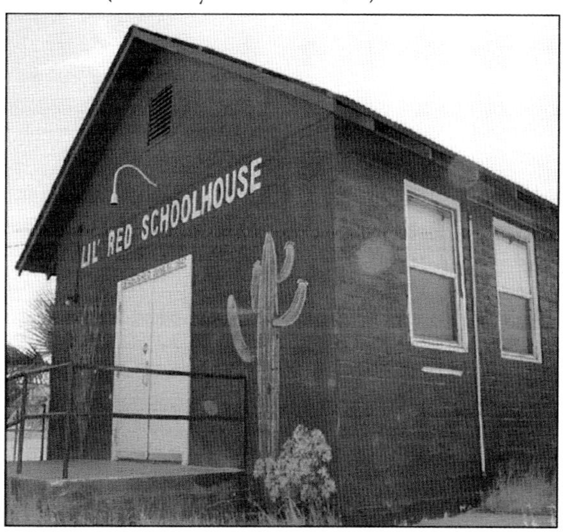

The school's gray brick exterior was painted red in the 1990s when Bashas Grocery donated $1,000 for the project. At that time, it became known as the "Lil' Red Schoolhouse." The school currently sits on its original site on Lee Avenue, off Second Street, but plans are being made to relocate it to Bullhead Community Park, north of Original Bullhead. (Author's collection.)

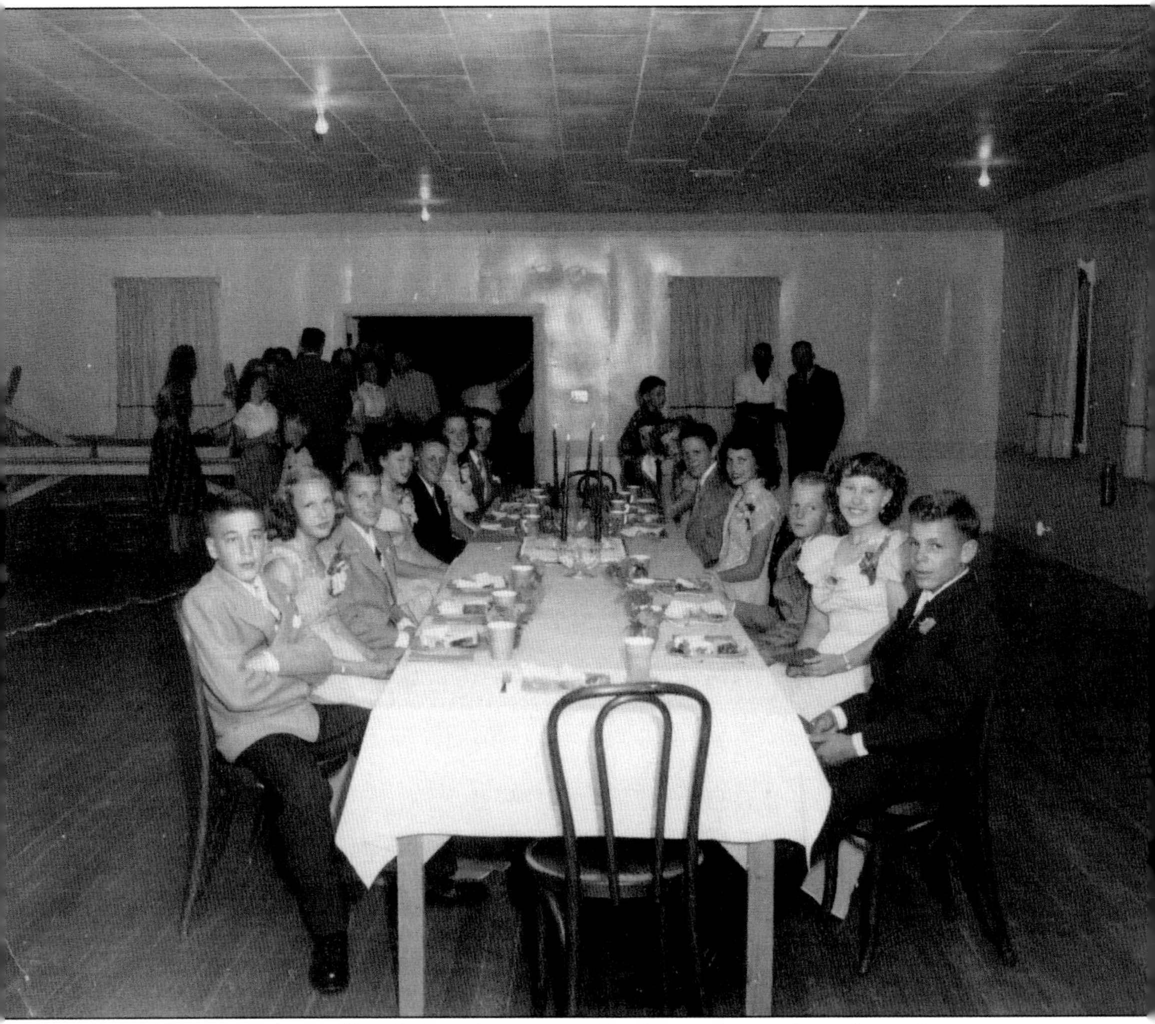

Students from the Bullhead City Grammar School attend a sixth grade graduation ceremony at the US Bureau of Reclamation Recreation Hall at Davis Dam on May 17, 1951. Seated at the table are, from front to back, (left) Rylie McDowell, Linda Wilkas, John Wallace, Carol Wood, David Laffoon, Sharon Loose, and Donald Graham; (right) Robert Dell, Patricia McIntyre, Gerald Bryan, Joanne Davidson, Dick Henson, Donna Olea, and Richie McDowell. (Courtesy of Robert Dell.)

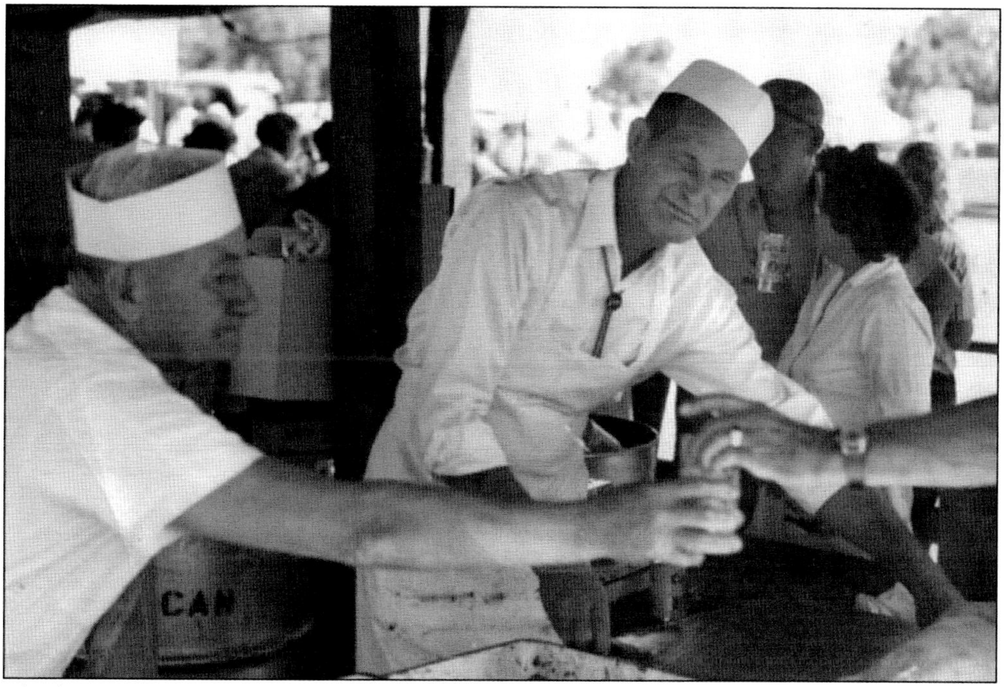

The first Burro Barbeque was held in 1954, when O.C. Buck and some friends decided to throw a party for the community to drum up business during the slow month of April. Buck and friends hunted and killed wild burros, roasted them in underground pits overnight, and served them up with side dishes. The first few years, the barbeque was free, until burro meat was replaced with beef. The annual event was turned over to the Bullhead City Rotary Club in 1965, and they have continued the tradition to this day. (Both, courtesy of Larry Ford.)

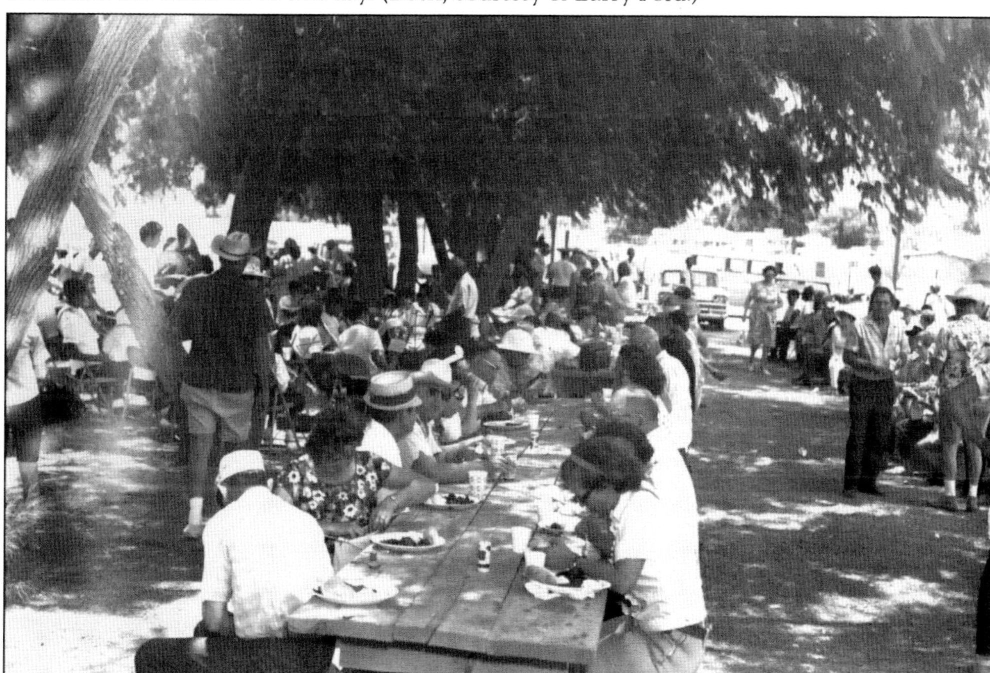

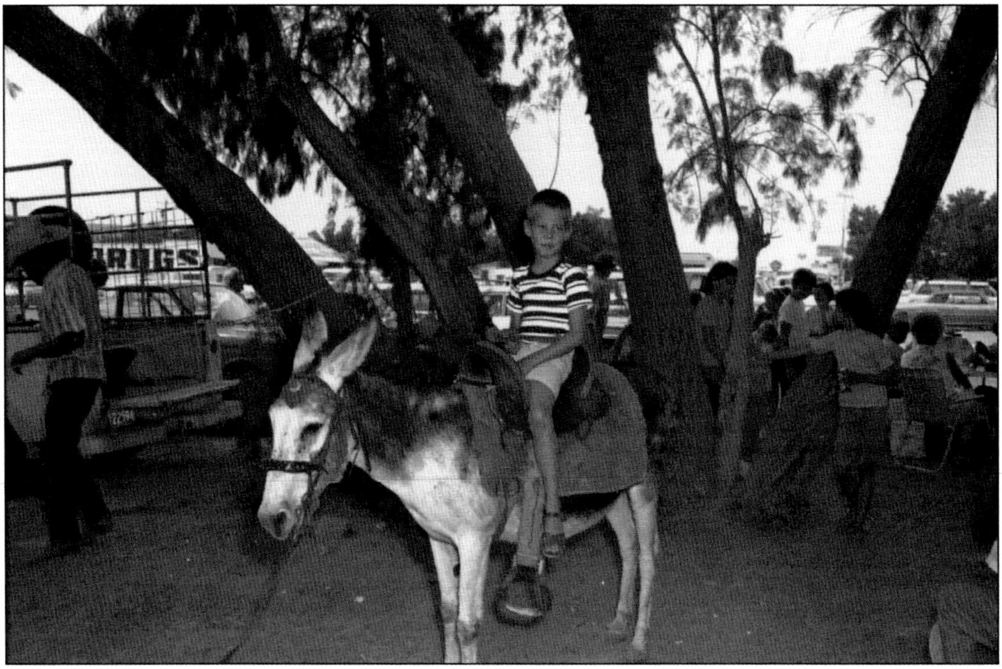

Around 1966, a boy has saddled up on a burro at the annual Burro Barbeque, but he looks just as unhappy as the burro. (Courtesy of Larry Ford.)

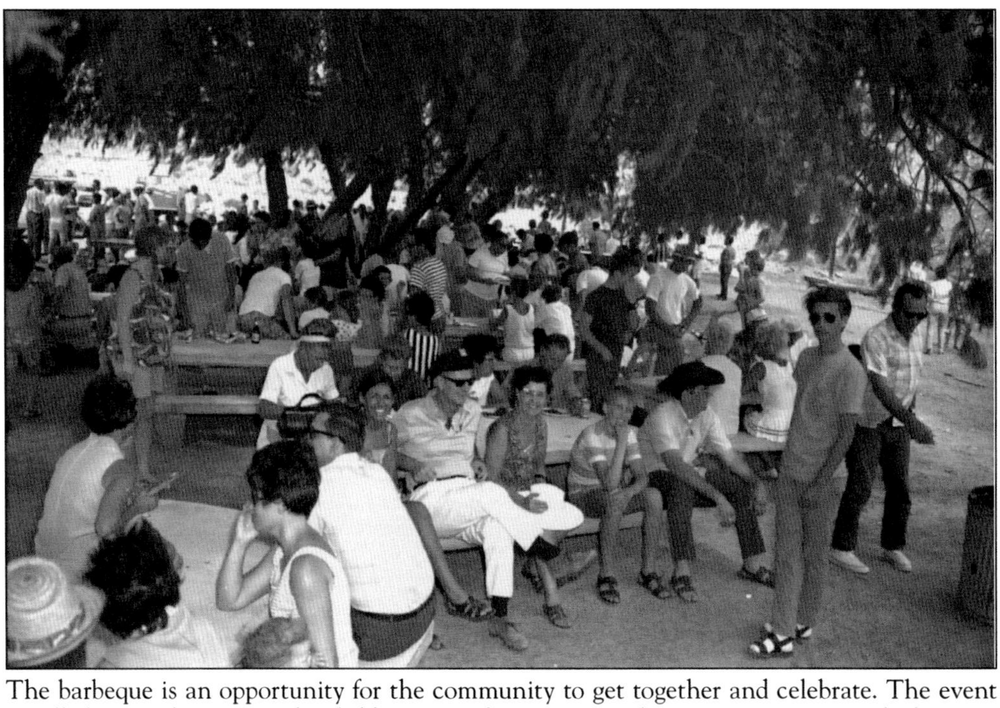

The barbeque is an opportunity for the community to get together and celebrate. The event usually has vendors, games for children, tug-of-war contests, live entertainment, and of course, the beef barbeque. (Courtesy of Larry Ford.)

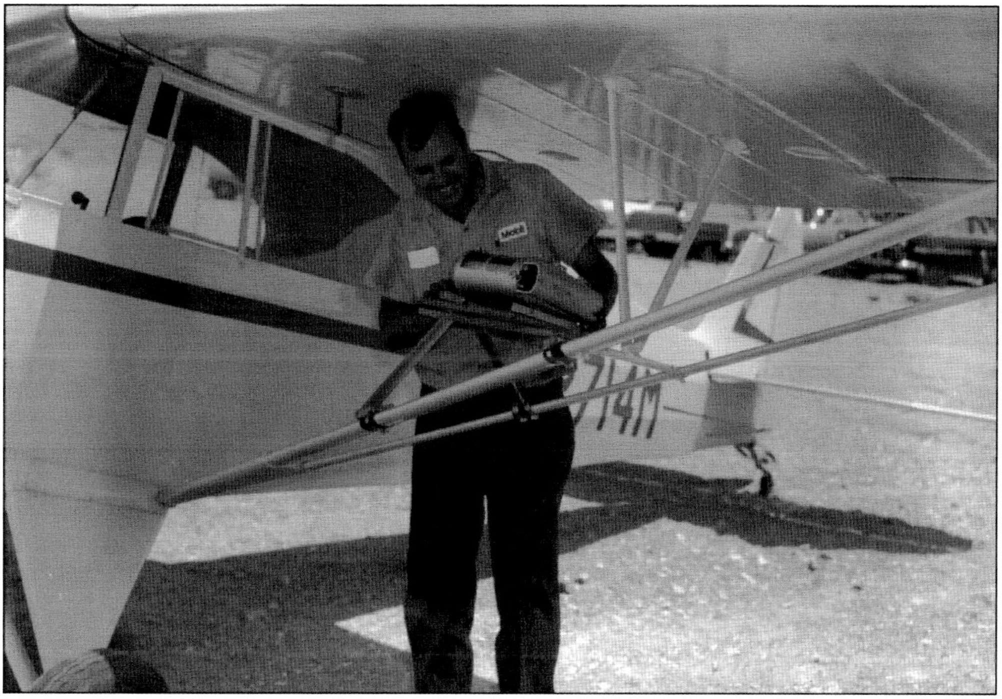

Pilot Don Zurcher inspects special equipment installed on the wing of his airplane to measure inversion layer levels in a c. 1965 image. He was conducting tests for Southern California Edison to determine how high the exhaust stacks needed to be built on the Mohave Generating Plant being installed across the river in Laughlin. (Courtesy of Larry Ford.)

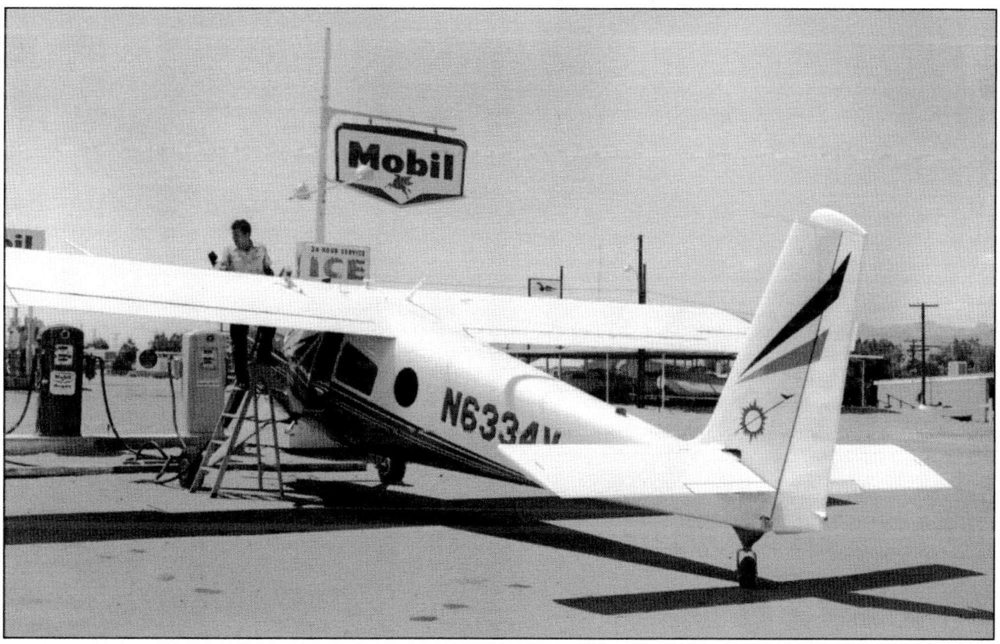

Zurcher pumps gas for an airplane at the Mobil station in Bullhead City. The station straddled Highway 95 and the adjacent airport runway. It was not unusual to see automobiles, boats, and planes all filling up at the same time at the local gas stations. (Courtesy of Larry Ford.)

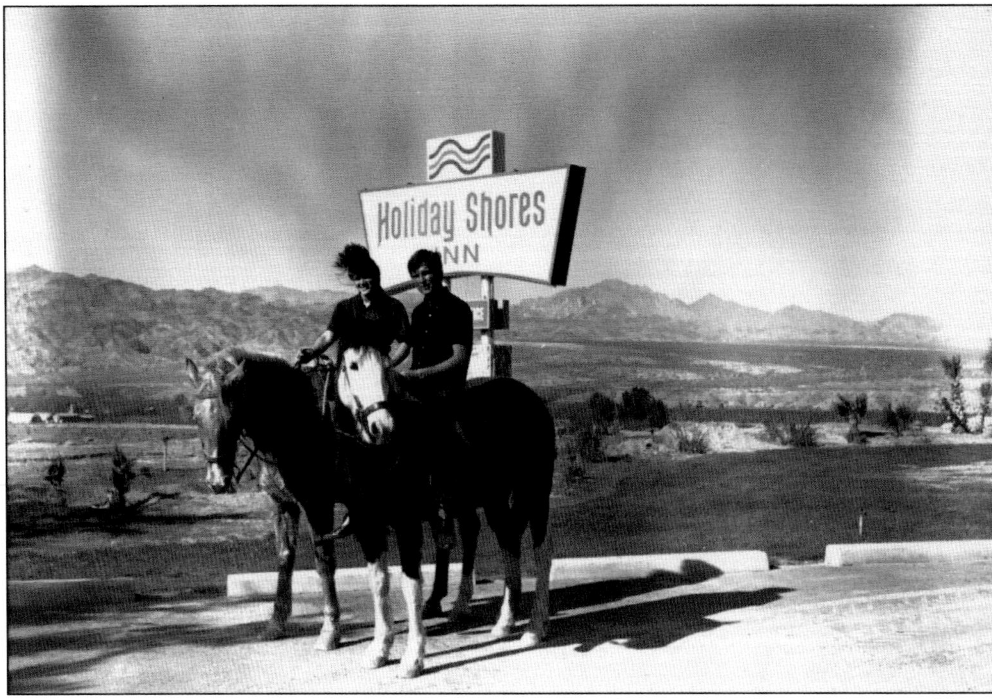

Holiday Shores was another large development company that promoted land sales in Bullhead City. They marketed Bullhead City to the Southern California market and possibly coined the advertising slogan "Where the Hell is Bullhead City?" This startling but effective question appeared on bumper stickers, print media, and television commercials in Los Angeles. (Both, courtesy of Larry Ford.)

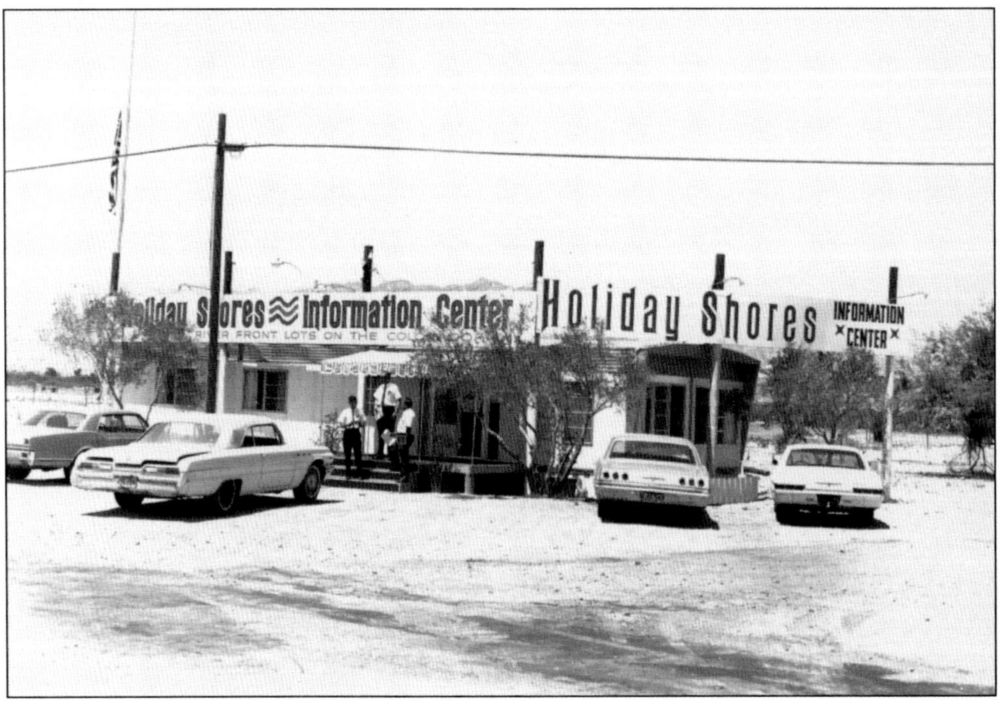

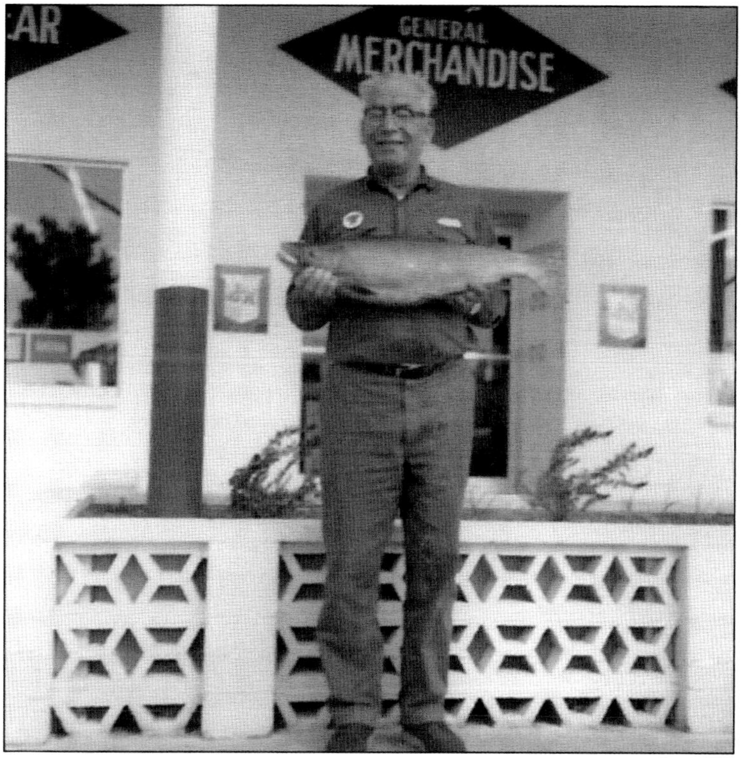

Standing in front of his Peyton Place general merchandise store, O.C. Buck proudly displays a fish he caught. Bullhead City catered to fishermen and held an annual striper bass tournament with large cash prizes for the winners. The tournament was discontinued in the late 1900s. (Right, courtesy of Donna Zurcher; below, courtesy of MMHA.)

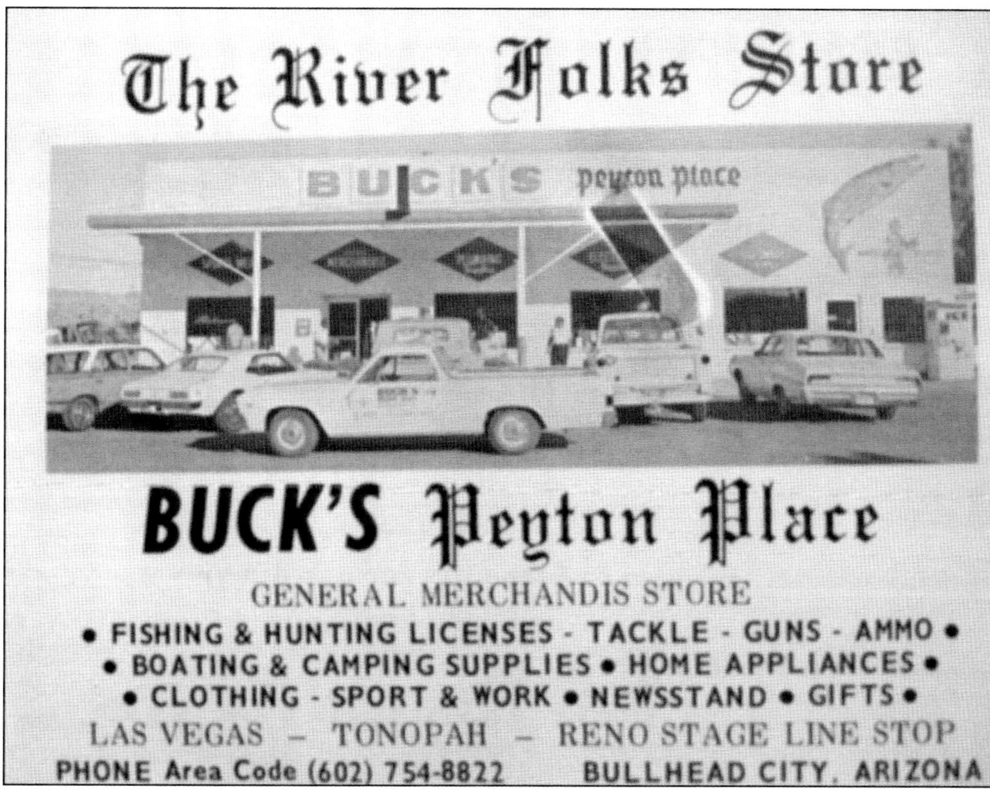

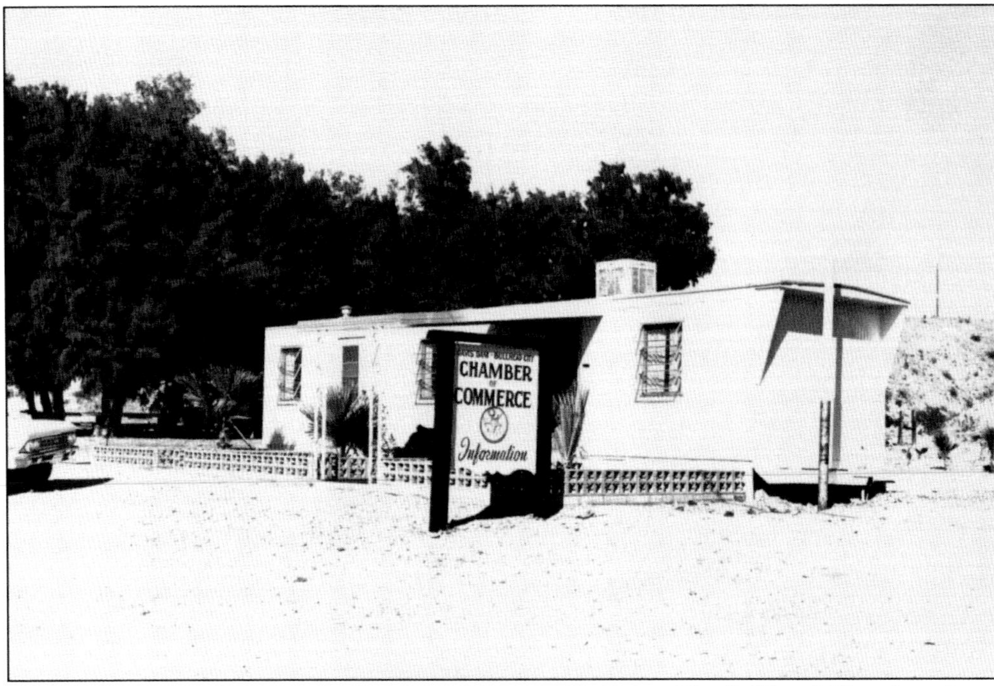

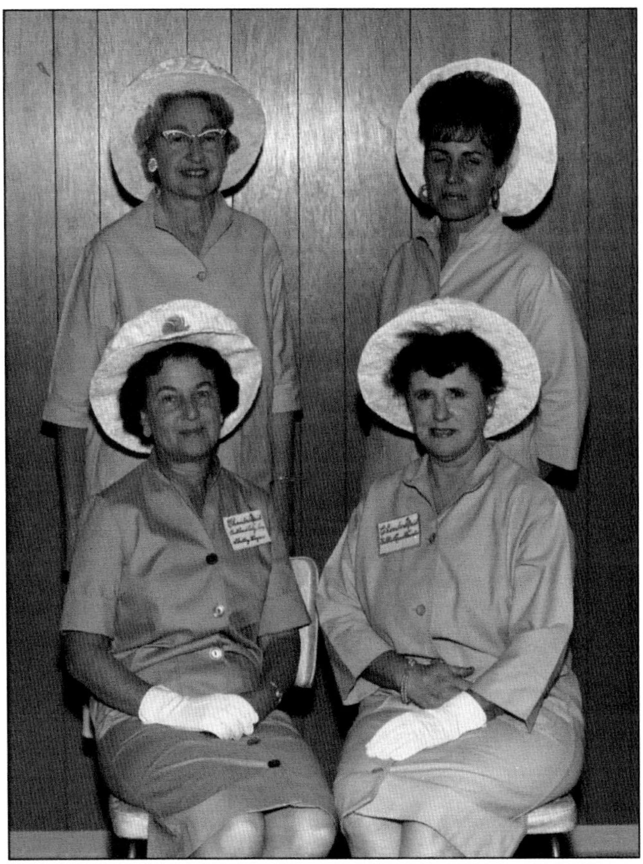

The Bullhead Chamber of Commerce operated out of a single-wide trailer from 1965 until their building was completed in 1969. The chamber was instrumental in promoting Bullhead City as a fishing and boating mecca, encouraging the growth of local businesses, and marketing Bullhead as a place to raise a family. The women's auxiliary, the Chambermaids, formed in 1965. From left to right are (seated) Dorothy Bryan and Billie Ann Fancher; (standing) Lura Dunlap and unidentified. (Both, courtesy of Larry Ford.)

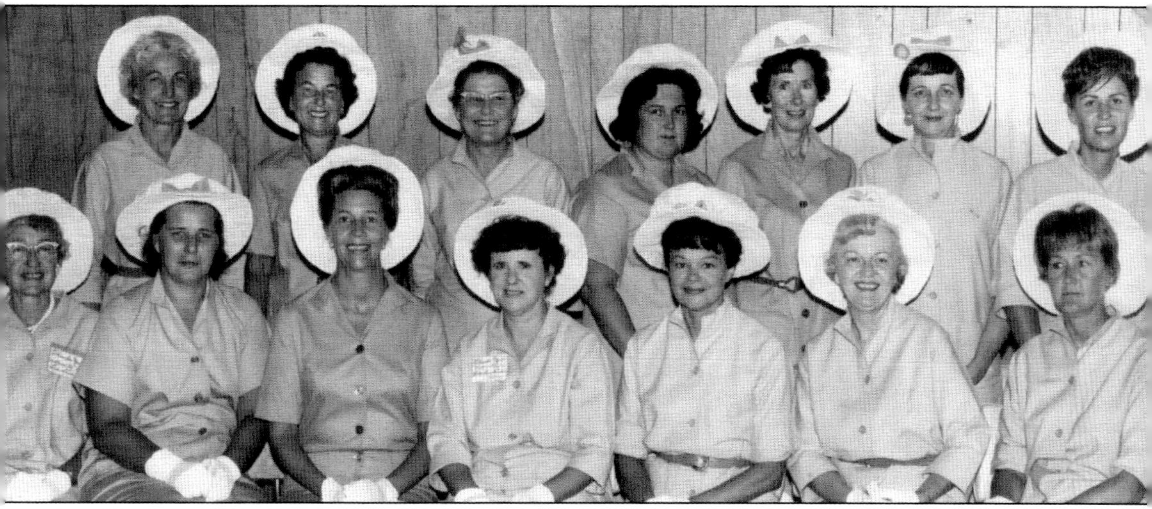

An officer installation of the Chambermaids is pictured here around 1966. Members are, from left to right, (first row) Lura Dunlap, Rosemary Smith, Maggie Jones, Billie Ann Fancher (president), Jill Foster, Eunice McKellips, and Dorothy Erickson; (second row) Laura Crooks, Dorothy Bryan, Evelyn Scoutland, Sherill Medlin, Charlotte Winter, Nancy Walker, and Ethel Swan. The Chambermaids eventually changed their name to the Colorado River Women's Council. Throughout the years, the organization has continued to work to help the less fortunate and build a better Bullhead City through numerous programs. The Western Auction, held in May, is the council's main fundraiser for projects such as the Colorado River Leadership Program (to promote community leadership and preserve the highest quality of life in the river communities) and Women Helping Women (to help abused women return to the workforce). They also sponsor the Holiday Boom Box Parade and donate to the Shop with a Cop program. (Courtesy of Louise Zaborsky, Colorado River Women's Council.)

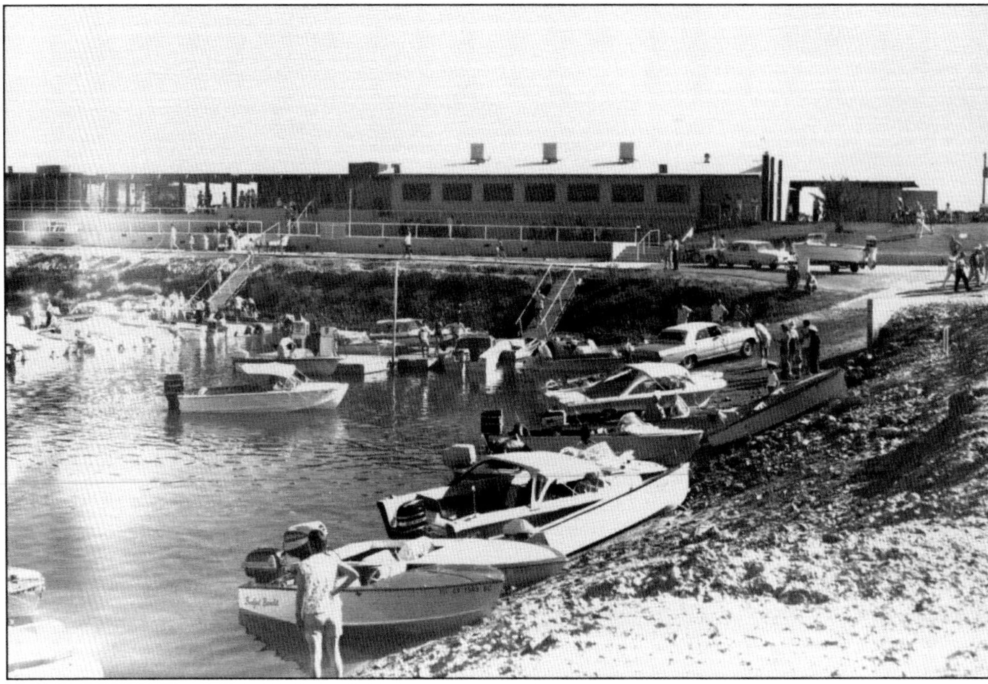

Sunshine Marina has boating and swimming amenities, including a launch and clubhouse. The Willow Beach National Fish Hatchery stocks the Colorado River every year with various fish, such as trout, sunfish, and catfish to provide anglers with ample fish in the waterways. Below, fish are stocked at the Sunshine Marina in the Riviera community in the late 1960s. (Both, courtesy of Larry Ford.)

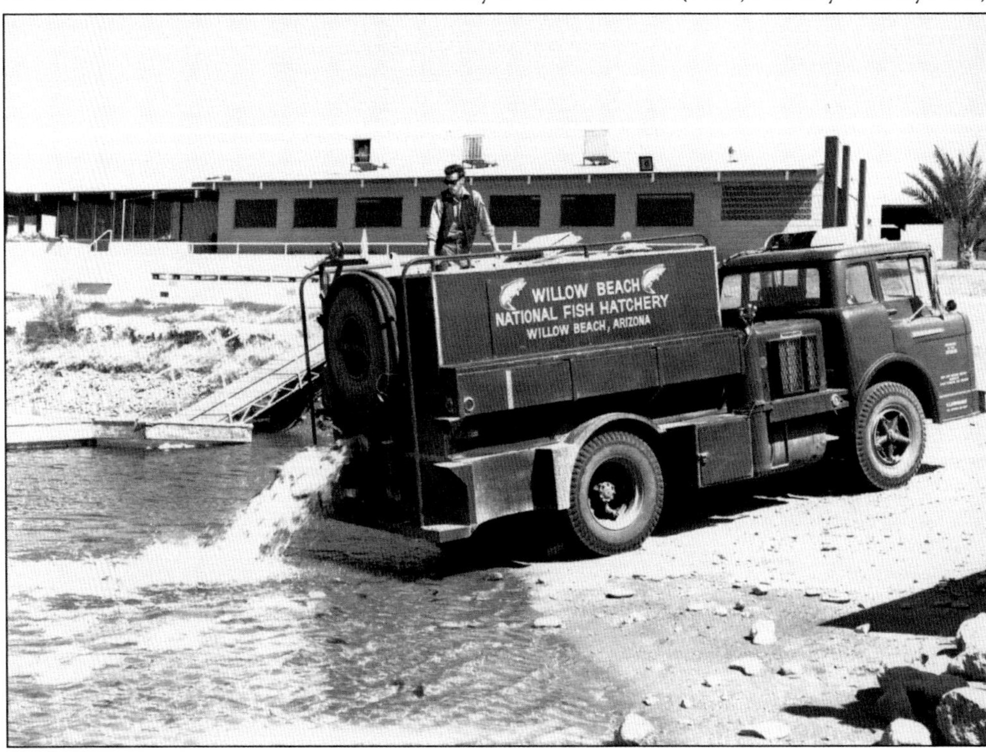

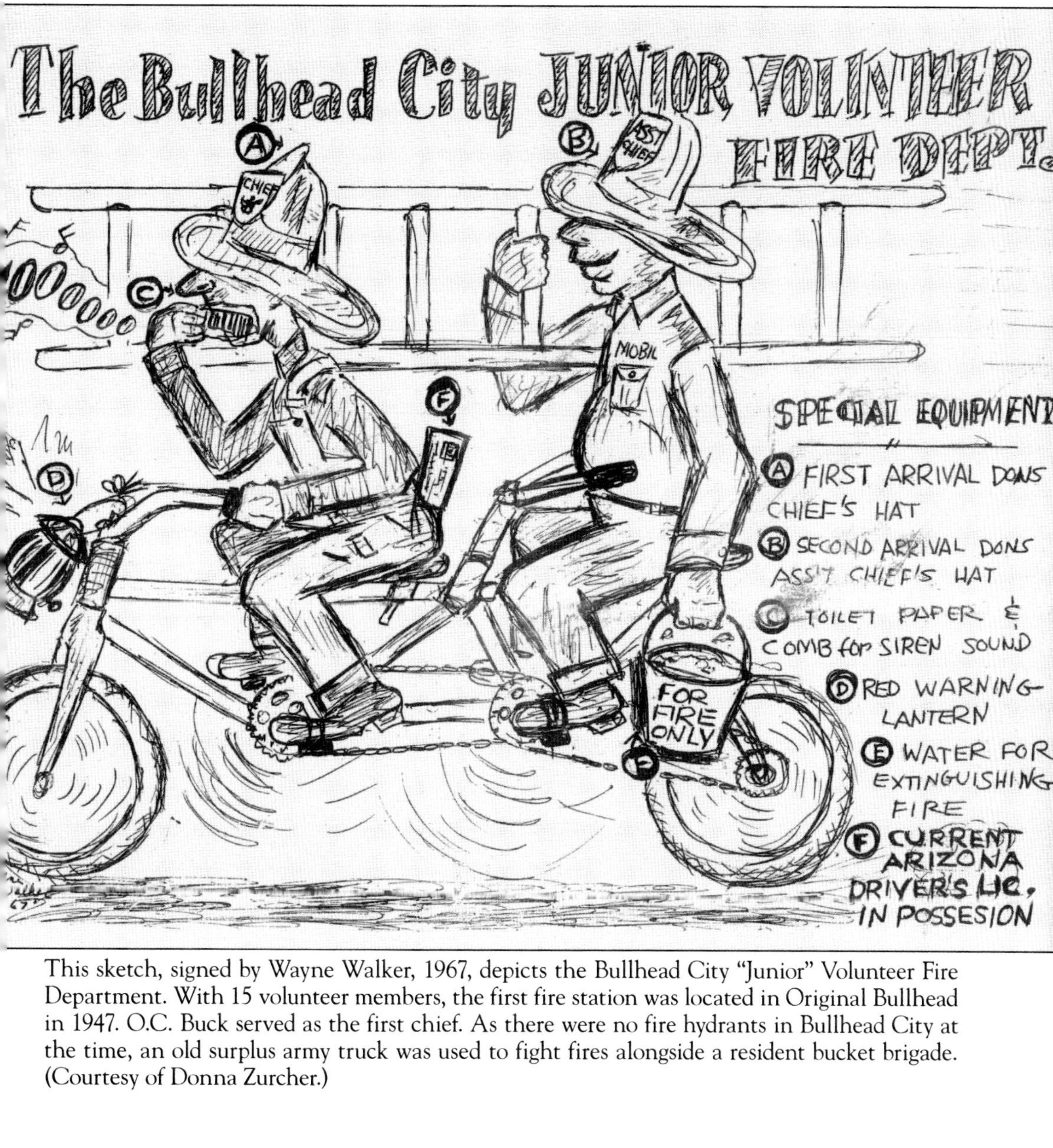

This sketch, signed by Wayne Walker, 1967, depicts the Bullhead City "Junior" Volunteer Fire Department. With 15 volunteer members, the first fire station was located in Original Bullhead in 1947. O.C. Buck served as the first chief. As there were no fire hydrants in Bullhead City at the time, an old surplus army truck was used to fight fires alongside a resident bucket brigade. (Courtesy of Donna Zurcher.)

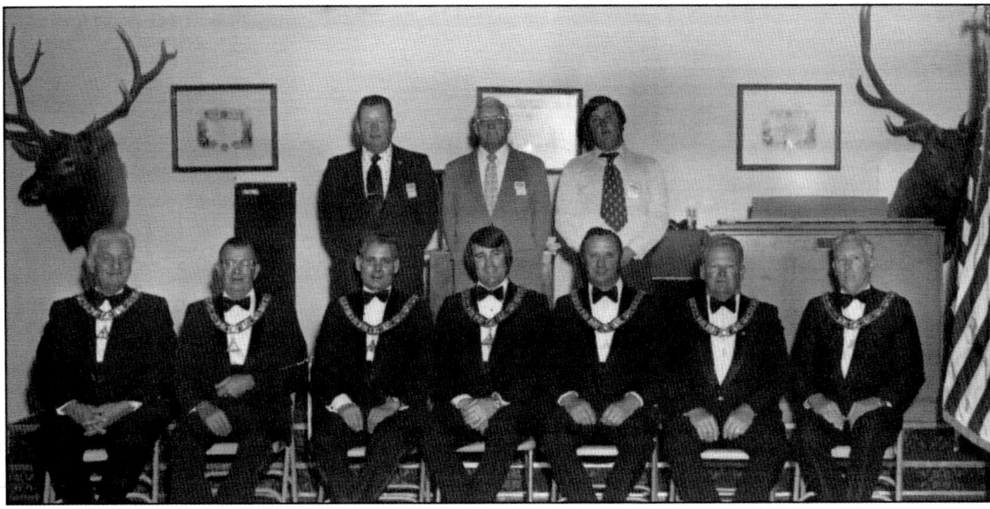

Pictured in this c. 1969 image of an Elks officer installation are, from left to right, (first row) Robert Ricketts, exalted ruler; Robert Murasko, esquire; James Belmor, esteemed leading knight; Thomas McCraley, esteemed loyal knight; unidentified; Walter Betts, chaplain; and unidentified; (second row) unidentified member; unidentified esteemed lecturing knight; and unidentified inner guard. The Elks have a long history of philanthropic work in Bullhead City. They sponsor college scholarships for high school students, a drug awareness program, the Hoop Shoot youth basketball program, and the Elks Veterans Memorial. (Courtesy of Elks Lodge 2408, Bullhead City.)

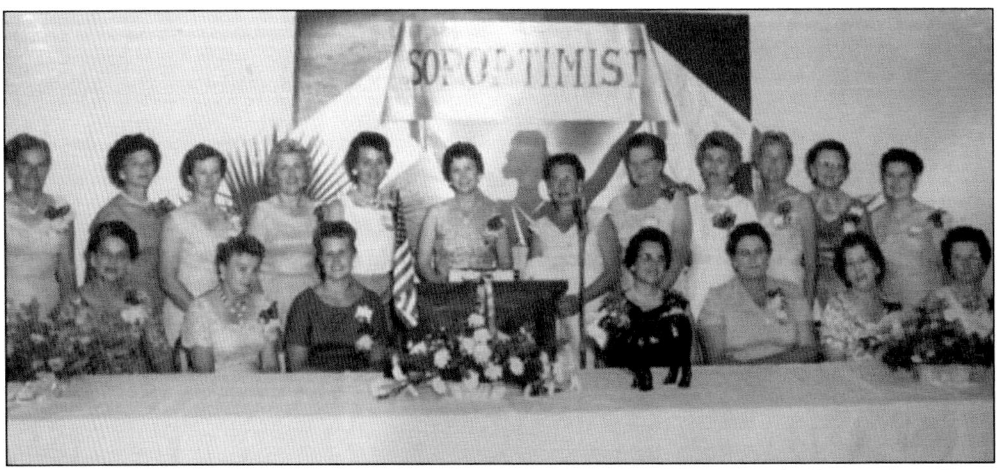

Shown here is an officer installation of the Bullhead City Soroptimist in the late 1950s. Those pictured are unidentified. Soroptimist supports the education of young girls, along with role models to enable them to reach their full potential. Programs include S-Teen College Scholarships, the Women's Opportunity Award (to provide resources to women who are the primary earners for their families), and recognition for young women involved in volunteerism. Their major fundraiser is the sale of See's Candies during the holiday season. (Courtesy of Donna Zurcher.)

Homer Fancher and his wife, Billie Ann, were prominent citizens in the community. Homer was one of the earliest postmasters of Bullhead City, and Billie Ann was president of the Chambermaids, in addition to having her own local radio show. Both were very involved with civic matters and staunch supporters of Bullhead City. (Courtesy of Larry Ford.)

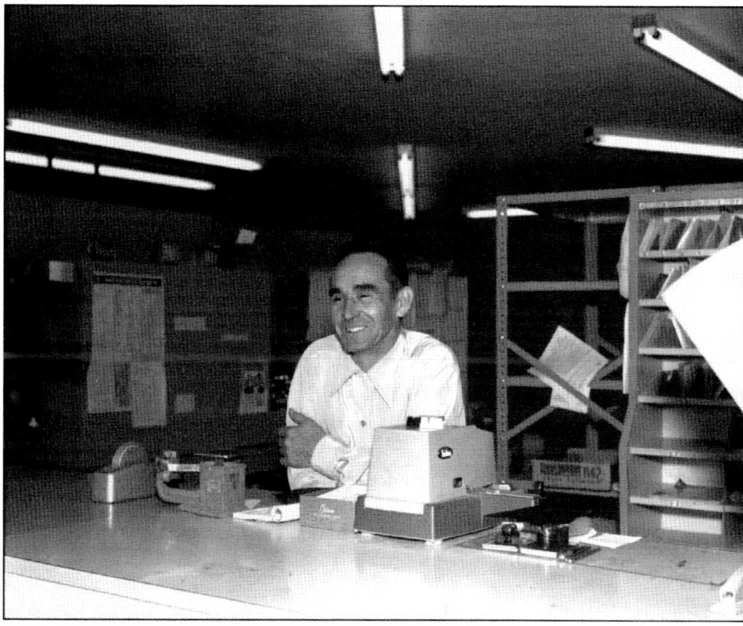

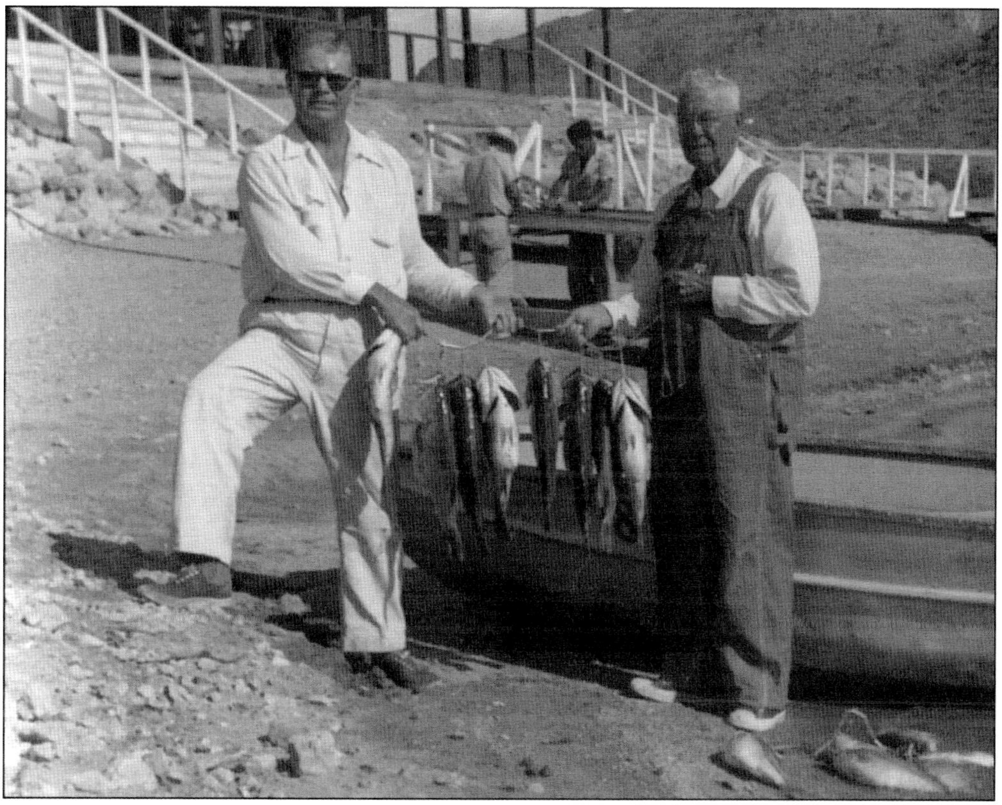

Buster Favor and his father, Fred Favor, display the fish they caught from Katherine Landing at their Lake Mohave Resort. The Favors left a lasting imprint on Bullhead City. Development of the lakeside property allowed Bullhead City to grow into a resort destination and a permanent home for thousands. (Courtesy of Donna Zurcher.)

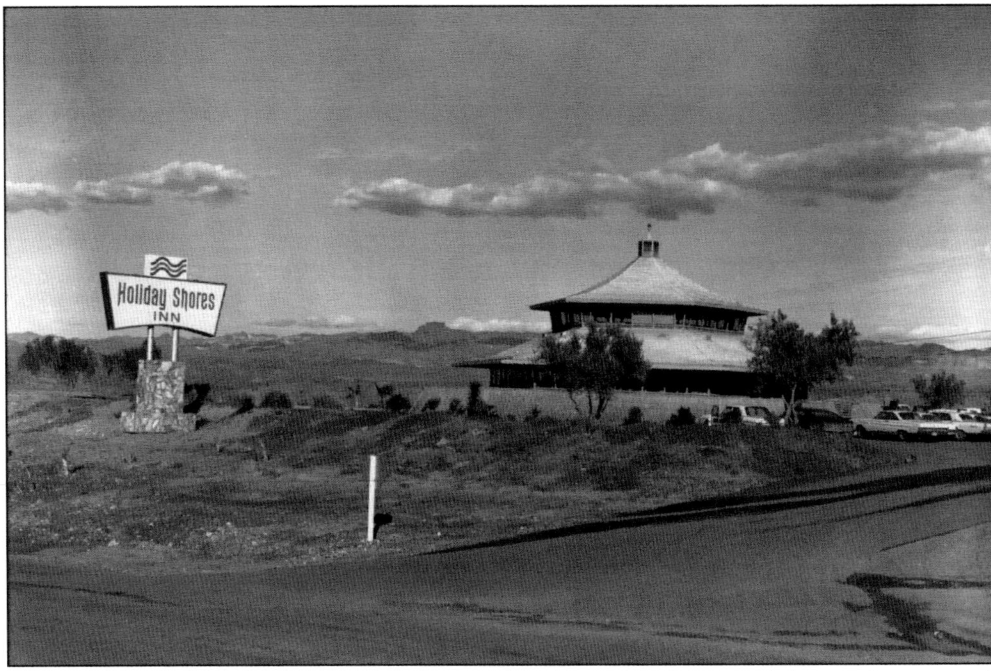

By the 1960s, Bullhead residents were enjoying more entertainment and dining choices, such as the Holiday Shores Inn (above). Situated on a bluff overlooking the city, its location on Highway 95 at Ramar Road is now home to a Wild Wings restaurant. Another local favorite was the Sportsman Club (below) in Original Bullhead. (Above, courtesy of Larry Ford; below, courtesy of MMHA.)

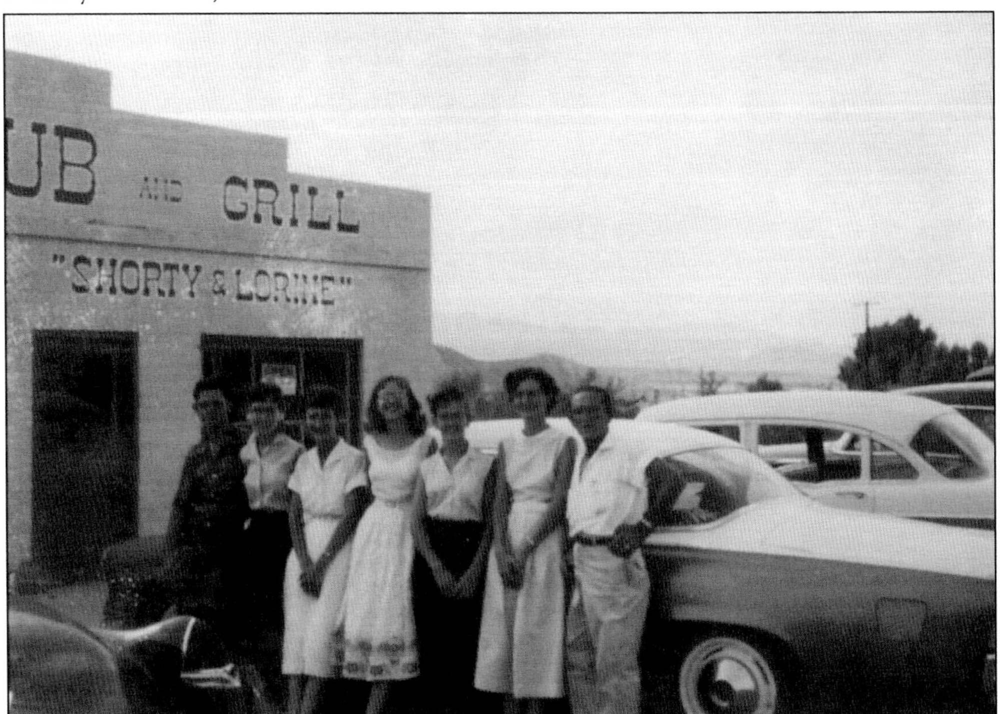

Nine

Life in the Desert
A River Runs through It

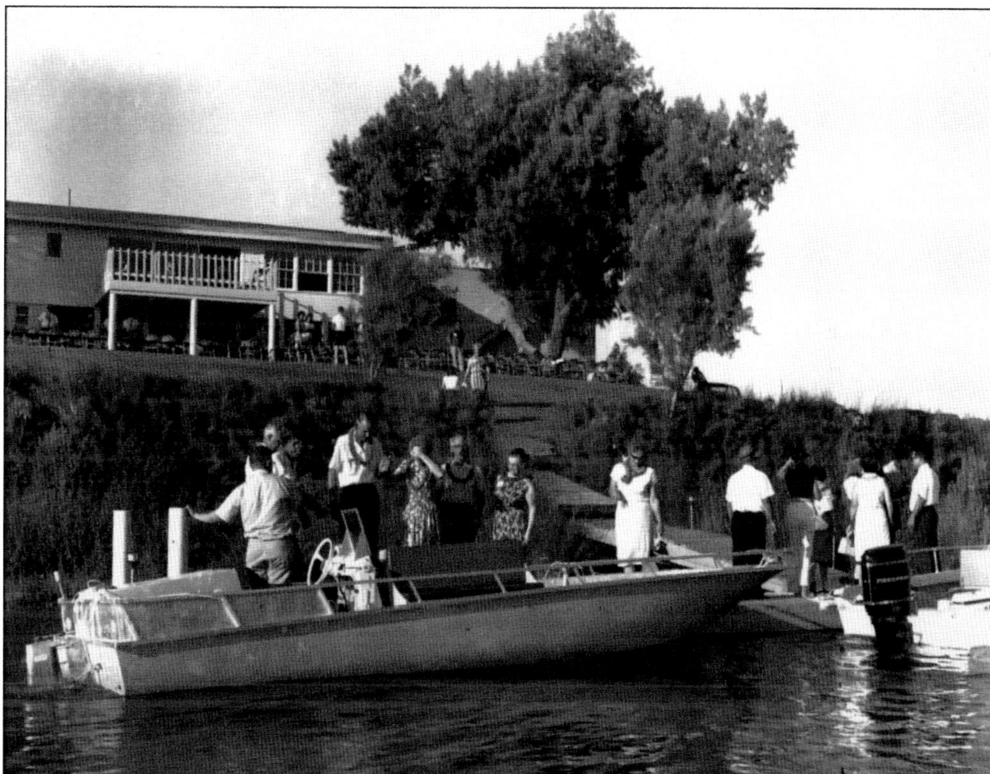

Guests of the Langford family enjoy an outing on the river. Their home was one of the early riverfront properties in Holiday Shores with a boat dock. Leonard C. Langford, their son, became a superior court judge in Kingman. (Courtesy of Larry Ford.)

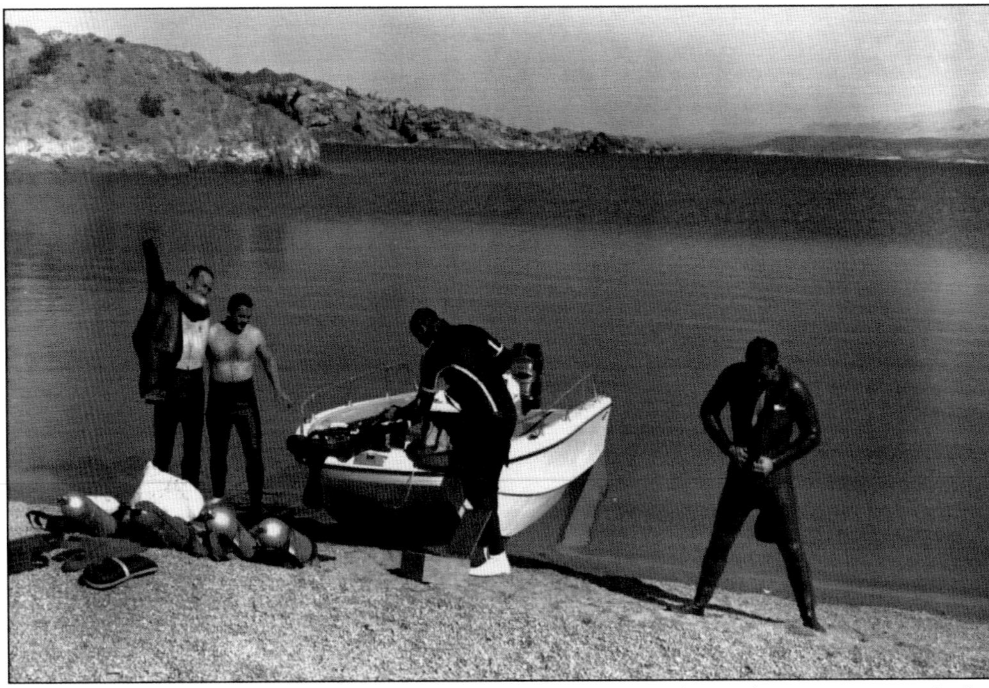

Scuba diving became a popular water sport on Lake Mohave. Above, these men suit up before a dive at Katherine Landing. Below, Bullhead City's first pharmacist, Jon Dalke (kneeling), is pictured with divers Al Kyle (left), a subdivider/land developer, and Alan Walstead, manager of Holiday Marine Boat Supplies. (Both, courtesy of Larry Ford.)

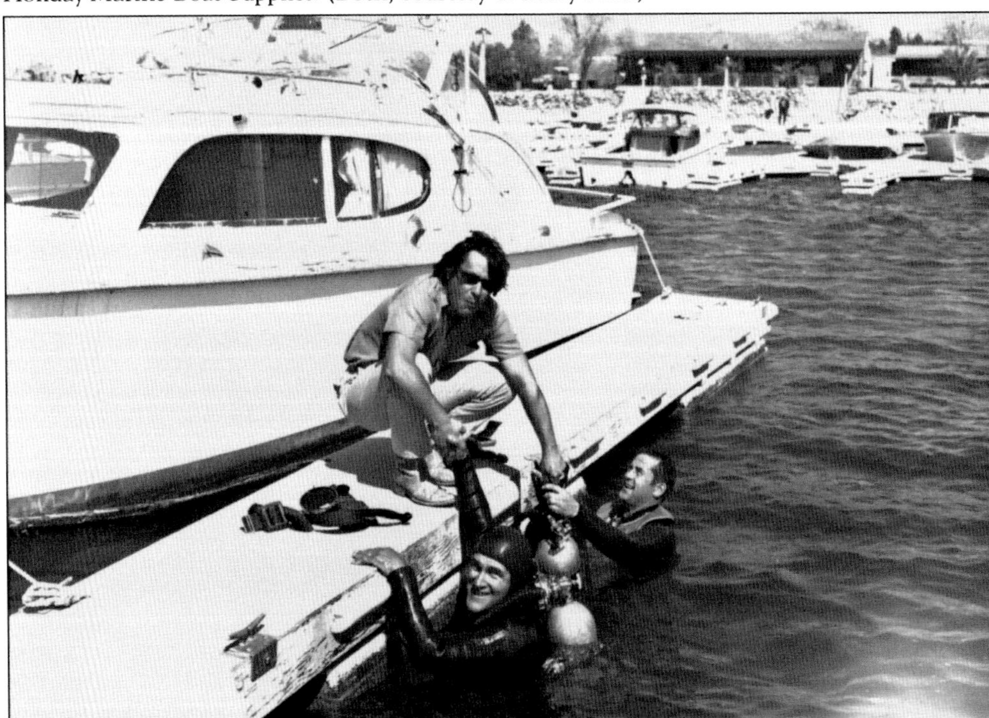

Rodney Head, motorcycle police officer in 1986, became chief of police in 2001 and held that position until he retired in 2014. (Courtesy of Rodney Head.)

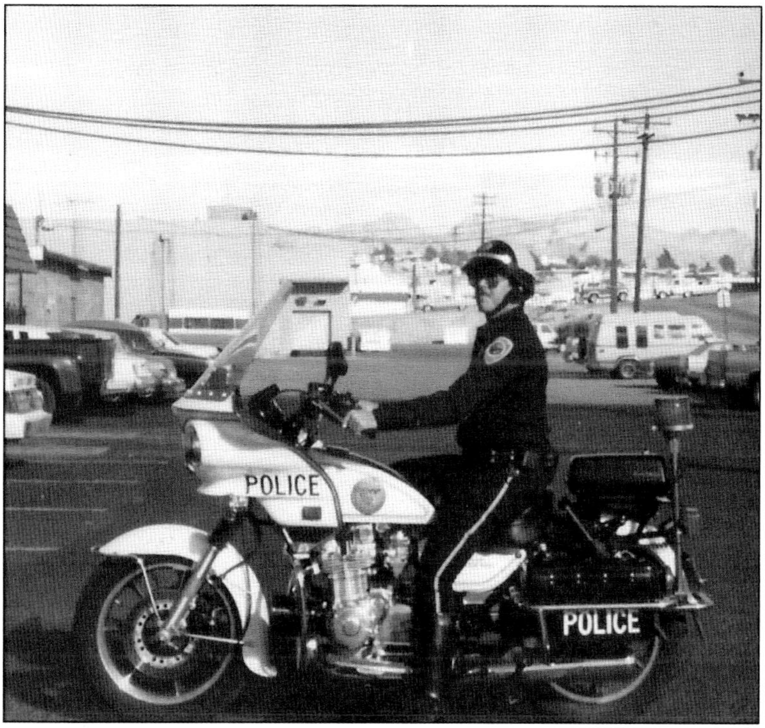

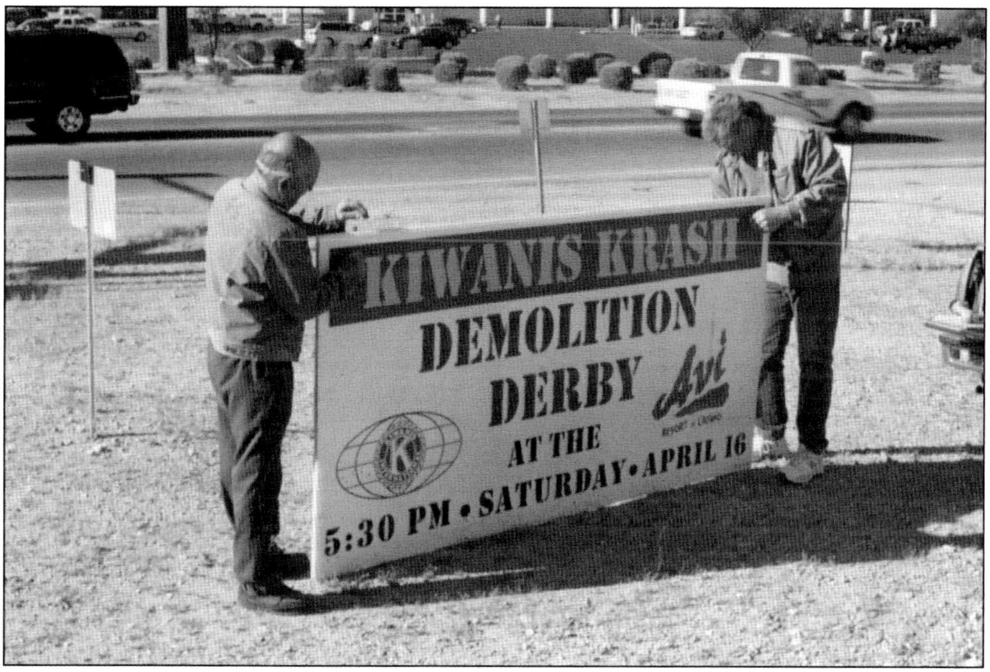

The Bullhead City Kiwanis Club holds its annual Kiwanis Krash in April; the demolition derby is their major fundraiser. Proceeds from ticket sales support the Morning Kiwanis Club's many local programs that benefit the area's youth, including free swim lessons offered through the Bullhead City Recreation Department, the city's first Splash Park, the Kids Need Coats drive, and the Boys and Girls Clubs of the Colorado River. (Courtesy of Karla Brady.)

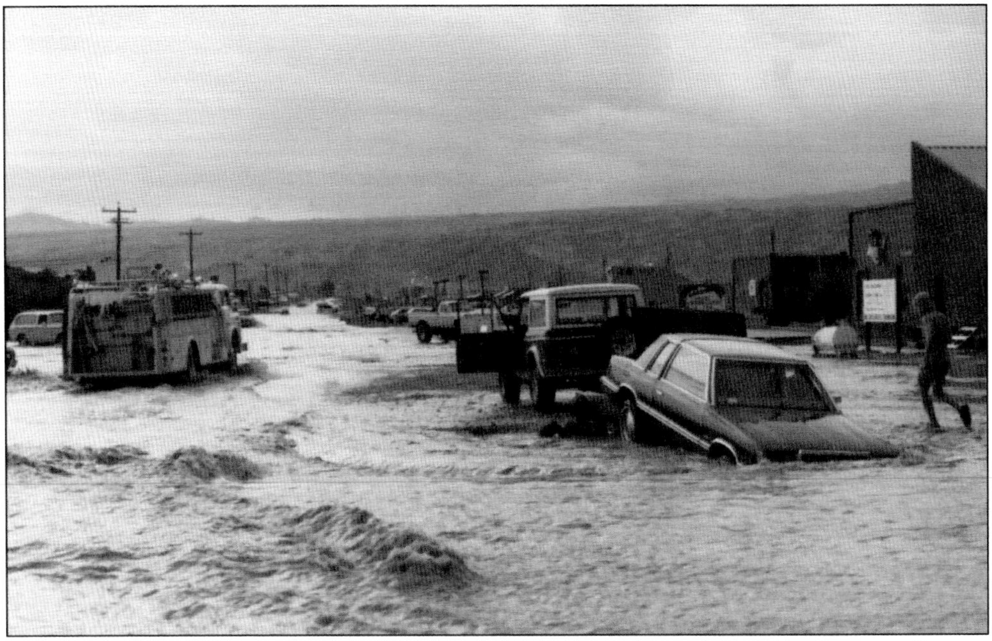

In 1985, heavy storms sent torrents of water downstream from the mountains, overflowing the spillways on Davis Dam. Automobiles on city streets were mired in floodwaters, and one street, Baseline Road (below), became a raging creek. Annual flooding from winter storms was commonplace until the late 1980s, when drought altered the weather patterns. (Both, courtesy of Mike Conner.)

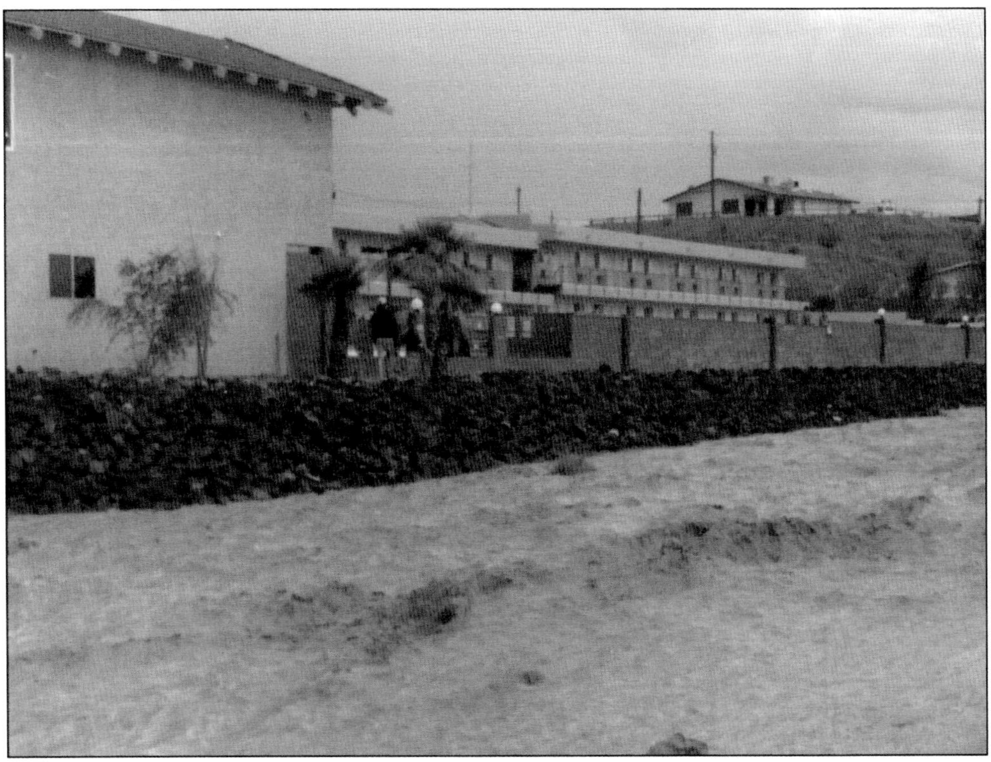

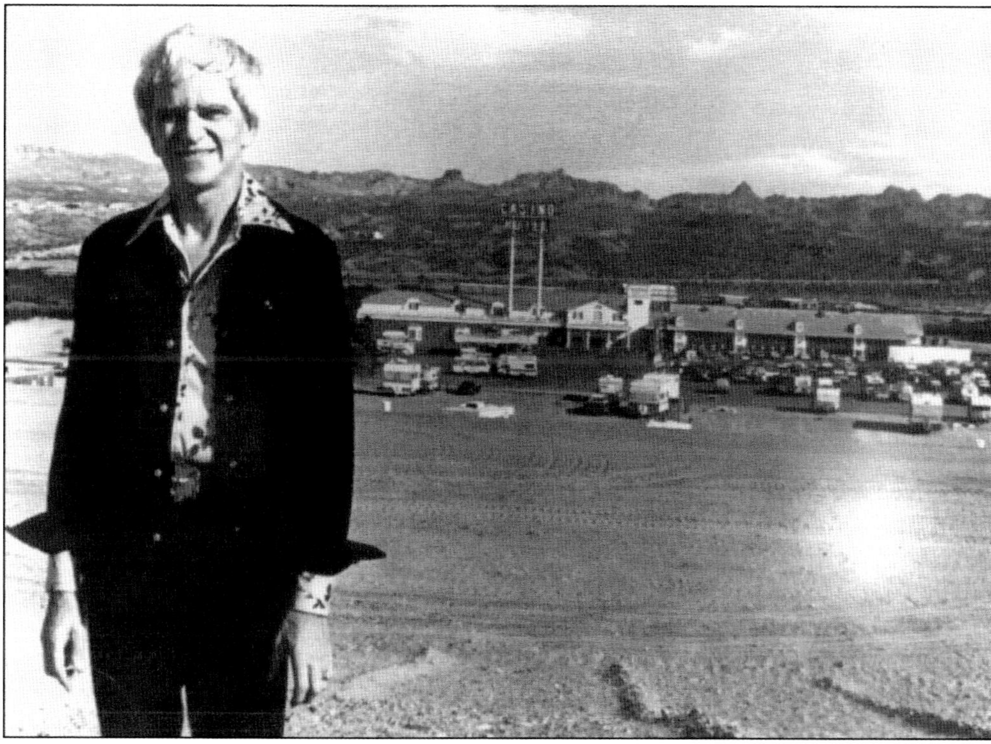

In 1964, Donald J. "Don" Laughlin discovered a piece of land on the bank of the Colorado River, across from what is now Bullhead City. He bought the only structure, an eight-room motel, and offered all-you-can-eat chicken for 98¢. The original Riverside Resort opened in 1966 with 12 slot machines and two gaming tables. Today, Don Laughlin's Riverside Resort & Casino features 1,404 guest rooms and employs 1,800 individuals. (Courtesy of Don Laughlin.)

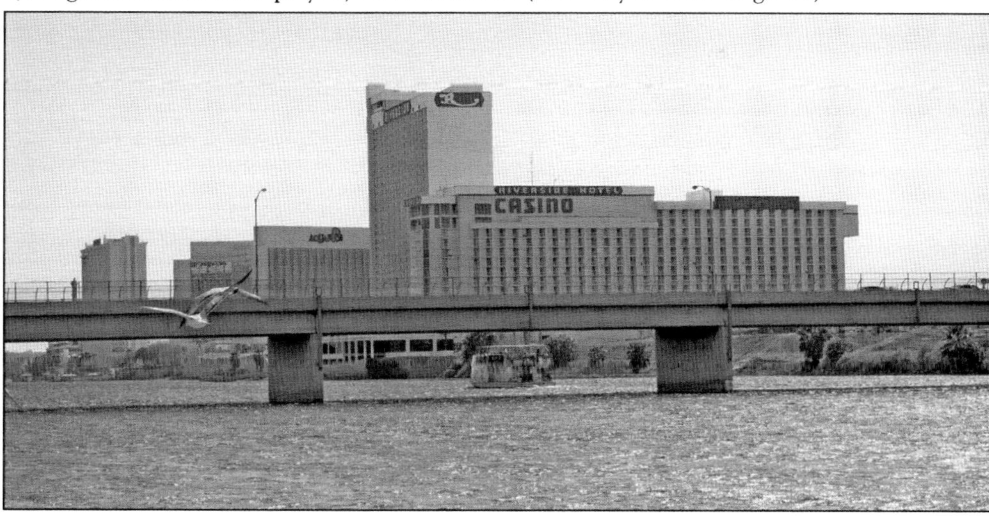

In 1987, Don Laughlin built the Laughlin Bridge at an out-of-pocket cost of $3.5 million, then donated the bridge to the states of Nevada and Arizona. Today, thousands of vehicles cross the bridge each day, representing tourists from all over the world and the more than 10,000 individuals employed by the hotel and gaming industries of Laughlin Township, Nevada. (Courtesy of Don Laughlin's Riverside Resort & Casino.)

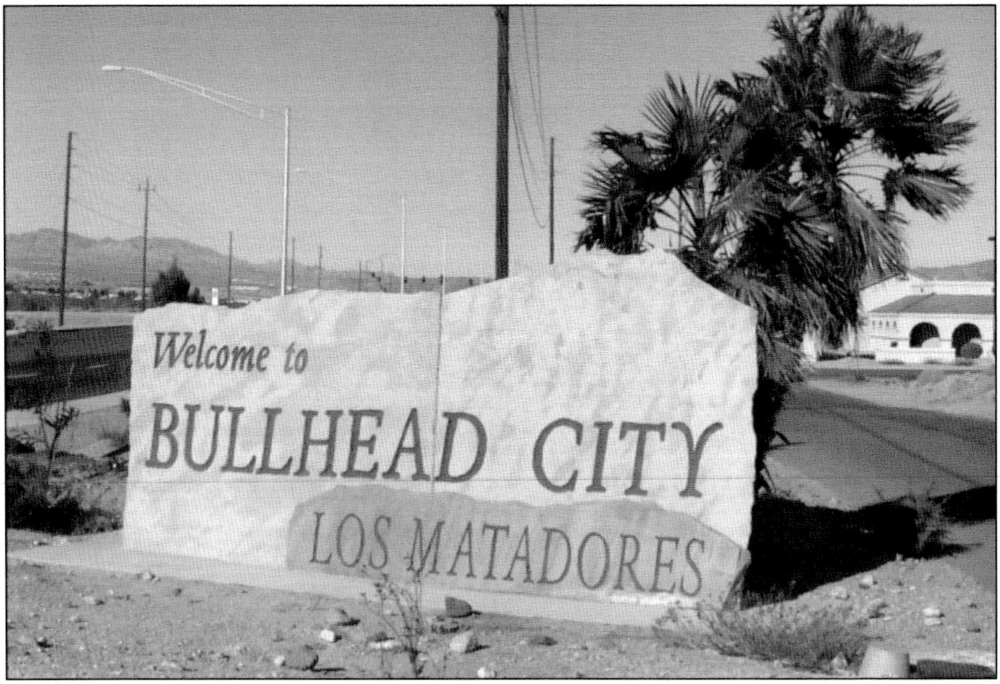

Los Matadores originated as an organization to greet dignitaries visiting Bullhead City. It also operates as a nonprofit, assisting the community with charitable donations and, most notably, providing signage to welcome visitors to Bullhead City at both the north and south city limits on Highway 95. Pictured below around 2003, Matadores install the large sign at the north entrance to town, next to the Laughlin Bridge. From left to right are Larry Morse, Dan Oehler, Scott Merrill, and Pat Burright. (Both, courtesy of Rodney Head.)

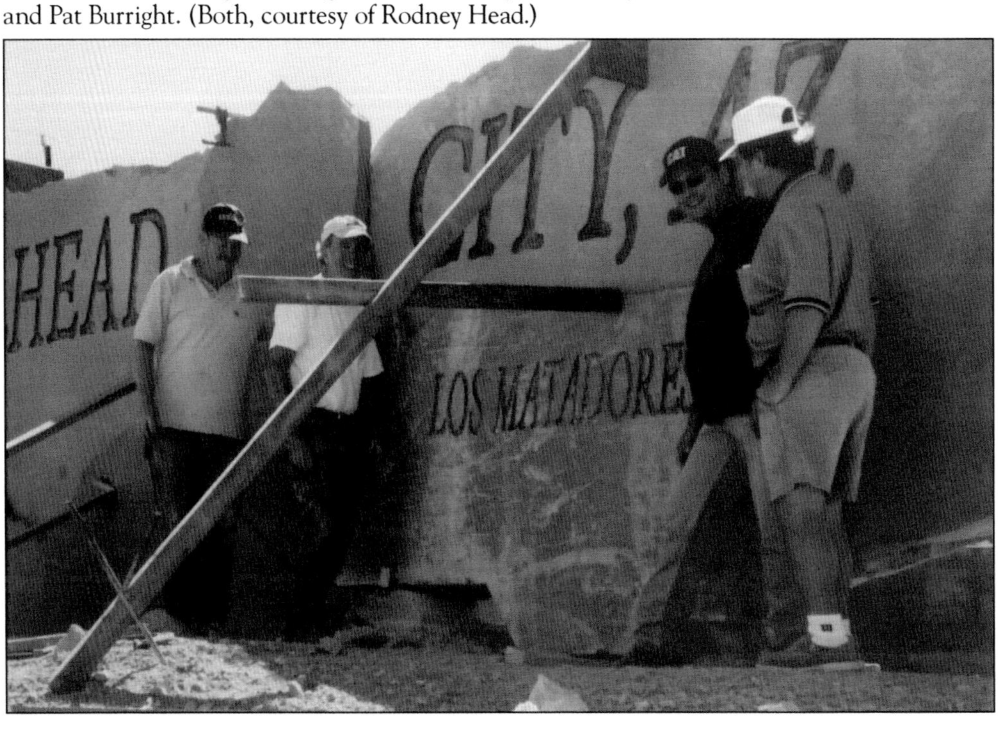

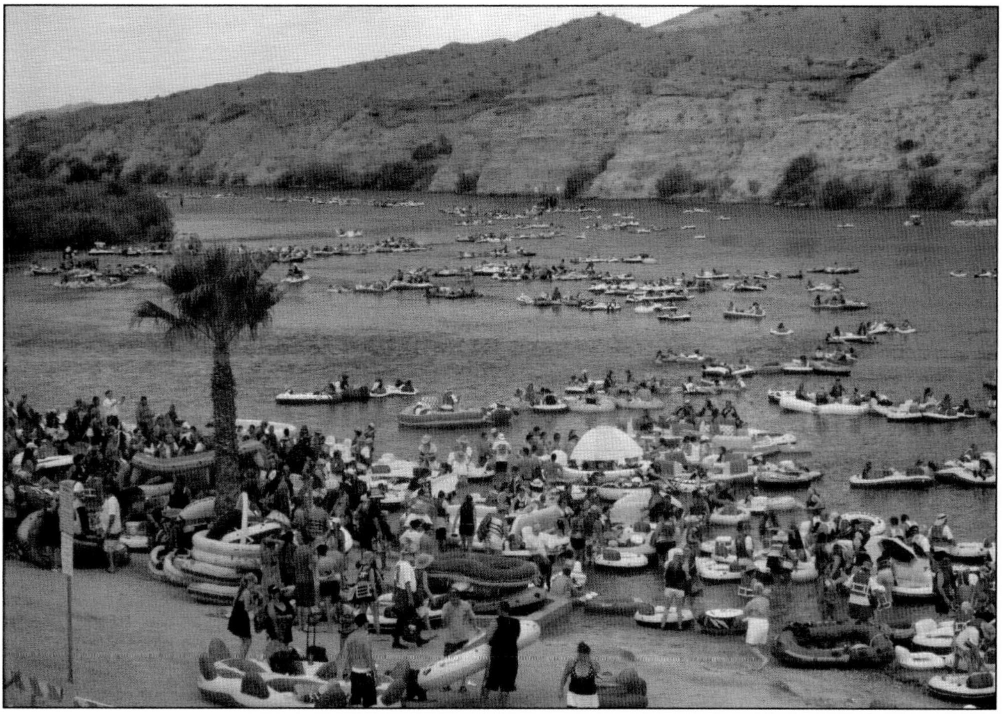

Bullhead City's annual River Regatta, which began in 2007, is now the largest event in the area. The first year, 900 people floated down the river in nonmotorized rafts, the second year more than quadrupled to 4,000 participants, and it has been growing ever since. The 2014 regatta attracted more than 28,000 people from all over the United States, Canada, and the world. Jack Hakim, Bullhead City's mayor, spearheaded the event to attract new visitors to the area. The Laughlin resort casinos all participate in the event. (Above, courtesy of Bullhead City; below, author's collection.)

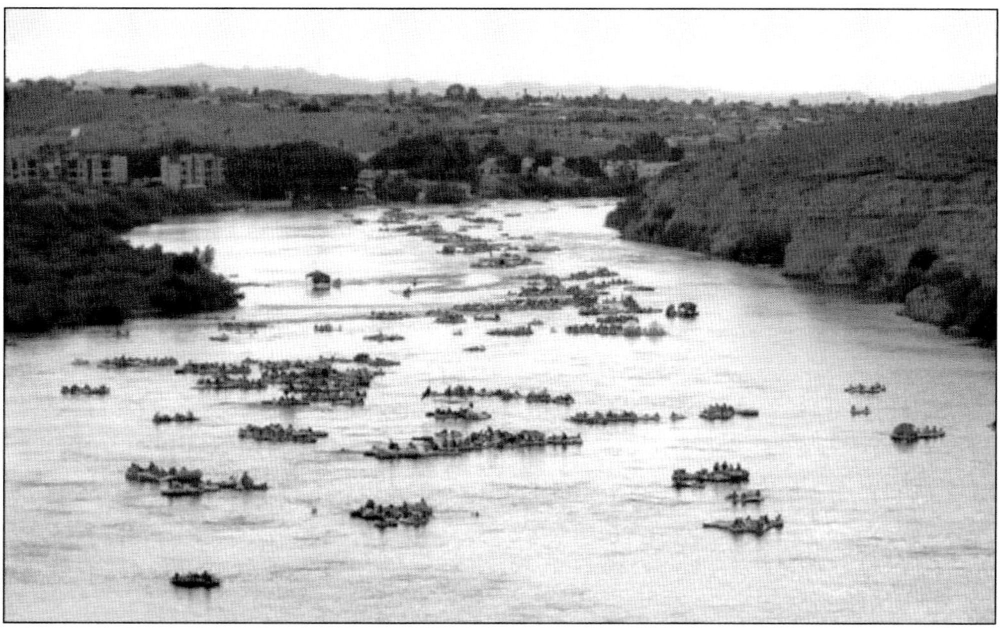

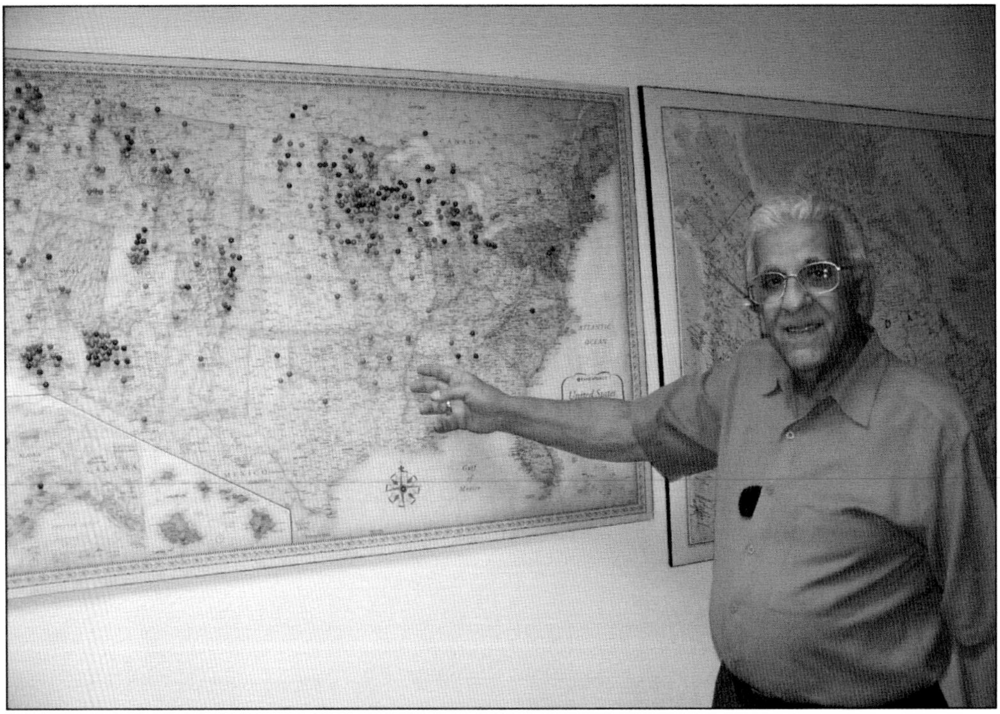

Mayor Jack Hakim started an annual Winter Visitors' Expo to welcome the snowbirds who flock to Bullhead City from all over North America during the winter months. Maps of the United States and Canada are dotted with pins representing the people who visit each winter, many of whom have second homes in the area. (Author's collection.)

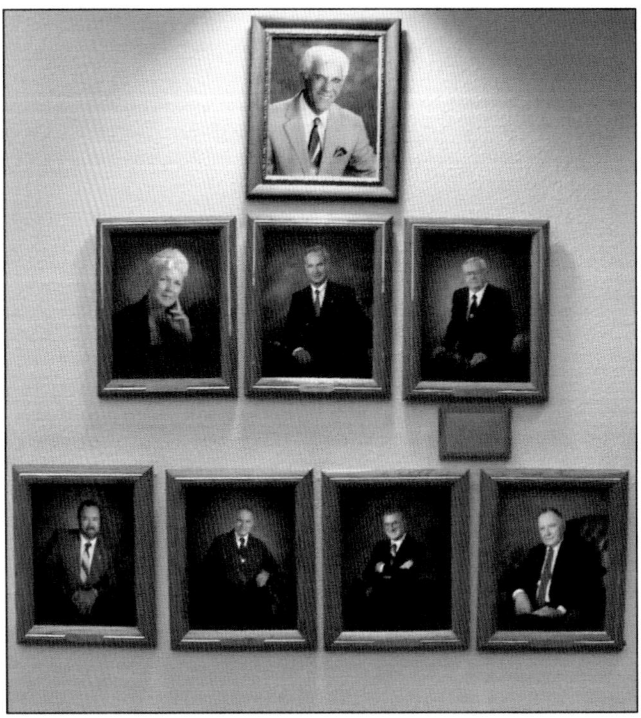

The "Wall of Mayors" at city hall displays photographs of Bullhead City's mayors since the city incorporated on August 28, 1984. In order of service are, from right to left, (first row) Arvid Hoppas (August 1984 to June 1985), Glenn Tudor (June 1985 to June 1987), Dean Hackett (June 1987 to September 1988), and Rob Rogge (January 1989 to May 1991); (second row) J. Michael Love (May 1991 to May 1995), Norm Hicks (June 1995 to May 1999), and Diane Vick (June 1999 to June 2007); (third row) Jack Hakim (June 2007 to November 2014). Not pictured is Mayor Tom Brady, who took office on November 11, 2014. (Author's collection.)

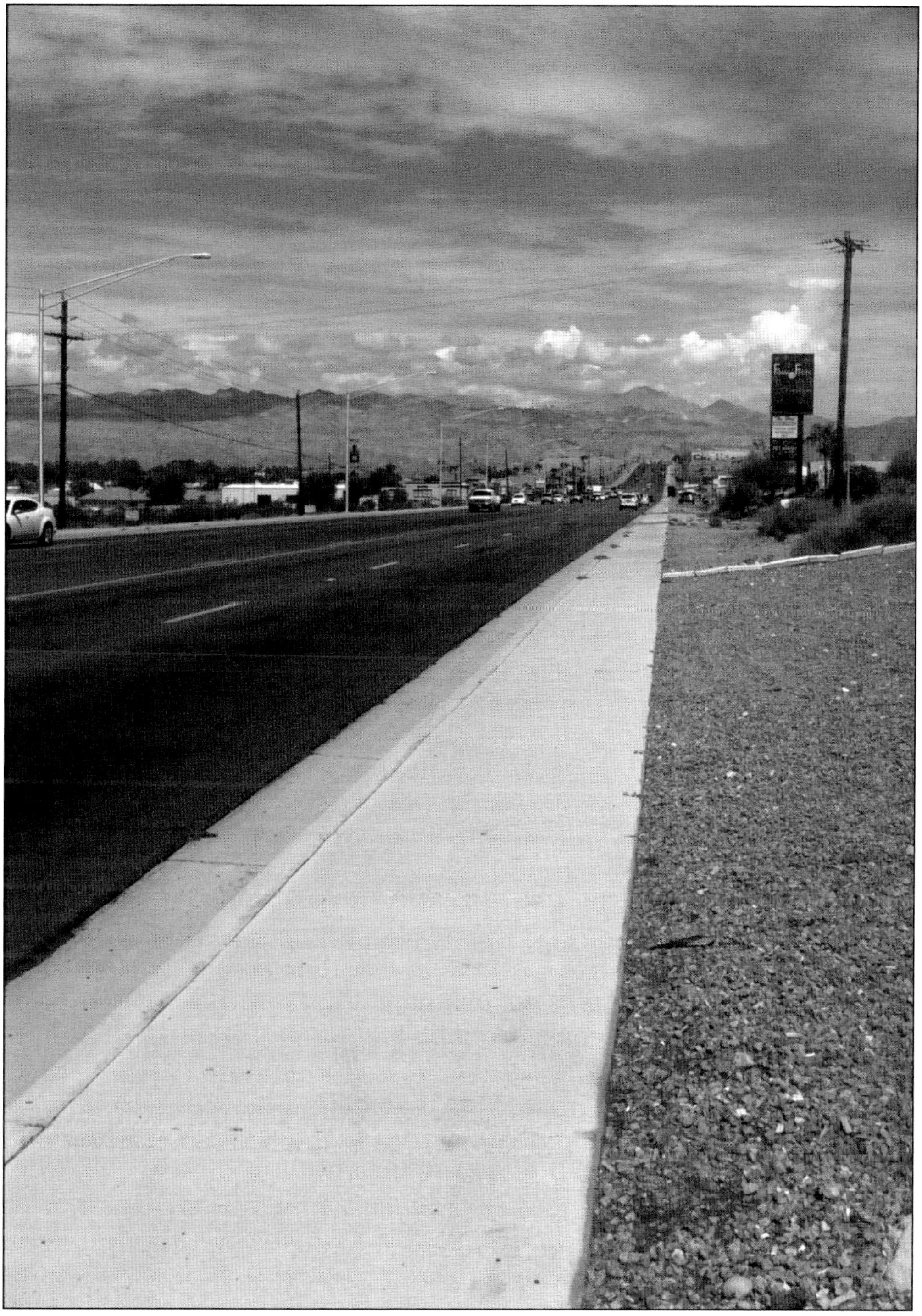

Looking north on Highway 95, Spirit Mountain looms above the city under a blanket of clouds, reminding us of the area's rich history and all those who have lived in the shadow of the mountain. (Author's collection.)

Bibliography

Baker, Jere. *Claude Compton Indian Trader: Fort Mojave, Arizona, 1899–1904*. La Cañada, CA: Blue Oak Books, 2013.

Casebier, Dennis. *The Mojave Road (Tales of the Mojave Road No. 5)*. Essex, CA: Tales of the Mojave Road Publishing Co., 1975.

Clark, Hal and Doris. *The Oatman Story*. Kingman, AZ: H&H Printers, 2002.

Fox, Theron. *Arizona Treasure Hunters Ghost Town Guide*. San Jose, CA: Nevada Publications, 1964.

Heckethorn, Ada Fancher. *The Toll Road: Prescott to Fort Mohave*. Chino Valley, AZ: Pioneer Heritage Publishing, 1997.

Jenkins, Minnie Braithwaite. *Girl from Williamsburg*. Richmond, VA: The Dietz Press, Inc., 1951.

Lingenfelter, Richard E. *Steamboats on the Colorado River, 1852–1916*. Tucson, AZ: University of Arizona Press, 1978.

Malach, Roman. *Adventurer John Moss*. Kingman, AZ: Mohave County Board of Supervisors, 1977.

———. *Bullhead City, Land of Early Gold Mining*. Kingman, AZ: Mohave County Board of Supervisors, 1975.

———. *Military Posts in Mohave County*. Kingman, AZ: Mohave County Board of Supervisors, 1980.

Messersmith, Dan W. *The History of Mohave County to 1912*. Kingman, AZ: Mohave Historical Society, 1991.

Peterson, Samuel E., and Harold K. Reed. *Northwest Arizona Coast*. Bullhead City, AZ: Colorado River Historical Society and Museum, 1997.

Sherer, Lorraine M. *Bitterness Road, The Mojave: 1604 to 1860*. Menlo Park, CA: Ballena Press, 1994.

Williams, Jack S. *The Mojave of California and Arizona*. New York, NY: Rosen Publishing Group, 2004.

About the Author

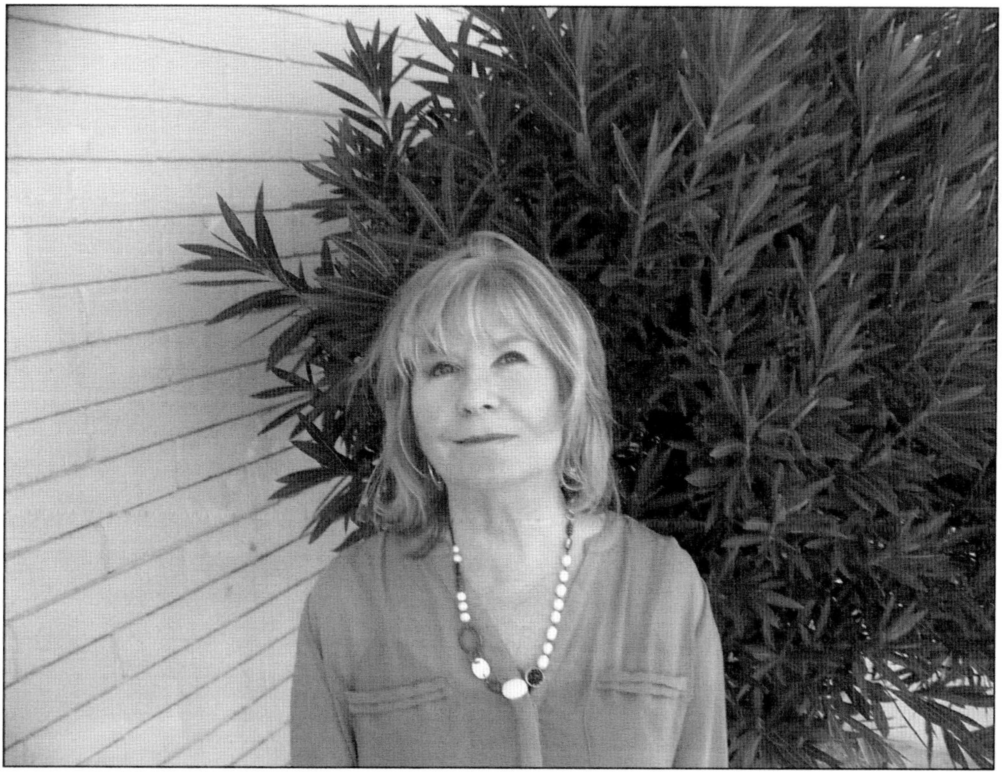

Author Shirín McGraham is editor and co-owner, with her husband Thom McGraham, of the *Bullhead City Bee* and the *Economic Development Journal of Mohave County*. She is a graduate of UCLA and former member of the Los Angeles Press Club. She has lived in Bullhead City and the Mohave Valley for 15 years. Prior to moving to Arizona, she worked in Los Angeles as a teacher, professional dancer, photojournalist, publicist, and the director of development for a television production company. She also served as vice chairperson of Planning and Zoning for the City of Big Bear Lake, California, where she owned and operated a bed-and-breakfast. (Photograph by Mark Randall.)

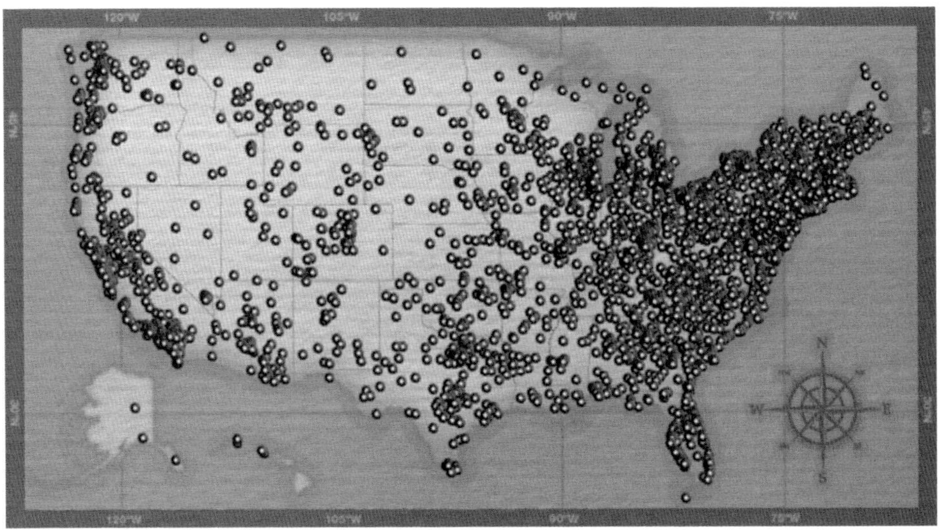